Smart Love

Nancy Van Pelt

Straight talk to young adults about dating, love and sex.

Dedication

Dedicated to all young adults who are in love, will one day fall in love, or wish they were in love, and all who want the best for their dating years.

'There are four things that are too mysterious for me to understand:
an eagle flying in the sky,
a snake moving on a rock,
a ship finding its way over the sea,
and a man and a woman falling in love.'
Proverbs 30:18, 19, GNB

First published in 2003 by Review and Herald Publishing Association.
Revised, updated and published by The Stanborough Press Ltd. © 2010

British Library Cataloguing in Publication Data.
Catalogue record for this book is available from the British Library.
ISBN 1-904685-61-7
Published by The Stanborough Press Limited, Grantham, Lincolnshire.
Printed in China.
Designed by Abigail Murphy.

Other books by Nancy Van Pelt, all published by The Stanborough Press Ltd.
Highly Effective Marriage
Train Up a Child
To Have and to Hold

All Scripture quotations are taken from the *New International Version* (Hodder and Stoughton) unless indication is given to the contrary.
Other versions used:
Good News Bible (Collins) = GNB
New King James Version (Thomas Nelson) = NKJV
New Living Translation (Tyndale) = NLT
New English Bible (Oxford/Cambridge University Press) = NEB

Reprinted 2012, 2014

Smart Love

Nancy
Van Pelt

*Straight talk to young adults
about dating, love and sex.*

contents

A Word with Mum and Dad and Significant Others

Did you know that the average child learns about the facts of intercourse from his parents five years after he has heard about them from his friends? Nine out of ten children learn the facts of life on the street, from the wrong people, in the wrong way, and at the wrong time. Only one in ten hears them from parents first, in the right way, from the right people, at the right time!

As your child approaches the early teen years, you are going to have to shift gears from talking about sex in general to more specific terms. *Smart Love* is my effort to communicate with this age group about the challenges they face during their dating years. In my typical, straight-from-the-hip style (as evidenced in over twenty of my previous books) I seek to provide biblical, yet practical information about the delicate matter of opposite sex relationships and sexuality.

Prior to 1960, most young people did not have sex until marriage. This included not only younger adolescents, but also university and college students. Sexual abstinence till marriage was the norm back then. But note, sexually-transmitted disease and pregnancy out of wedlock were also dramatically lower than today. A 2007 report in the UK showed that more young people have had sex by the age of 15 than in any other country and an estimated one quarter to one third of young people in the UK have had sex by the age of 16.*

With encouragement and instruction in appropriate abstinence skills, there is every reason to believe that the vast majority of young adults can make the decision to wait. Young adults enjoy the challenge of a goal and they can be highly disciplined in reaching

their goals. For example, students who want to achieve good grades, or excel in a sport, often achieve those goals.

In one of the most powerful reports ever published in the US about issues that affect young adults negatively, four top risk factors for sexual involvement have been identified and are the same for boys as for girls. They are as follows:

- alcohol use
- a steady boy or girlfriend
- no parental monitoring
- having parents who thought that adolescent sex was acceptable.

Maybe you think that your teens won't listen to anything you have to say about dating, love or sex. But this report identifies the influence of parents as key to avoiding risky behaviours. The study, funded by the US government, found that parental attitudes play a protective role in delaying sexual activity. Young adults responded positively to parental messages when feelings of warmth, love and caring were present.

The Safe Sex community that backs

promoting condom use says, 'Kids are going to do it anyway.' This is refuted by this finding that parental attitudes play the greatest protective role. Other important factors that were emphasised were parental disapproval of adolescent sex, and parental disapproval of adolescent use of contraception. You can clearly see that sexual activity does not occur in a vacuum, but instead is often associated with parental neglect. Kids will and do listen to their parents!

School connectedness also plays a protective role in delaying sex. This was connected to perceived caring from teachers and high expectations for student performance. Students in parochial schools or schools with high average daily attendance were positively influenced. Of significant importance was the finding that 88% of the students interviewed reported having a religion and placing an importance on prayer.

Another influencing factor was making a pledge of abstinence from sex until married. If teens had made that pledge, they were statistically far more likely to avoid early onset of sexual activity than those who had not taken such a pledge. But the strongest message above every other factor influencing positive choices was a good relationship with their parents. This does not mean that young adults will do what their parents would like, but the chance that young adults will complete their teen years without engaging in risky sex is higher if parents take a firm stand on issues, and communicate that stand to their children.

Two of the most significant problems we have in society today are the twin epidemics of sexually-transmitted diseases (STDs) and out-of-wedlock pregnancy. Despite years of government funding on programmes advocating the use of contraceptives, there has been a continued devastating effect on society from these two problems which have continued to grow significantly.

I believe it is time for a new sexual revolution – what is called *character-based abstinence education*. To be effective, this education must begin with instilling a strong foundation of values in our youth. From the very beginning young people must be encouraged to be abstinent until marriage. First, parents need to be the primary role models. But parents must be supported by the community, schools, medical professionals and church as they work to guide their children towards sexual purity till marriage.

The next step is to understand what your teenager is going through. Preteens and younger teens face some of the most volatile years of their lives. This age group lives more in and for the moment than do older teens or adults. And they don't have the ability to think like adults until they are fifteen or sixteen. In general, they are incapable of making decisions based on knowledge of future consequences, because their brains haven't

developed the connections that allow them to think this way. These characteristics can be potent if they become sexually active, as they often don't connect sex with the consequences of pregnancy or STDs or other risk.

And girls who don't have effective male role models during their early to mid-teen years become vulnerable to the attention of older men from whom they seek 'fathering' as much as they seek romance and intimacy. In *Smart Love* I refer to some shocking studies establishing that the fathers of babies born to teen mothers are at least four years older than the girls, which means that most of these men are adults, not teens.

In *Smart Love* I also have to be very open in discussing sexual practices other than vaginal intercourse, since many young adults are adopting alternatives to intercourse, such as mutual masturbation, as well as oral and anal sex. The *Journal of the American Medical Association* (JAMA) published a survey of American college students who were asked what was meant by 'having sex'. It showed that 59% of the students said oral-genital contact did not count as 'had sex' with a partner. What may be even more shocking is that 19% expressed the same opinion about penile-anal sex. Other studies show that *47% of those who took an abstinence pledge considered oral sex to be a form of abstinence, and 61% put mutual masturbation in the same category!* What is meant by abstinence must be spelled out clearly, which I attempt to do.

In *Smart Love* I lead young adults to make a pledge towards abstinence or what I call *sexual purity*. Research shows that some abstinence strategies help delay the onset of sex particularly among young adolescents on the average of about eighteen months.

However, researchers who have been tracking pledgers have also found that *those who broke their pledge were about one third less likely to use contraceptives!* According to the researchers, 'pledgers are less likely to be prepared for an experience that they have promised to forgo.'

On the other hand, evaluations of programmes that combine abstinence education with contraceptive information find that they can help delay the onset of intercourse, reduce the frequency of intercourse, and the number of partners, as well as all the health risks! The evidence clearly shows that contraceptive information is not inherently harmful and that abstinence information can include contraceptive messages. A US national study by the Kaiser Family Foundation found that 97% of the surveyed parents with teenage

children want both abstinence and birth control information for their young adults. I have adopted this philosophy in *Smart Love* and give limited contraceptive information.

Abstinence programmes, of course, do not promote oral or anal sex. But young adults are very creative in stretching the boundaries of all rules. Some attempt to remain 'technical virgins' while engaging in oral and/or anal sex. But those who do not know about safe sex practices are more likely to contract STDs than are sexually active young adults who know what they are doing and act to prevent infection. So the gap between terminology and sexual practices must be stopped. Therefore you will find that in my straight-talk style I can help young adults set comprehensible boundaries when they get into 'touchy situations' or petting. Boundaries are clearly defined.

Recently I heard the music from the ever-popular classic film *Fiddler on the Roof*. The words from 'Sunrise, Sunset' contain poignant lines about parents' feelings over their child's growth. Memories flooded in and took me back a few years to a time when I dressed and carried a little girl and watched with pride two rumbustious boys at play. The little girl has become a beautiful young mother of four, and our sons have matured into caring fathers. Yet it seems like only yesterday when they were small children at play. I don't remember getting older. How did our children mature so quickly? I guess it happens to all of us. The months and years flow by us, even though the past seems like only yesterday.

Hopefully you will purchase *Smart Love* for your own children, but it is not meant to replace your role as a parent. But if you have remained painfully silent, embarrassed, or ignorant about what and how much to tell them and when, this book will provide a welcome bridge to open communication. And remember, the information you give won't be nearly as important as your attitude when talking about each subject. Your attitudes – unspoken as well as spoken – will be passed on to your teen. Your teen will listen to what you say, but he will copy your attitudes.

Please do not think that your teen is too young or innocent to learn the facts of life. Some parents think that they can let their preteens and early teens enjoy a few more years before exposing them to the harsh realities of life. Innocence is entirely different from ignorance. Innocence implies purity of heart and freedom from sin. Ignorance is lack of information.

Capture the right opportunity to reach and prepare your young adults for the challenges ahead. This book is designed to assist you. If you miss it, you may never again have another chance.

Nancy Van Pelt

*Report: 'Sex, Drugs, Alcohol and Young People' by Independent Advisory Group on Sexual Health and HIV, [pub. 2007].

The First Word

You come to adulthood searching for ways of building successful relationships with members of the opposite sex. Remember, half the fun is getting there.

Ready,

Set,

Go!

Dating For Beginners

One of the biggest problems facing young adults today revolves around dating, love and sex. I find them very interested in the subject yet suffering from confusion and frustration over the multitude of choices that must be made when dating. Most young people begin dating with no purpose, direction or know-how.

Dating in such a manner reminds me of a story I read about a funny insect called a processionary caterpillar that feeds on pine needles.[1] These insects move in a group through the trees in a long procession, one leading, the others following, each with his eyes half closed and his head snugly fitted against the extremity of his predecessor.

Jean Henri Fabre, a French naturalist, experimented with a group of these caterpillars. He enticed them to the rim of a flowerpot where he succeeded in getting the first one connected with the last one, thus forming a complete circle which started moving around the rim with no beginning or end.

The naturalist thought that eventually they would catch on, get tired of their march and start off in a new direction. Not so. Through sheer force of habit the creeping circle kept moving around the rim of the flowerpot, keeping up the same pace for seven days and would undoubtedly have carried on longer had it not been for ultimate starvation and sheer exhaustion. Incidentally, an ample supply of food was close at hand and plainly visible, but it was outside the range of the circle, so they continued along the beaten path. They stupidly followed by instinct, habit and custom, blindly following the one before them.

Just as these caterpillars blindly follow in the path of the one before them, so many young adults muddle through their dating years with no direction. They, too, go around in circles, doing what their crowd does without thinking it through. Others are depressed because they struggle with sexual temptation or they have no dating life or they have a crush on someone who doesn't know they exist.

You, too, may be floundering because you don't know how to manage your dating life. This is what *Smart Love* is all about. I have researched the

subjects of dating, love and sex and measured them all against biblical standards. One thing I've learned is there's a lot to learn about dating, so you feel good about it and yourself.

Anyone can date, but not everyone can

date and be really successful at it. There are a lot of finer points to learn so that you can handle all the emotional aspects, as well as the pressure and proper rules of etiquette that will help you become an intelligent dating partner. Drifting along with the crowd, blindly following where others are going, won't suffice for those of you who want only the best from your dating years.

This book will show you how to date and be sensible about it. What could be more fun? It will help you:
• Develop healthy feelings of worth in yourself
• Learn what the opposite sex wants in a dating partner, where to go, what to do, and how to act on a date
• Decide when and how to end relationships
• Learn the difference between real love and infatuation
• Discover how far too far really is
• Choose a life of purity and obedience.

Think About It . . .

Many young adults spend less time thinking about what they want out of dating than they spend on what clothes they will wear the next day. If you want to enjoy your dating years, find someone to love you, you need a game plan. *Smart Love* is a game plan for anyone wishing to follow God's plan for dating, anyone attempting to live a pure life in the midst of a sexual jungle, and anyone seeking forgiveness for foolish dating mistakes in the past.

Most of you have had very little instruction in how to date intelligently and yet you are

expected to make brilliant choices. Statistics on premarital pregnancy show how often those choices are stupid. *Smart Love* is my attempt to make a difference, beginning with you. As a Certified Family Life Educator, I will deliver straight talk about how to establish healthy dating patterns before problems develop. Unlike a counsellor, who helps people find solutions to problems after mistakes have been made, I will help you learn skills so you can make wise choices in the first place and be more successful in love than you ever dreamed you could be.

The probability of your having a happy marriage is much greater if you follow this biblical game plan. Those who drift with the crowd and who count on luck or doing-what-comes-naturally are those who are going to end up going in circles like the caterpillars – either in a divorce court or with disappointing marriages.

The theme of *Smart Love* is prevention – preventing stupid dating mistakes – hurtful break-ups, premarital sex, out-of-wedlock pregnancy, and heart-rending decisions about abortion and adoption. This is similar

to how a computer programmer operates. The sooner the programmer catches the programme glitches and corrects them, the cheaper it's going to be. Errors caught after the implementation of the software project are going to be a lot more expensive.

Tina's Story – A Cry for Help

I stress taking time to allow friendship to develop before falling in love. The best way to prevent unhealthy and hurtful relationships is to slow things down. Slowing romantic involvement allows time to analyse your

have seen too much pain.

Healthy relationships develop over time and with a little savvy. The following letter from a teenager I'll call Tina illustrates what I hear too frequently:

Dear Mrs Van Pelt

I have read your book and attended the Dating seminar recently at _____. I want to thank you for both. They've been very helpful. I only wish I'd had your material much sooner than I did.

I have a question. But I'll tell you my story first. Please give me a straight, honest answer. I dated for the second time when I was 17. I'll call him Tim. At first I was only infatuated with Tim, but then slowly I fell deeply in love with him. Up to the time that I dated Tim, I had been completely innocent of anything – even kissing. I had no idea what petting was all about until I met Tim. I knew I wanted to save my virginity for marriage, but I hadn't really set my standards on petting because I knew nothing about it. Then Tim started touching me below the waist. Of course, it was a new feeling for me and I enjoyed it. But then he made me touch him. Being afraid that I would lose him if I didn't, I continued it for a while.

One day when we were alone on a walk, Tim pinned me on the ground and tried to get me to have sex with him. When I refused he pinned down my arms and continued trying.

Let me explain the details – his penis was just inside my labia. I couldn't move so I begged him to let me up and he did, apologising. I know I should never have been in the situation where he could even try to make love to me. Since then, mostly because of the awful guilt I feel, I've broken up with him.

Now for my question. I want to know if I'm still a virgin or at least a technical virgin. I have now decided not to date, at least until maybe college. Actually, I'm so ashamed that I have no desire to date.

Please reply.

Hopefully still Virgin

'Hopefully Still Virgin' broke nearly every rule of good sense while dating this boy. To name a few:

involvement with this person and make choices regarding where the relationship is heading and where you want to go.

I have a real problem with those who jump into serious relationships too quickly. I

• she never set her standards on petting

- she never educated herself on how to handle a 'touchy situation'
- she allowed Tim to touch her below the waist
- she touched Tim below the waist (because he 'made' me. Explain to me how a guy 'makes' you do that!)
- she went with him alone where a 'close encounter' could occur
- she allowed him access to her body repeatedly
- she encouraged his behaviour
- then got upset when he tried to act out what she led him to believe could happen
- she did this against her will because she was afraid she would lose him (she wouldn't be suffering from guilt now if she had said No and had lost him!)
- will forever wonder if she really is a virgin
- suffers from guilt and shame
- has no desire to date.

Like 'Hopefully Still Virgin', most young adults rush to sex to find intimacy. Closeness is the goal; sex is the means. They assume doing 'the ultimate' will make them happy. Often the greater their problems, the faster they rush. But sex does not automatically bring intimacy or solve problems. Sex doesn't produce closeness or prove intimacy. It can only celebrate the intimacy that's already there. Sex just can't deliver what doesn't already exist. It's more likely that sex clouds the realities of the problems that must be faced. One of the biggest mistakes young adults make is thinking that having sex somehow proves love. Sex outside of marriage is little more than lust.

Sex is a thrill. I'll not argue that point. But the true pleasure of sex cannot be enjoyed unless each person can be completely open with the other – where you have complete trust, total commitment, and unconditional acceptance. Such attitudes are possible only in marriage. And it is worth waiting for.

The wise crowd doesn't just do what makes them feel good right now, but rather asks, 'What are the long-term consequences of this?' before hopping into bed. You don't have to be a stick-in-the-mud, but you must refuse to make stupid choices. You decide not to settle for a cheap imitation when you know the real thing is waiting for you just ahead.

The wise crowd wants guidelines and restrictions. When asked about it, they snort, laugh and roll their eyes. But deep inside, they want guidelines. Because few have thought through their choices, they tend to make up their own rules to the game as they go along, which leaves them not knowing which direction to take. Caught in a crush between everyone making up their own rules, they find themselves in chaos.

Going for Gold

Someone used a champion swimmer as an example – a swimmer who has trained, competed and proven herself to be a world-class athlete. She is ready for the Olympics and has a chance of the gold. She goes to the starting block to begin her race. But something has gone wrong! Then she notices that some of the starting blocks are at one end of the pool, some at the other end, and some along the sides! Some of her fellow competitors are already in the water and racing ahead of her. There are no lanes, only arrows painted on the bottom pointing in all directions. Everyone takes off at different times in different directions, bumping into each other. What chaos!

The Olympics aren't set up in such a haphazard manner. If they were, it would be a demolition derby. In a swimming competition, the pool must have lanes and officials watching to make sure everything is fair. Rules govern starting and stopping times. Without these parameters and rules which govern the competition, no one can win. Rules make it possible to win. Rules protect competitors from others in the race who might hinder them. In the same manner, dating has rules to keep us in our lanes, to keep others in their lanes, and to protect us from hurt.

But without a standard of right and wrong, how can one decide where those lanes are and what is right? Our culture says, 'If it feels good, do it.' God says, 'Follow me.' Both of these philosophies cannot succeed. One is false and must fail and every young adult must decide which side he or she is on. One young woman told me her boyfriend pressured her by saying, 'What's the matter with you? Everyone else is doing it.' Without hesitation she shot back at him, 'Everyone but me.' She made her choice. God is not 'out to get us' or spoil our fun through these rules. He is only trying to protect us so we can be winners.

The second force working against youth today is the breakdown of the family. Without role models in Mum and Dad to show how values are determined and acted upon, we are swept along with the mudslide of the culture. Without guidelines, without restriction, we wander in a maze. Without guidelines we have no reason to say No to anything. Rather than giving increased freedom, this lack of values makes us indecisive.

Without a biblical point of reference, you will be confused and empty, which leaves you powerless. This in turn leads to insecurity and the need to hold on to something or

someone. It will drive you to fill up your empty spots with just 'anybody' or settle for temporary closeness. Without guidelines, you can't recognise right and wrong. You may find something that you call closeness that makes you feel good for the moment.

But when you have guidelines and can follow them, you have learned to obey. And when you can obey you learn self-control. Self-control and the ability to make wise choices are two important elements of maturity – powerful tools that will help you make sensible dating decisions and deal with sexual temptation surrounding you.

When our lives are out of sync with biblical truth, our actions will be also. That is why the Bible tells us not to be conformed to the garbage the world offers but rather to be

transformed by the renewing of our minds, that we may understand God's good, pleasing and perfect will for our lives. And when we get a grip on his will for our dating life, we can act in accordance with it.

My prayer is that God will use the guidelines in *Smart Love* to help you learn, more easily and sooner than others, how to build and maintain successful dating relationships. We serve a magnificent God. Regardless of your past, with God as your partner you can have a great dating future. I can't promise that as a result of reading this book you will find the perfect boy or girlfriend and live happily ever after. But I know that we serve a God who has a master plan for your life. My prayer is that his Spirit will speak to you on every page about his will for your life.

Smart Love

chapter ONE

Part 1: Loving Yourself Comes First

Mike is a student who desperately wants to be like the rest of the guys he knows. His friends seem to be able to have fun with the opposite sex, talk, laugh, joke, and date girls. But every time Mike thinks about dating, his mind plays reruns of all his failures. No girl has ever liked him, wanted to sit by him, singled him out to talk with, or showed an interest in going out with him. One day he met Susan through a friend and they went out for something to eat. He knew their time together would be disastrous, and sure enough it was. He liked Susan. She was pretty, had a pleasant personality and seemed to like him. But Mike was so self-conscious he was miserable. He said all the wrong things,

laughed at the wrong times and couldn't think of anything clever to say. Mike's lack of self-worth had already cost him several relationships, and it was about to cost him one more.

Amber has had a couple of casual dates with a guy she is beginning to like. Since he said he would call this evening, she anxiously waits by the phone. An hour goes by, then two. He never calls. Amber is devastated. She begins running herself down. 'Every relationship I've ever had ends like this. . . . I knew it wouldn't last. . . . He probably didn't like me at all . . . I'm too fat. . . . He's probably already got someone else. . . . I'll never have a boyfriend. . . . There must be something seriously wrong with me.'

Here's a message for all the Mikes and Ambers of the world: If you don't change how you think and feel about yourself now, you'll end up dating the wrong person. If you date the wrong kinds of persons, you'll end up making a multitude of wrong choices – moral decisions, as well as whom to marry. The poor image you have of yourself will most probably attract someone who will try to control, parent, or use you. Worse still, because you don't like yourself, you may allow someone to abuse you physically, emotionally, sexually, or all three.

If you want a healthy dating relationship, first you need a positive self-image. Unless you like yourself, you aren't capable of making intelligent decisions about love, nor are you ready to date.

The way we view ourselves is the basis from which we make our choices and react to situations. It determines how we choose our values, select our life goals, and formulate our belief system. Our response to life events is shaped to a large extent by who we are and what we think about ourselves. Remember: Self-image is not what we actually are. *Ninety percent of our self-image revolves around what we think others think of us.* In effect, we allow others to determine our self-image!

Sometimes our perception of what others think about us is false. It is possible to be loved by parents and friends and still not love yourself. You could be voted most popular at school and still feel worthless because of other experiences that have had a negative impact on your self-image. Honours and awards can be won even by those who feel useless, because self-esteem comes from within. Success in the eyes of friends does not spell success inside.

The self-concept, then, is formed from a combination of all past experiences and relationships, our successes and failures, and what we think others think about us.

But . . . Sometimes I Hate Myself

Your major task as a young adult is to establish a healthy self-esteem, while at the same time major changes are taking place. The body changes; interest develops in the opposite sex; sexual feelings emerge; peer acceptance supersedes parental opinion. Because so many dramatic changes occur in your life, earlier evaluations you made of yourself no longer fit. You are developing and maturing so quickly that the former concept you had of yourself must change also. So you begin the difficult task of reworking your previous identity.

The early teen years from 13 to 15 might be described as the most difficult thirty-six months of teen life. This is when inferiority and doubt of personal worth reach an all-time high. You feel as if your worth as a human being hangs on whether a certain group accepts you (and groups are notoriously fickle). Even a minor evidence of rejection takes on major significance to those who already feel like failures. The impact of having no one to sit with on a school bus trip, not having an invitation to an important school event, being laughed at, of waking up to six shiny, new pimples on your forehead, or falling down in front of someone you like, take on larger-than-life proportions.

Furthermore, this age group can be brutal to one another, attacking and slashing each other's self-esteem in such a vicious manner that the victim may never recover. Early senior school years are critical to the development of healthy self-esteem. It isn't uncommon to see a bright-eyed, happy youngster enter senior school and emerge three years later broken and discouraged. He hates his physical body, feeling he has no appeal to the opposite sex, and wishing he'd never been born. Teens desperately need help during this critical period of intensive self-doubt.

Throughout your teen years you bring with you all the experiences and feelings from the years that have gone before. You tend to evaluate yourself against these past experiences.

During childhood your self-concept is not firmly fixed and can be changed more easily. But by the time you reach adolescence, your self-concept is less flexible and the judgements you've already made about yourself become more fixed. As a result, you think of yourself as the class clown, the shy type, the 'big mouth', a geek, a leader, a sports star, Miss Popularity, or a wallflower.

Once you accept an evaluation as valid, it is extremely difficult to change. Your parents, teachers, even friends, may attempt to help you improve your self-worth, only to have you reject their efforts. The reason is simple: Once you begin to think of yourself as a 'slow learner' or whatever, you will put up steel-like resistance to prove everyone else wrong. The results of this belief system are found, for example, in the beautiful girl who believes she is ugly because she grew up with the idea she is ugly. She rejects any information that is contrary to her fixed ideas about herself. Many teens do not understand that some of these feelings are influenced by the mood of the moment or by a recent experience.

Teens of all ages could be helped tremendously through this traumatic period of life if they could only realise the transitory nature of the physical and emotional changes they are going through. But the present takes on exaggerated importance, and they think it will last forever. It is usually only during later maturity that some of these things can be viewed objectively.

And remember – the closer your evaluation of self matches how others see you, the better the adjustment you will make to life and the greater sense of belonging you will enjoy, as well as a greater sense of personal worth.

Dr James Dobson tells the story of Julie,

whom he hadn't seen in over ten years. He was the teacher of this 13 year old with sad, brown eyes. She seemed especially embarrassed by her ethnic heritage and because she was slightly overweight. During that year her only friend moved away. Then, ten years later, Julie called, inquiring where Dr and Mrs Dobson attended church; she too began attending there. Over the next few months, Julie became a vibrant Christian. She participated in the choir, and many in the congregation commented on how she radiated a glow whenever she sang.

One day after church, Dr Dobson asked her why she had gone to so much trouble to obtain his unlisted telephone number more than ten years later. Julie thought for a moment and then paid him a great compliment. 'Because,' Julie said, 'when I was 13, you were the only person in my life who acted as though you respected me and believed in me . . . and I wanted to know your God.'[1] When we treat people with this kind of respect, we have found the best way to treat people of all ages, as well as lead them to Christ.

Each of us has the opportunity and ability to build others up or tear them down. Let's purpose to build up and encourage self-esteem. After all, this is what Jesus would do.

What It Means to Like Yourself

Many definitions of self-esteem have been given, but a simple one that spells it out clearly is how warm and loving you feel towards yourself. Healthy self-worth is genuine love of yourself, based on a total and unconditional acceptance of yourself as a worthy and important person. Self-worth allows you to feel 'equal to' others, not 'better than', as in pride.

When you feel like this about yourself, you will be able to have healthy dating relationships, handle daily responsibilities, make rational, intelligent decisions regarding your future, bounce back from pain and hurt, and pursue worthwhile goals.

Self-worth is the centre of emotional and mental health. If you genuinely know and respect yourself, you have laid a solid foundation that equips you to handle the daily challenges of life. When you possess a poor self-image and shaky self-confidence, you cannot maintain control of your life.

A dating relationship can only be as healthy as the two persons involved. A critical question for two young people to answer before going steady is: How healthy is my self-worth? If either has a fragile or

poor sense of self, the couple will be susceptible to endless emotional turmoil. It takes energy and maturity to manage the inner life. When one or both aren't healthy there is high probability that their relationship will be damaged or not survive.

But Where Does It Come From?

Feelings of worth are learned, not inherited. Originally, these are formed during childhood. When parents love and value a child and such feelings are conveyed in a positive manner over a period of time, the child learns he is loved and special. The opposite can also be true. When a child is repeatedly ridiculed, he thinks that's what he deserves, and accepts this evaluation as valid. A lack of affirmation from parents who are too busy or lack knowledge and skill to provide it can be just as devastating. The effects of this early programming can last a lifetime.

Young people from dysfunctional homes – those who have alcoholic parents, physically, emotionally or sexually abusive parents, or parents who neglect them – are at particular risk. Such young people begin to believe the message that they are no good – that if they had been good enough, their parents wouldn't have got drunk, abused or neglected them. If they had been good enough, their parents would have loved, nurtured and affirmed them.

Society also plays a part in promoting feelings of inferiority. Prizes are offered to winners, honours given to the most intelligent, and awards to the most beautiful and popular. Commercials tell us that to be accepted we must use certain products, wear certain brand-name clothing, and look a certain way. A person may feel inferior because he had to wear hand-me-downs, has a large nose, is part of a minority race or religion, or has a physical handicap.

Mirror, Mirror on the Wall . . . I'm Not the Fairest of Them All!

The most highly prized attribute affecting the self-concept is physical attractiveness and it becomes all-consuming during adolescence. Society places a high value on a beautiful physical appearance. A survey by *Psychology Today* on body image showed that more than 60% of both sexes feel their looks are a liability to them. Actors and actresses depicted on the screen are chosen for their photogenic qualities which are further enhanced by film techniques to magnify the beauty of the already beautiful. It is most probably against such standards that you judge yourself.

Making Friends With Yourself

During senior school the beautiful girl enjoys many advantages which have nothing to do with beauty. Handsome boys receive 'breaks' from peers and adults alike. Girls with low self-esteem, it has been determined, try to be inconspicuous, shun leadership, and never like to be up front. Such girls stay away from social activities and lack confidence in their abilities. They bemoan their lack of popularity, failing to recognise they are bringing it on themselves.

Two thousand girls between the ages of 11 and 18 were asked, 'What would you most like to change about yourself if you could – your looks, your personality, or your life?' Fifty-nine percent mentioned some aspect of their physical appearance, with most complaints centring on facial defects and skin problems. The things that concerned the girls most were their height, weight, late development, thinness, large arms or legs and glasses. Boys were more concerned over being short, wearing glasses, obesity, poor physique, lack of muscles, skin blemishes, and lack of shoulder width.

Sometimes just an unguarded comment about size leaves an everlasting impression. One boy had been excessively tall even in early senior school.

His mother was once asked how she could find him in a crowd. 'I just look for the kid who's sticking up above everyone else,' she replied. These words made such a lasting impression on him that he could remember them three decades later – even though chances are he could not remember one other thing which happened that month.

The clothes you wear can either add to or detract from your appearance and prestige in the group. But many young adults don't possess enough savvy about clothes to understand how to use them to improve their appearance. A youth with low self-esteem will conform to peer pressure by adopting the prevailing style, whether or not the style is becoming.

Those who were teased about their appearance as children are much more likely to carry the residual effects into adulthood than those who did not like their appearance but were not teased about it.

Psychology Today's survey, as well as numerous other studies, confirms that self-worth is deeply affected by appearance. While there are exceptions, generally speaking, the higher you rate your looks, the higher your self-worth. The less satisfied you are with your personal appearance, the lower your feelings of worth.

What Happens When You're a Failure

The consequences of a poor self-concept are far-reaching. Not only will a poor self-concept warp your feelings about yourself, but it will also reach out and affect all your friendships – including your dating relationships.

A poor self-concept limits your capacity to love and accept others. It's a simple fact. You cannot really love someone else until you first love yourself. You can genuinely love and receive love from others in direct proportion to how you feel about yourself. If you cannot like yourself, then you cannot like others. If you do not feel secure and worthwhile at the very core of your being, you cannot like, respect or love others. This doesn't always show up early in relationships, but later in the ability to sustain long-term relationships.

One girl who finally 'got her act together' said, 'From now on, no more sex until I'm married. What I've done in the past is wrong. Before you can love someone else, you first have to love yourself. If I had respected myself, I wouldn't have done what I did. Things are different now. I've gained the maturity and self-worth I need to live by the standards I've chosen. Now that I like myself, I am free to like and love someone else.'

A poor self-concept influences your choice of dating partners.
The one who lacks self-respect often dates someone who criticises or puts them down. Why? Because this treatment recreates the feelings to which they have become accustomed from their parents.

They feel comfortable with it.

A poor self-concept may cause you to use sex to prove your worth. Love and security are often sought through premarital sex. With a poor self-image brought on by a lack of acceptance from their peers, teenagers often grab for the first thing that

resembles security. Often this means sex.

Such teenagers feel so lonely and depressed, feeling nobody really cares whether they live or die that they use sex to connect with someone . . . anyone. They want, at least for a few moments, to be held and feel cared for or important to someone, even if it means giving sex to get it.

A lonely, insecure girl may feel she has nothing to offer a guy . . . she believes she has no personality, she's not popular, and not even very attractive. But if she can get a guy interested in her, she'll offer him her body so she doesn't lose him, to prove that someone wants her, desires her.

Any girl who thinks she has to have sex to prove she's 'cool' or 'liberated' or grown up places a very low value on herself. Such viewpoints not only demonstrate a lack of self-worth but also show that people have very misguided ideas of what constitutes masculinity and femininity. Once such young people recognise that worth and dignity are not based on sexual performance, they can place a new value on themselves and recognise how special they are to God. In turn they will begin to treat others with respect.

Guys often do likewise. They try to be 'macho' or prove their masculinity through sexual activity. Their view of manhood is a guy who can out-drink everyone else and make it with the girls. They selfishly use females for their own gratification and show no respect for others. They have such a low opinion of themselves that they think they have value only as long as they live up to their warped 'macho' image.

Should a girl seem hesitant in responding to their masculine charm, they see the chance to be persuasive, domineering and the 'conquering hero'. Each sexual encounter proves to such a guy that he is a real man, and such experiences provide something to brag about in the locker room. He'll laugh a lot, joke and share crude talk about sex with his friends. His main objective is self-gratification – all feeble attempts to bolster his own shaky, immature ego. The consequences of his actions do not concern him. Even the physical thrills are not as important to such a male as exerting his masculine charm on a female. He looks to sex to bolster his self-image instead of looking to his Creator to find worth.

Disobeying God and choosing to have sex once damages self-esteem. But continuing down this path in deliberate defiance further destroys self-esteem. Such a young person may feel cheap, used, and unworthy of God's love. One girl commented that God could never use her because she had lost her virginity, so she might as well 'blow it' again. She was miserable since she had lost all sense of worth. She will continue to feel this way until she accepts God's forgiveness and can forgive herself.

Within marriage sex includes love, trust, security and freedom. Within a permanent commitment there is no need to prove anything or use the other as an ego booster or a security blanket. God provided a perfect arrangement, but we still try to sidestep his plan and improve on it.

A poor self-concept may cause you to tolerate abuse. Liz is 30 now, but began her self-destructive behaviour early. By the age of 13 she was having sex regularly with a boyfriend so she wouldn't lose him. At 14 she was pregnant and had her first abortion. By 17 she was on a binge of sleeping with anyone. By her own admission she hated herself. 'I was attracted to guys who would emotionally abuse me, physically use me, and eventually reject and abandon me. I would put up with anything. My experience with men taught me that I'm not worth much. I subconsciously set myself up, time after time, by becoming involved with men who would treat me this way.'

A survey showed that 52% of the teens surveyed said that they experienced abuse in their dating relationships.[2] The abuse included repeated insults, isolation, extreme ignoring and destruction of possessions as well as threats of physical harm. *Three quarters of these kids were aged 14 to 16!* Thirty-three percent had been threatened with physical

violence while in a dating relationship and yet very few ever told anyone.

Those with a poor self-concept put up with abuse and other destructive behaviours because they don't think they deserve better. They believe they are worthless and look for and feel comfortable in love relationships where this idea is confirmed. Because of their low opinion of themselves and the tendency to repeat self-destructive behaviours, they will date anyone who shows an interest.

A poor self-concept may cause you to resist authority. Whenever we don't like the way we are made or the way we act, we begin thinking that life has somehow cheated us.

Consciously or unconsciously we can develop the attitude that the world owes us something. This attitude produces a bitterness against parents, school authorities, police, employers, rules and laws. Whenever an authority figure comes along and lays down further restrictions that get in the way of what we want when we want it, we resent it and lash out.

Teens with low self-worth not only feel that others don't like or respect them, but they are also convinced that they lack likeable qualities. Rarely do they consider themselves easy to get along with, pleasant, popular, or good-natured. Yet it hurts to admit how they really feel, so many act out their feelings through rebellion and hostility. In its most severe forms, some even consider themselves unworthy of life and commit suicide.

A poor self-concept is a hindrance to forming genuine friendships. Hating ourselves not only hinders our response to others but also hinders others' responses to us. If you are over-sensitive about your appearance or what you believe others think of you, you can become unable to focus on the other person's needs. You are too wrapped up in worrying about their response to you! If you feel that everyone is against you, treats you unfairly, belittles and disapproves of you, your self-esteem is showing. You will automatically bow to the decisions and opinions of others, even though 'others' have no more knowledge on the subject than you do. You may also persistently judge yourself by unreachable standards and feel worthy only when you surpass others. Those with low self-worth may also pretend to be something they are not, or go out of their way to boast and impress others.

Another symptom of low self-esteem is to plunge recklessly into one scrape after another, actually inviting punishment and disgrace, when there is nothing to gain and everything to lose. The only way to build genuine friendships is to forget about yourself and concentrate on the needs of others.

A poor self-concept increases vulnerability to peer pressure. If you truly feel you are worthless in certain areas, you may try to gain acceptance by achieving goals that will bring the acceptance and approval of others. Teens who struggle with low self-worth are particularly vulnerable to peer pressure. Peer pressure isn't negative if the morals of the group involve doing what is right. But when friends exert a wrong influence, there is danger. It makes sense to choose like-minded friends and steer clear of the wrong crowd. Avoid people who don't share your basic ideas about how to live, regardless of how attractive or popular they are. Instead, choose friendships with those who share your values and convictions.

A poor self-concept will hinder spiritual growth. Young people frequently feel troubled about their inability to trust God. Try as they will, they feel they lack faith. This inability to trust God can often be traced to a deep rejection of self. One young woman reasoned this way: 'God created everything, didn't he? He is supposed to be wise and everlastingly loving. If what I see in the mirror is an example of his creation and his love, then I'm not interested in God.'

Such feelings are usually not conscious. More often than not, they are unconscious murmurings that we have never knowingly voiced or explored. But they are widespread among young people whose self-rejection hinders their relationship with God.

Part 2: Private Pain

A person can suffer more from a lack of self-respect than from physical pain. These people are much more sensitive to criticism and deeply disturbed when laughed at, blamed or criticised. In other words, they are much more touchy and easily hurt and deeply concerned over the reaction of others to them.

The one with low self-esteem indulges in severe self-criticism. When someone makes a critical remark of a general nature without reference to any one person, the person with low self-esteem assumes that he/she is the one referred to. He often believes that others are noticing, laughing at, or talking about him when in fact they are giving him little or no attention at all. Inferiority gnaws at the soul through the conscious mind by day and haunts dreams by night. So painful can the lack of self-respect become that our entire emotional system is designed to protect us from its oppression. A great proportion of our lives is devoted to protecting ourselves from the inner pain of inferiority.

A father had been extremely critical of his son. After trying to straighten out this wayward boy through constant criticism he realised his son was only becoming more withdrawn. At the point of desperation one day he searched through his son's desk for a piece of paper and came across a poem in free verse the boy had written. A few excerpts are included here:

Hello out there, world;
It's me in here . . .
The outside shell is very thick;
I'm having trouble getting
out.
Who am I? You say I don't
sound like myself?
That's because you've never heard me. . . .
I can't be hurt here.
You see, my shell keeps you away . . .
I can't hear too well inside this shell. . . .
And it's so comfortable in here, world.[3]

If you wish to understand yourself, your friendships, as well as the progression of your dating relationships which eventually lead to marriage, you must investigate your own cover-ups as well as the ways other people cope with personal inadequacies.

Great Pretenders

Let's see if you recognise any of these cover-ups:

The clown act. The clown deals with inferiority by laughing it off. He conceals his self-doubt and makes an enormous joke of everything. Art Buchwald once said, 'Humour is a mask. It is a way of hiding emotion.' Yes, humour is a mask comedians often use to cope with the pain and hurt from their past. Many famous comedians have amassed fortunes by poking fun at their own physical appearance or something else about themselves. The class clown, the one who comes in late, always falls down, or acts stupid to keep you and others laughing is the one we're talking about. This person has discovered that by keeping people laughing he can have friends but keep them at a distance. You see, if someone got too close, he might not like what he finds. So he'll keep you laughing.

Conformity. Those with self-image problems find it difficult to go against the crowd. These young adults usually have parents who do not communicate well with them and are unaware of their stunted self-worth due to family stress and instability. Through conformity to their peers, these young adults find a haven for their insecurity.

It is very difficult for this group to make positive moral choices, even if they intellectually and morally understand a course of action may be wrong. Their need for acceptance is expressed by dressing, talking and acting like a part of the crowd. Their lack of security and poor self-worth will cause them to follow the crowd, regardless of the consequences, because their sense of self has not yet matured. They do not yet possess what it takes to go against what their peers say.

The fighter. The fighter has learned that it hurts less to fight back than to withdraw, so instead of surrendering when he feels threatened or rejected, he gets mad. He carries a chip on his shoulder and dares others to knock it off. Insignificant issues can trigger his temper, and he lashes out cruelly at others. He is a temperamental, nasty and angry person who is always ready to take a swing at anyone in his way. Take pity on anyone who marries a fighter.

Withdrawal. The one who chooses this route surrenders completely and totally. She measures herself against others and concludes that she is worthless. Mary is like this. She's never been successful at dating so she concludes that she'll never have a boyfriend. With this evaluation of herself firmly in place, she must protect this belief.

Therefore she withdraws from all social situations, even though she's lonely. She will not take any chances or assume any unnecessary emotional risk. She fears initiating a conversation, speaking up in a group, entering a contest, running for an election, or even defending her thoughts and ideas. She proceeds through life, coping with inferiority by withdrawing into a shell of silence and loneliness. She has learned that the best way to face life is to button her lip.

There is a striking relationship between self-worth and involvement in extra-curricular activities. The lower a person's self-esteem, the less likely he is to participate in activities.[4] A whopping 70% of those with low self-esteem in one study belonged to no clubs. Yet those with high self-esteem participated in three or more activities and spent five or more hours every week at such activities. Among those with high self-esteem, 60% had held some elected office at school, compared with only 33% of those with low self-esteem.

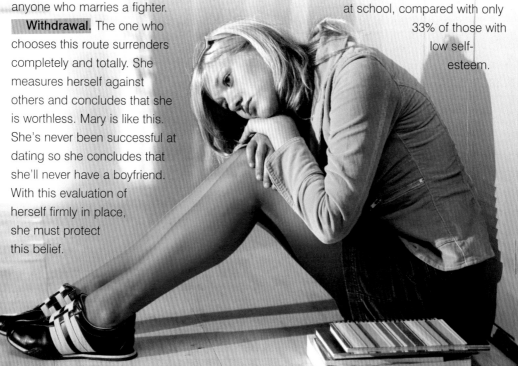

Girls with low self-esteem, it has been determined, try to be inconspicuous, shun leadership, and never like to be up front. Such girls stay away from social activities and lack confidence in their abilities. They bemoan their lack of popularity, failing to recognise that they brought it on themselves.

This lack of participation occurs because those with low self-esteem turn their interests inward. They spend a good deal of time daydreaming, for example. They also doubt their ability to be as successful as others.

Denial of reality. A person who cannot seem to erect a good defence to hide behind might choose, as a last resort, to deny reality. Such a person pulls down a mental shade and creates his own dream world. He copes with problems by refusing to believe they are there. Experimentation with drugs and alcohol are popular ways of denying reality. In most cases, such persons have not yet learned mature ways of coping with problems so try to escape or hide behind a drug-induced stupor. Excessive amounts of television or movies, novel reading and like entertainments can be used to deny reality.

I'll Do Anything for You if You'll Only Love Me!

When your self-image is positive, you tend to seek dating partners who will reinforce your positive feelings. The opposite is also true. When consumed by negative feelings about yourself, you look for dating partners who confirm this feeling. When you feel like a nobody inside, when fearful and easily depressed, you will be easily swayed by the attentions of anyone who flirts with or flatters you, regardless of who it is. When you lack the ability to validate your own worth, you tend to follow others around like a puppy, totally dependent on them to make you feel like anything.

Some are so lacking in self-worth and are so afraid of being abandoned, they cling desperately to any relationship, even a rotten one or one that brings pain. It doesn't have to be this way. To avoid getting into a destructive relationship, you must be ruthlessly honest about any hurt or pain from the past, any unfinished business with parents or previous partners, or you will have a self-image so poor you will permit abuse. You must deal with these issues before you can have a healthy dating relationship. Dating is beyond your capabilities for now. Back off from all emotional involvement.

Building positive self-esteem, learning to feel entitled to a healthy, happy relationship, and expecting good things to come your way are important elements in being ready for romance. Some people appear from outward appearance to have a healthy self-image. Others must struggle to find it. Still others must spend long hours in therapy to heal hurt and pain from the past.

You can often tell by the way someone

looks and acts that he does not like himself. Charlie Brown from the *Peanuts* series depicts inferiority. The slump of his shoulders, hands in his pockets, and down-turned mouth all tell a story without the caption: 'Nobody cares if I live or die.'

Just as this attitude holds Charlie Brown back from being all he can be, so will a weak self-image keep you from achieving all that you really want. It will force you to stick with the safety of the known and familiar rather than challenging you to achieve new and worthwhile goals. If your aspirations are low, you won't achieve much. But the higher your self-esteem, the higher your aspirations will be for achieving success – emotional, financial, intellectual, spiritual and romantic success.

The poorer your self-image, the greater is the urge to prove something just to impress others. The better your self-image, the easier it is to be yourself without having to put on airs. Low self-concept will cause defensive and inappropriate communication patterns.

If you hope to achieve a healthy, happy dating relationship with a member of the opposite sex, this factor of self-esteem is the most important. *The greatest barriers to successful dating are feelings of worthlessness, inadequacy and failure.* So the first love relationship in which you must achieve success is a love relationship with yourself. You must first feel you are worthy and lovable. Then you are more likely to enjoy healthy dating relationships. Only when you can first love yourself will you be able to accept love from others.

Part of loving yourself is being happy with how you look. This has a lot to do with how you present yourself to the opposite sex. And how you present yourself has a strong impact on how successful you are in attracting dates. If you feel you are ugly or physically unattractive, you may be afraid to approach or respond to someone who catches your attention.

How you feel about yourself and how you present yourself also determines what kind of person you are likely to attract. It is hardly surprising, then, that those with a scruffy, sloppy appearance rate themselves as dissatisfied with their dating life.

When evaluating your self-esteem you must look at what relationships you currently have that validate your worth and which are destructive to your feelings of worth. Whenever a relationship becomes destructive and negative, you must choose to end it.

Detours

A much-publicised report on teen pregnancy by the National Research Council of the National Academy of Sciences in the US draws one important conclusion. *Sexual activity among young adults is definitely connected with the issue of self-image.* The sense of what and who one is and can do, and wants to be is at the heart of sexual decision-making.

Unless you feel good about yourself, you'll be insecure. When you feel this way, you need  some kind of jump-start from someone in order to feel right about yourself. Sex is a common tool used by such people to function. An insecure male uses sex to prove he is macho and attractive to girls. An insecure female uses sex to hold on to and be appealing to a guy – all to provide security for herself and prove she has some value.

Terrific expectations are placed on sex. People think sex can work miracles, make them feel secure, wanted, needed, achieve a better view of themselves, or even look better in the eyes of someone else. Another expectation people place on sex is that it establishes intimacy and closeness. Often people have low self-esteem because they have trouble establishing an intimate relationship with anyone. They think sex will help them find emotional intimacy and make them feel better about themselves. In reality, what they usually find is guilt and a broken heart and a deepening spiral of lower self-worth. But even when people find sex pleasurable, it doesn't help them become more capable of intimacy.

Premarital sex can fool us into marrying the wrong person. Sex produces strong emotional and physical bonds between people. The bond between them often makes them think it is deeper than it really is, that they know each other better than they really do; or because a couple has had sex they sometimes hang on to a relationship just to 'save face'.

God asked us to reserve sex for marriage to protect us. He knew that a person's self-esteem would only be damaged, not enhanced, by sex outside of marriage. He understood that the artificial high produced during the experience quickly wears off, leaving one with no sense of closeness afterwards. Therefore God established boundaries in which sex could be used to make it fulfilling and bring lasting pleasure – within the boundaries of matrimony.

So remember, your life will be sweeter if you wait for sex till marriage.

How to Be a Winner

Self-worth should be an honest appraisal of self. 'Do not think of yourself more highly than you ought, but rather think of yourself with sober judgement,' Romans 12:3. We should not rate ourselves too highly, neither should we underestimate our value. Some people try to make low self-image a virtue by identifying it with humility rather than pride or arrogance – their definition of self-esteem.

But high self-worth is not arrogance. When we have high self-worth, we feel equal to, not better than others – able to cope with the responsibilities of life.

There is no bragging, nor do we run ourselves down. We accept our weaknesses as well as our strengths and feel we deserve the respect of others. We learn to build on strengths and not berate ourselves for our weaknesses. We learn to live with the limitations we have been unable to change. We fail sometimes but are able to pick up the pieces and move on. We try to be honest and open and we consider that we are worthwhile.

Feeling good about ourselves frees us to pay attention to the needs of others. We can then be as tolerant of their weaknesses as we are of our own. We can appreciate their differences instead of putting others down or ridiculing them because they are different. We realise that differentness makes each human being unique. Healthy feelings of self-worth also free us spiritually, for we can more fully appreciate God's acceptance of us just the way we are and the potential for good within us.

Those with low self-esteem are usually drawn to each other and form destructive, unhealthy relationships. Develop high feelings of worth – this is how to become a winner in love!

Help! My Boyfriend Has Low Self-esteem!

If after all you've learned about self-esteem you recognise that your self-worth is fairly solid, but your boy/girlfriend's self-esteem is low, what should you do? *Slow down! Danger ahead!* You must recognise that someone who is unhappy with himself while dating will still be unhappy in all the years to come – even after marriage. Since you have positive self-worth, you are able to give love freely, be compassionate, forgive when it's called for and accept others as they are. When problems and disappointments weigh you down, you will still be able to manage.

But the one with a poor self-image has difficulty solving problems constructively because he is buried in self-loathing and self-defeating patterns. When a problem surfaces he reacts in desperation. He doesn't possess the coping mechanism to resolve his problems or the ability to put new skills to work, and will sink deeper into a cycle of defeat. As he spirals downward, anyone close to him will be caught up in his despair. He is often unhappy and will be likely to sink into states of depression and indifference or lash out at you with blame for the hurt and pain he feels. In spite of your efforts to pull him out of it, nothing helps.

Should you recognise any of these symptoms in your dating partner, you can save yourself a lot of trouble by moving on to someone who feels good about himself. Why risk your future hoping he will change? You can avoid a lifetime of heartache and gain a lifetime of happiness by being sure that both you and your dating partner have high self-esteem. You deserve a dating partner who is capable of nourishing a relationship.

It's more difficult than ever to find an emotionally healthy partner because so many young adults are growing up in dysfunctional homes – families that have been ravaged by divorce, alcoholism, drug abuse, and emotional, sexual or physical abuse. Though few recognise it, such young people carry devastating wounds. Their pain drives them to search for someone who can heal that pain, soothe their wounds, and put together all the broken pieces of their lives. But you cannot heal such wounds. So when you enter the dating arena, carefully evaluate each dating partner. Look beneath the surface. Rush into nothing. Take your time. Keep things cool. Some people are experts at hiding behind cover-ups.

If you ever hope to have a happy love relationship that will last a lifetime, no factor is more important than self-esteem – in you

and in your partner. There is no greater barrier to successful dating relationships than feeling you are unlovable. The first love affair you must negotiate is a love affair with yourself. Only when you have accomplished that are you really ready for romance. Only then will you be fully able to love another person and allow the other person to love you. Unless you can fully appreciate how lovable you are, the other person's love will never be quite real or convincing to you. You will always question why and how he can really love you – insignificant, ugly you – and you will unknowingly attempt to undermine your relationship.

Part 3: Learning to Be the Best 'Me' You Can Be

Samantha felt she had a million problems but only named a few. She plays in a basketball league and can send a ball through the hoop every time during practice; but in a real game gets so nervous she forgets which end of the court belongs to her team! She liked a boy in her class a lot, but after only two weeks he broke up with her. To make matters worse, she is tall and about thirty pounds heavier than she should be.

The boys her age (14) are mostly shrimps, so she feels unpopular. She feels clumsy, awkward and inferior, and longs for someone to wave a magic wand over her.

Recognising you have low self-esteem and struggling to overcome its crippling effects are two different things. So if you have been condemning yourself because of past failures and rejections, it is time to free yourself. The sooner you make friends with yourself, the sooner you will be ready for healthy friendships.

There are no easy solutions for deep-seated inferiority, but change is possible! Since a large portion of the self-concept is learned from past experience, it can be unlearned. You simply replace negative feelings about yourself with positive ones. The good news is you don't have to stay the way you are today.

There is no magic wand, and it won't happen all at once. And certainly you can't undo years of self-hate in one step. But you can begin now to take small steps to free yourself of past failures. Your progress depends entirely on how much effort you are willing to put into it.

Now let's see what can be done to help Samantha and all the others like her to feel better about themselves. Let's combine your desire to change and Christ's power to change us with some practical suggestions.

Step 1: Inventory Your Strengths

First, Samantha was in desperate need of a little confidence in her abilities. She named only one thing she could do well – sink a ball through the hoop – and then only during practice. Samantha did a fantastic job of describing her failures. What she really needs to do is count her successes rather than all her failures, to get a better picture of her talents and abilities. Samantha also needs to develop a broader picture of what her talents and abilities are so that when she outgrows basketball she will have the necessary confidence in other areas of her life.

Like Samantha, we rarely take time to look at our strengths. If I asked what you dislike most about yourself, you could probably name several disgusting attributes. Instead of focusing on what you don't like, however, let's focus on the positive – what attributes and positives you have to work with.

Shown here are five areas of life. In each category you are to list at least three strengths.

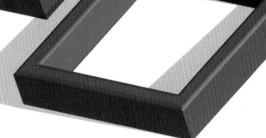

Under 'Achievements' think of awards and honours you've won, offices held, and any other personal successes. Under 'Appearance' guys might list: tall, broad shoulders, athletic appearance; girls might list: attractive, pretty eyes, good figure, clear skin. Under 'Personality' you might include: good sense of humour, calm nature, friendly, pleasant disposition. Under 'Talents and Skills': What natural gifts and aptitudes do you possess? Include musical or artistic ability, cooking, organising, scholastic and athletic abilities. Under 'Character and Spiritual Abilities' list such things as high standards, integrity, honesty and excellent moral values. Serving as a youth leader, on the drama team or as a youth prayer warrior would be spiritual abilities.

Use the chart below to list your strengths:

Achievements

Appearance

Personality

Talents and Skills

Character and Spiritual Abilities

After completing your list contemplate the personal attributes you possess. Then you will recognise that 'we are God's workmanship, created in Christ Jesus to do good works, which God prepared in advance for us to do.' (Ephesians 2:10.) By listing your good qualities, you are not bragging about yourself but simply recognising that God has begun a good work in you. This list of positive traits should help you recognise that you have tremendous potential and many talents with which to work. If you have trouble getting three qualities in each category, ask a friend what they admire in you.

Step 2: Rebuild Your Thought Patterns

A researcher conducted an experiment with three groups of students who were instructed to sink basketball free throws. One group practised daily for twenty days. The second group did not practise at all. The third group threw no balls, but spent twenty minutes a day sitting on the free-throw line visualising that they were sinking free throws. If in their imagination they missed the hoop or failed to make the free throw correctly, they were to correct their aim accordingly. The researcher tested the three groups on the first and last days of the experiment. The first group, who actually practised every day, improved in scoring 24%. The group with no practice showed no improvement. The third group, who practised *only in their minds*, improved in scoring 23%!

Thinking positive thoughts about yourself and your abilities really works!

Wow! Think what this would have done for Samantha on the basketball court! She already possessed natural ability. Her failure during real games was due to negative thinking patterns. Once she made a stupid move during an actual game, she began to think she would always make stupid moves during games and the only time she could be successful was during practice – negative thinking that crippled her ability to play well during a game.

Once negative thoughts take hold, they can be hard to change. We actually look for proof to confirm what we already think about ourselves. So if you think others don't like you, you will look for evidences to prove this.

Some examples of negative self-talk might sound like this:

• I'm so ugly no one will ever like me.
• I can't think of anything to say to others.
• I'll never have a boy/girlfriend.
• The only ones who ever like me are nerds and geeks.
• I can't do anything right.
• No guy (or girl) will ever like me.
• My mother always told me no one would ever want to date me.

The good news is that you can change negative thinking! The first step in changing negative thinking is to become aware of negative thoughts. Begin catching yourself thinking negatively as these thoughts parade through your mind. Then replace negative thinking with positive self-talk.

• I am an attractive person who will attract the right person some day.
• I can smile, be friendly and try to talk to others.
• Some day I will have a boy/girlfriend who will care about me.
• Some day I will meet someone special who will be as interested in me as I am in him/her.
• I choose to ignore negative messages from the past and will focus on positive messages that will help me prepare for healthy dating relationships in the future.

Some experts estimate that 75% of the thoughts we have daily are negative and counter-productive. They work against us instead of helping us build strong self-esteem. Whether we tell ourselves positive or negative thoughts plays a tremendous part in shaping what really happens in our lives.

When Wilma was a young girl her left leg became paralysed. Her doctors told her she would never walk again. But Wilma decided she didn't want to be an Invalid. Instead of saying to herself in dismay, 'I'll never walk again,' she changed that message to 'I will walk again.' Not only did she want to walk again, she wanted to run. She

began telling herself she would be one of the fastest runners in the world. In high school she entered every race but always finished last. But one day Wilma came in next to last. Finally, she won a race, and another and yet another! Less than five years later Wilma Rudolph became the first American woman ever to win three gold medals in the same Olympics.

Wilma's story is an amazing example of the powerful influence our thoughts have over our success or failure in life. Positive, happy thoughts produce chemicals that actually strengthen the body. Negative thoughts produce chemicals that weaken the body. Words like 'I *can't*' or 'I *never*' limit what you can do. Replace all self-defeating thoughts with thoughts that will build your self-esteem. Instead of saying, 'I can't do anything right!' say, 'I am confident I can succeed at whatever I choose to do.' This is more than a meaningless phrase. You are actually refocusing your thoughts. If you tend to get depressed, refocusing will help you get over symptoms common in depression.

Those of you who are really serious about reprogramming your mind may wish to carry little cards on which you have written scriptural or inspirational messages. You can keep such cards in your Bible, your bag or your wallet. You can paste them on mirrors, dashboards, or by a light switch. Here are some Bible verses that will help you meditate

on the worth that God places on you. Romans 8:31-39; Psalms 56:9 (last part); 100:3; 139:14: Isaiah 40:11, 28-31; 41:10; 43:1, 2. If you set your will in the right direction, your emotions and feelings will follow.

According to the experts it takes twenty-one to forty-five days of repetition to change a habit. If you consistently work at rebuilding your thought patterns, you'll feel better about you in twenty-one to forty-five days! Don't expect miracles overnight. Give yourself time to change. Be gentle with yourself while waiting for old attitudes to disappear.

Step 3: Learn to Compensate

If you have a bad knee and through doctor's orders cannot participate in active sports, you can compensate by developing an interest in something else – design web pages, take photographs, produce your own video, or create oil paintings. Or perhaps you're overweight; this does not mean you are inferior. It certainly didn't mean Samantha was inferior. Yet she felt unpopular, clumsy and unattractive – all because she was thirty pounds overweight.

Samantha needs to accept and like herself with the thirty extra pounds of weight, remembering that people come in all shapes and sizes. God did not create one human being and insist we all be the same height and weight. Either Samantha must accept

Know this:
God is God, and God, God.
He made us;
we didn't make him.
We're his people,
his well-tended sheep.

love because of the way that Jesus
our Master has embraced us.
lived one day.

ready to go into action.

arms. H

them, leading the nursing
ewes to good pasture.

herself the way she is or, with the help of a sound weight-loss programme, shed those extra pounds and get a new mental picture of herself as being normal weight.

Don't exaggerate your poor qualities just because others remind you of them. Instead, call attention to some other attribute – beautiful eyes, broad shoulders, naturally curly hair, or some other feature.

When compensating, make sure you know your limitations. Don't stake everything on trying to overcome one handicap. If you were born with one leg shorter than the other, don't weep because you can't take first place in track events. If you are plain in appearance, don't expect to win a beauty contest. Instead, compensate by developing a dazzling personality, by becoming a good listener, and an entertaining conversationalist. Learn how to dress to make the best of your body build, and how to style your hair. Some things just cannot be changed – being tall, small-framed, large-framed, short, blind, deaf, racially different or bowlegged.

A handicap didn't stop Julia Wallace, however. Julia was an Olympic triathlon champion who excelled in three sports. One day she was in a tragic car accident where one leg was severed and her husband killed. To make matters worse, she lost one lung, a kidney and part of her stomach to cancer. After this blow she lost the will to live and attempted suicide twice. Her life as an athlete was over.

A single event changed her life. While shopping in a supermarket she met a friend who invited her to go swimming. Julia was almost insulted by the invitation. She knew she couldn't swim. After all, she had lost a leg. But later that day she found herself in the swimming pool with her friend. By placing a weight between her legs she found she could compensate for the loss of her leg. At this point she stopped saying, 'I've lost a leg and can't swim or participate in sports.' Instead she began training in a wheelchair for distance events and became an Olympic champion all over again – only this time in the Paralympics. She compensated for her handicap and reprogrammed her mind to think like a winner rather than a loser.

If you are honest with yourself about your limitations or things you can't do, you will not need to dislike or resent others if they remind you of them. You are already aware of your limitations. They no longer hurt you, because you can compensate for them. This then frees you from having to invent cover-ups to protect yourself. It frees you to develop genuine friendships since you no longer have to worry so much about yourself. You are free to give, love, accept, respect and share with others. Your limitations cannot ruin your life unless you allow yourself to be defeated.

Step 4: Develop Admirable Qualities

Learn what you need to know to make the best use of the abilities you already possess. Take any one talent listed in step 1, anything you are already good at, and begin to develop it. You'll have to practise, of course, for no one learns a skill without practice. And you must invest the time necessary for such practice. Wishful thinking won't help you become a winner. It certainly wouldn't have helped the all-time basketball great, Pete Maravich.

At a young age, Pete became obsessed with the game. He practised all the time. When his mum came in to kiss him goodnight, she'd find him lying in bed shooting balls at the ceiling. Instead of using the family car he would walk two miles to town so he could dribble all the way, alternating hands to become equally good with both. He also practised dribbling while riding his bike. At the movies he would take an aisle seat and dribble through the film to get more practice time in. He talked his dad into driving the family car at varying speeds while he hung out of the window – still practising his dribbling. Now that's dedication – and also just what it takes to be really good at something!

If you are shy and want to learn how to speak to people confidently, take a speech class or join a club that will force you to do just that. If you are plain in appearance, learn what you can about posture, social graces, clothes and conversation. If you wear thick glasses or cannot make the gymnastics team but have the ability to write short stories, take a class that will help you develop that talent.

Samantha needs to do this. At 14, much of her world revolves around basketball. But basketball can't carry her forever. She needs to think of developing a new skill, another talent or ability that can serve as a self-esteem booster after basketball season, after school. Samantha needs to be open to new experiences and get out of the rut she created for herself.

As you develop some new skill and practise doing it well, you will gain confidence in yourself. Skills will give you the self-confidence you need to be optimistic, to show friendliness and be patient with the disagreeable. The confidence a boy gains on the football field can help him be self-assured when talking with girls. Serving on the school newspaper staff will help a girl overcome feelings of embarrassment because she is taller than most of the other girls.

All-round personal adjustment improves through the development of talents and abilities. Gradually you will emerge from behind your cover-ups to become a more genuine and interesting person. But don't expect miracles overnight. Give yourself time to change. You can rid yourself of fear and thoughts of failure only by replacing them with confidence. So be gentle with yourself while waiting for old attitudes to slough off.

Step 5: Never Compare Yourself with Others

The biggest single cause of low self-esteem is comparing oneself with someone else. We tend to judge and measure ourselves not by our own standard but against someone else's.

Samantha constantly compared her heavier, more muscular legs to other girls' legs, and her wider waistline to their tiny ones. This constant comparison really took its toll on her self-esteem. Samantha was particularly envious of Kate, who was tall and willowy and moved across the court with grace. Even her hair bounced gracefully. And she was pretty and popular too – and class president to boot. When Samantha compared herself to all that, she felt even worse.

As long as you do this, you will always come out second best. The end result of such reasoning is that we believe we are not worthy, that we don't deserve happiness or success, and that it would be out of place for us to express our own abilities or talents.

You do not have to look or act like anyone else. Be yourself. You are not in competition with any another person on Earth. The truth is you are not inferior; you are not superior. You are simply you, equal to others. And that you is unique. So stop comparing yourself with others.

Step 6: Give of Yourself to Others

Our own problems seem less threatening when we help someone else handle theirs. One study showed that those who get involved in helping others experience relief from depression and headaches as well as other aches and pains. Researchers call it 'helper's high'. This has to be something you want to do, however. If someone forces you or 'assigns'

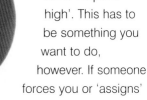

you to help and you do it only because you have to, you will experience little benefit. And you also have to have close personal contact with those you help; in other words, be closely involved.

For every one of you who feels rejected, unloved and unworthy, there is someone else who is worse off than you. Get busy and visit the sick, sign up for volunteer work at the hospital or hospice, listen to someone with a problem, feed the homeless, run an errand for a friend, collect clothing or food for a needy family, work with a youth centre. The world is full of lonely, hurting people who need someone to care about them. And while you are doing all this, your own inadequacy won't seem so important. The best medicine for self-pity is to give of yourself to others.

Step 7: Ask God to Make Something Beautiful Out of Your Life

Kathy became the object of much concern in her early teens. She continually criticised herself. When drying dishes, she would throw down the towel in disgust and say, 'I can't even dry dishes right!' Then she would go to her room and spend hours berating herself, depressed and isolated from everyone. Her lack of response to those who tried to help her soon destroyed many friendships and caused her more hurt. As this problem increased, she gave

evidence of living in an imaginary world.

One day her youth pastor asked her if she felt God was concerned about her problems. 'Yeah, I think he is,' Kathy responded.

'Do you think God has the answers to your problems?' he asked.

'I guess he does,' she responded hesitantly.

'Would you like to discover some of God's answers to what you're dealing with?'

'Sure,' Kathy said.

The pastor then asked her to answer two questions: 'Is there some boy at school whom you like very much but who doesn't seem interested in you?' and 'If you were standing in front of a mirror and had the power to change anything about the way you look, would you use that power?'

Kathy's answer to both questions was, 'Yes!' She had a long-standing interest in a boy at school, but he showed no interest in her. To the second question, her response was quite emphatic: 'I'd change my height. I'm too tall.'

Her height had been the source of much concern and this became painfully acute when Kathy concluded that the boy she liked did not return her affection because he was shorter than she. This accounted for her continual self-criticism and the creation of an imaginary world in which she was shorter than the boy.

After learning about her frustration and resentment over being 'too tall', the pastor suggested that many of her problems stemmed from a deep distrust and bitterness towards God. This idea shocked Kathy. She had never associated bitterness towards herself with bitterness towards God. As she thought about it, however, it became quite clear to her that this was actually the case.

Now the pastor shared several insights to show the value God placed on her appearance:

1. God described exactly how she was to look even before she was born. 'I will praise, you, for I am fearfully and wonderfully made; marvellous are your works, and that my soul knows very well. My frame was not hidden from you, when I was made in secret, and skilfully wrought in the lowest parts of the earth. Your eyes saw my substance, being yet unformed. And in your book they all were written, the days fashioned for me, when as yet there were none of them.' (Psalm 139:14-16, NKJV.)

2. She learned that God's intention for her appearance was logical if he had something special he wanted her to accomplish. 'What sorrow awaits those who argue with their Creator. Does a clay pot argue with its maker? Does the clay dispute with the one who shapes it, saying, "Stop, you're doing it wrong!" Does the pot exclaim, "How clumsy can you be?" ' (Isaiah 45:9, NLT.)

3. Kathy came to understand that God was not finished with her yet. 'Being confident of this very thing, that he who has begun a good work in you will complete it until the day of Jesus Christ.' (Philippians 1:6, NKJV.)

4. She also learned that her feelings of inferiority over being too tall were caused by comparing herself with others. 'We should not dare to class ourselves or compare ourselves with any of those who put forward their own claims. What fools they are to measure themselves by themselves, to find in themselves their own standard of comparison.' (2 Corinthians 10:12, NEB.)

5. Her pastor explained that her outward appearance was only a 'frame' around inner qualities. When we purchase a picture, our primary concern is the picture, not the frame. The frame only enhances the quality of the picture. In the same way, Kathy's outward appearance was only to emphasise and enhance her inner qualities which God wanted to develop in her. 'Do not let your adornment be merely outward – arranging the hair, wearing gold, or putting on fine apparel – rather let it be the hidden person of the heart, with the incorruptible beauty of a gentle and quiet spirit, which is very precious in the sight of God.' (1 Peter 3:3, 4, NKJV.)

It took Kathy a little time, but after a while she gained insights into the subject of self-worth. The pastor took her a step further – to acknowledge her bitterness towards God for the way he had made her. She also asked God to forgive her for not recognising his workmanship in her.

Secondly, she thanked God for making her just the way she was. She even thanked God for her height!

Now she was inwardly free to commit to the Lord her interest in the boy at school. True commitment involves thanking the Lord whatever the outcome may be. She purposed to thank the Lord for whatever response this boy would have to her.

A sense of personal freedom was immediately evident in Kathy's personality. Later her father, a doctor, visited the pastor and with tears of joy exclaimed, 'I want to thank the Lord and you for what happened to my daughter. I have never seen her so happy.'

If you've had negative attitudes about yourself, ask God to forgive your past attitudes – resentment of your appearance, lack of talents and abilities. Ask God to forgive you for the bitterness you have held towards his creation – you.

When you are over this obstacle, thank God for creating you just the way

you are. This will not be an easy step. You may feel that you cannot thank God for creating you tall when you hate being tall. You might think that that this would make you a hypocrite, that you can't thank God when you don't feel thankful yet. But you can do it. Giving thanks is an act of the will. Being thankful is a feeling or emotion. You can discipline your feelings of thankfulness and give thanks even though you don't feel like it. Do not let your emotions control you. Set your will in the right direction, and in time your emotions will follow.

Kathy finally got to the point where she could do this. She went to the mirror every day and said with a grin, 'You're OK, kid.' At first she had trouble looking herself in the eye, let alone smiling at herself. But rather than giving up, she winked at herself and smiled every time. In addition, she turned her negative attitude over to God. She began thanking God for creating her just the way she was. She looked over the list of talents and abilities she had and decided to develop her artistic abilities. To prove how serious she was about making a change, the next term she signed up for an art class. She also began working with a teen drama group at the church which presented programmes to schools and youth groups in her area. By the time Kathy was 15, she looked, felt and acted like a different person. She partnered with God to make a difference, and came out a winner.

When you know that God accepts you and loves you just the way you are, you don't have to feel as though you must change, act sanctimonious, become a religious fanatic or even act pious in order for God to love you. He wants you as you are. The only things God dislikes are the things that would destroy you. He is interested only in helping you leave destructive attitudes behind.

If you take God at his word, believing that you are loved and worthwhile, then you have laid a solid foundation from which to operate. You will have a firm centre to your life. You will be free to put the same kind of love and respect you have for yourself to work in your relationships with the opposite sex. Remember, you can never experience a true love relationship with someone else unless you first take care of any inferiority problems within you. This does not mean that you have no room for improvement. There will always be room for improvement. You recognise you're not perfect, but acceptable to God and others. A beautiful sense of peace and relief should come over you at this point. Not only does God count you as acceptable, but he stands ready to work miracles in you, to change your worst failures into successes.

You don't have to be born with talent, ability or money to develop self-esteem. Oprah Winfrey, the world's most popular TV talk show host, was born to poor, unwed teenage parents in rural Mississippi. During her teens she was sexually molested and at the age of 14 gave birth to a premature baby who died. With such a beginning, she wasn't exactly served popularity and success on a silver platter.

But Oprah had an indomitable spirit, an unshakeable faith, a belief that she was born to greatness, and she worked hard to turn this belief into reality. To a college graduating class she once said, 'It doesn't matter what you've been through, where you come from, who your parents are, or what your social or economic status is. None of that matters. What matters is what you do with what you've got at your fingertips.'

Take the talents and abilities God gave you. Work hard to develop them. Make something out of what you have. This is exactly what Oprah did. Now she is

one of the world's most influential women. It didn't come easily. She worked and worked hard for it. All of this originated in her thinking processes. She thought she could do it. She believed in herself and kept pushing herself until she achieved success in her field.

Over a period of time you too can develop a more solid sense of worth, even if you have a poor self-concept right now. When this happens you will be able to make a more realistic appraisal of your abilities and combine this with appreciation for your own worth without feeling conceited. You will be able to maintain your standards with a degree of assurance without bowing to the opinions of your peer group. You will be able to make a realistic analysis of your own limitations without irrational self-condemnation.

You will be able to view yourself as a person of worth, one liked by the majority of others. Such an opinion of yourself will show up in positive, well-adjusted behaviour. You will suffer neither from delusions of grandeur regarding your worth nor undue humility. You will see yourself for what you are and value yourself in accurate and realistic terms. When you have achieved this, you will experience an inner peace.

The bottom-line once again: if you possess high self-worth, you will be more likely to feel like a million dollars. If you feel like a million dollars, you are more likely to act and think like a million dollars. If you feel, think and act like a million dollars, you are more likely to attract those who also feel, act and think like a million dollars.

Smart Love

chapter *two*

Nicole tearfully shared her story. 'Andrew and I began dating and fell madly in love as soon as we met. For three months we spent every spare minute together. We were so in love it was difficult to keep our hands off each other because the physical attraction was so powerful. Then we began to argue a lot and get on each other's nerves. After discussing it, we decided it was due to the sexual tension of going so far but no further. We thought the arguments would stop if we got married. For two months after we were married, everything was perfect. Then we began having more fights than ever and now we are miserable.'

Married after three months of dating, Nicole and Andrew discovered that the initial rush of romantic feelings and sexual excitement doesn't continue forever. Four years and two children later, one disillusioned and angry couple separated. Unfortunately, Nicole and Andrew are not unique. Many couples marry before they have ridden out the wave of red-hot feelings that begin to burn during dating. Unless they learn to slow the pace, they will find themselves married to a totally unsuitable person. Society is quick to label this as another marriage failure when in reality it is a *dating* failure. There is no such thing as instant love. Strong, lasting relationships must be paced over a long period of time where 'getting to know you' is the major theme. This is why, for successful dating, I stress slowing down.

Part 4: The Game Plan

When I asked one teen to define the word *date*, she told me that she thinks of a date as a special experience when a guy calls a girl and they set a time and place to go somewhere together. They dress according to the occasion . . . and so on. Yes, that certainly is a date, but the term *dating* here refers not so much to going out on a date as the relationship between a guy and a girl.

A date, then, is a special type of friendship between two persons of the opposite sex that *may* lead to a steady relationship, love and eventually to marriage. Note that dating begins with friendship. Love and all the romantic stuff follow the developing friendship. Too often young people break the rules and get things backwards. They fall in love before becoming friends.

Think for a minute about the rules that control a sporting event. The rules state that the game or event will take place on a field or court within certain boundaries. The game also takes place within predetermined time frames. Certain rules govern the game which all players respect since an umpire or a referee limits foul play. The objective of most games is to display skill and win.

Dating will exist as long as males and females enter into relationships. The better each player understands and respects the

rules, the better the game they'll play. Unfortunately in dating, no outside force magically appears to monitor a couple's behaviour or calls 'foul' or 'time out'. But if both consult the rulebook for guidelines, and play fairly, the dating game can be a lot of fun and bring great rewards.

Just as a game of cricket or football contains innings or halves, so does dating. It progresses through seven stages. Each stage has a function and purpose. If any stage is rushed or skipped, there is a gap in the development of the relationship, and problems result. Let's take a close look at those stages.

Stage 1: Friendship

At the friendship stage, you get to know one another in a non-romantic way while participating in school, church and recreational activities. Most of these are group as opposed to couple activities. The friendship stage is more casual and less emotional than the later dating stages, since no romantic or sexual overtones exist. Dating usually refers to romantic involvement. When a couple leaves the group and pairs off, they are usually 'dating'.

Friends can see each other at their worst – when upset over a bad grade, covered with sweat after a game, depressed over the loss of a friendship. They get to know how the other responds to the ups and downs of life. There may be some flirting, which often happens in boy-girl relationships. But there is a fine line that friends choose not to cross.

Friends of the opposite sex are comfortable doing what they would do with same-sex friends. Because it's not a dating relationship, there is less 'game playing' and few, if any, sexual overtones. Friendships are definitely less stressful than dating relationships. Friends are often more honest with each other than are lovers and it is possible for friends to become closer emotionally than lovers.

Becoming friends before you begin dating makes a lot of sense. If you fall in love too fast and it doesn't work out, you will rarely be friends again. But if you take your time getting to know someone as a friend first, and let love grow slowly and gradually, you are more likely to have a friend for life, whether you marry this person or not. Furthermore, love affairs that flare up instantly usually burn out just as fast. And it is much more likely in such a relationship that you will be judged on superficial qualities like your appearance rather than your character.

Make no mistake. It is harder to remain friends than lovers. The easy thing to do when you find someone you are attracted to is to shift into high gear, give it all you've got and go for it. It is much more difficult to take your foot off the accelerator and move slowly. Strong dating relationships spring from strong friendships. The more you know about being a friend, the better you will be at the dating game.

Stage 2: Casual Dating

At this stage, two persons who have become good friends move away from the group to enjoy couple activities. They know they share common interests and now enjoy spending time together as a couple. Both are free to date others, since the degree of emotional commitment between them is low and they do not consider themselves to be 'in love'. Pleasant times are shared along with a friendship that may hold promise for the future.

Should they continue to enjoy one another's company, the relationship will probably include handholding and other romantic gestures. A couple should remain at the friendship and casual dating stages for six to twelve months, finding out about one another's likes and dislikes and learning about backgrounds, habits and behaviours. If what they learn at this unhurried pace checks out with what they are looking for, they can slowly move into the next stage.

Stage 3: Special Dating

Special dating is an in-between stage that means there is a growing attachment between them but they are not yet ready for the commitment of going steady. They spend more time together but are not officially 'going steady'.

It can also refer to a special event coming up at school. Sue has had her eye on a special someone for several weeks and has hoped he would ask her out. She can hardly believe it when she answers the phone and hears his voice. Butterflies flit around in the pit of her stomach as they small talk for a few minutes. When he finally gets around to asking her if she will go out with him, she casually says she'd like to. The minute he hangs up, she calls twenty of her friends to break the news. Sue buys a new dress and waits not so patiently for the big day. When it finally arrives, she spends hours preparing her nails, hair and makeup. This also is special dating.

Stage 4: Steady Dating

In steady dating two young people commit to dating only each other (or that's the way it is supposed to be, and is, as far as they know). They will spend more time together than in casual dating. For the first time, words like *commitment* and *exclusive dating* come into play.

This is an important stage during which a relationship can be thoroughly tested because of the amount of time they spend together. Steady dating tests their ability to remain committed to one relationship. At this stage a couple usually *think* they are in love but still may not be certain. Here they gain more confidence in interacting with a person of the opposite sex. They also get to know themselves better, as well as how they are perceived by the opposite sex.

Many personality traits can be observed during this stage. Is he a good listener or conversationalist? Does she have a good sense of humour? What about manners, thoughtfulness? It's during this stage that one can observe character traits such as dependability, spirituality, and maturity. Is he able to hear the feelings behind the words? Does she pout or use the silent treatment? Can hurt feelings be addressed openly, or are they stifled and avoided? How is anger handled and conflicts solved? Can differences of opinion be settled satisfactorily? Does one always win and the other lose?

When going steady is used correctly, it provides a serious trial period during which a couple can make an intelligent decision about their compatibility. It forms a natural bridge to the engaged-to-be-engaged stage and a formal engagement.

Stage 5: Engaged-to-be-Engaged

This term refers to the period between going steady and formal engagement when a couple begins discussing the *possibility* of a permanent relationship and makes *tentative plans* towards marriage. The understanding is private and personal and not final or binding. They make no formal announcement, set no wedding date, and no wedding plans are in progress. They do, however, plan to get married and talk of a future time someday when they will get married. Someday when we finish school . . . Someday when we have enough money . . . Someday after we have children . . .

Much of what used to be discussed only during a formal engagement is open here for discussion. This should reduce the number of broken engagements. It can also take pressure off couples who are not ready to announce plans to marry.

During this stage a couple can take an in-depth look at their personalities. They are more sure than they were when going steady that they have found genuine love, but still nothing is final or binding. It is now, before a formal engagement, that a couple should pursue relationship counselling by a pastor or counsellor and thoroughly explore their compatibility.

This is the last period – before a formal commitment has been announced – to bail out of a relationship without making it really uncomfortable for everyone involved. Love feelings are extraordinarily high, and they are more sure of the relationship's lasting.

Stage 6: Formal Engagement

The formal engagement follows the 'someday' talk of stage 5. It brings a deep sense of commitment and belonging that doesn't come with going steady or pre-engagement.

Several things separate the formal engagement from the engaged-to-be-engaged stage. A formal engagement serves as public notice to friends and family that a couple intends to marry. It provides an opportunity for others to adjust to the fact that a new family unit will form and a new member will join the extended family. A public announcement strengthens the commitment. The more people who know about the engagement, the more likely the couple will follow through and marry. *Thus a secret engagement is no engagement* at all. **Somebody is fooling someone about something!**

Traditionally the prospective groom presents an engagement ring or gift to his prospective bride which solemnises the engagement. This gift of love further strengthens the couple's commitment.

The third thing that makes an engagement formal is that the wedding date is set and *wedding plans are in progress*. Becoming engaged can be so satisfying and thrilling in itself that many couples do not pay enough attention to what it really stands for in relationship to their future. But engagement is not an end in itself: it's a commitment to marry. Therefore, plans for a wedding need to proceed. An engagement with no wedding date in sight destroys the value of engagement.

Engagements should not be long, because the couple's desire for intimacy will increase. Expressions of affection will become more intense because they are in a transition period from courtship to marriage. Because of this urgency to fulfil the natural desire for unrestricted intimacy, I recommend a short engagement of six to nine months. If a couple has spent two years getting to know one another before the engagement, this will be sufficient.

This is the last opportunity to check out the future partner before being locked in for life. Now they check and recheck their previous evaluations. This is the time to bring out any unresolved differences or reveal any hidden secrets. Remember also that engagement is not a sealed contract that forever links a couple's destiny. It is possible that as a couple get to know each other better they will decide not to marry. As many as 40-50% of all engagements are broken. As difficult as a broken engagement is, it is better than a broken marriage.

The most important task to be accomplished during engagement is not the planning of a wedding, but premarital guidance with a qualified pastor or professional counsellor. Every couple should have a minimum of six sessions prior to marriage.

Stage 7: Marriage

The seventh and final stage is marriage. Many people don't think of marriage as a stage of dating, but the friendship and love established during dating is the basis for a strong marriage. Marriage is final and binding. It is different from the previous six stages in that legal procedures and courts are necessary to dissolve the relationship through divorce. It is similar in that it should be a continuation of the romantic phase of the courtship evidenced through affection, attention, respect, courtesy and fun together.

Intimate Strangers

Unfortunately most couples go through these stages out of sequence.

They jump to steady dating or engaged-to-be-engaged without ever establishing real friendship first.

They are so eager to fall in love, they skip the preliminaries and jump into the romantic stuff.

Frequently I ask married couples if they consider themselves to be 'best friends'. Such an idea sounds bizarre to many, because they never thought about whether they *liked* one another. They just fell in love and got married. But liking one another and being friends goes a long way in contributing to happiness in marriage. All the romantic stuff does not necessarily produce lasting love if an enduring friendship has not first been established.

I recommend that every couple date two years prior to engagement. One whole year should ideally be spent at Stages 1, 2 and 3, slowly and carefully nurturing a friendship first. During the second year the 'masks' begin to slip and personality and character flaws emerge that had been hidden until then.

Many people are Great Pretenders and can successfully mask negative behaviours for a year. Such game playing can rarely go beyond that, however. But when a couple rushes to become engaged in three, four, five, six, seven or eight months, they haven't allowed sufficient time for the masks to slip. They pledge themselves to a virtual stranger, someone who may turn out to be stranger than they ever wanted to know.

Rushing through the stages of dating is so exciting that infatuation stays alive when it should begin to fade after a few weeks. As the euphoria intensifies, the thrill of being a twosome and doing enjoyable things together blinds the couple to reality. I have taught hundreds of dating and marriage seminars, read hundreds of books on the family, written twenty-five books, and counselled hundreds of couples whose marriages were in serious trouble.

The major contributing factor to the unhappiness of most couples was skipping steps and rushing too fast into marriage.

A study from Kansas State University proves my point. Researchers found a strong correlation between the length of time a couple spent dating their current spouse and marital satisfaction. Couples who had dated for *more than two years* scored consistently high on marital satisfaction, while couples who had dated for shorter periods scored in a wide range from very high to very low.[1] When couples date two years or longer, they have a much greater likelihood of having a great marriage.

Nothing gets my attention faster than hearing a couple talk about marriage who have not completed the two-year dating time frame. They are about to pledge 'till death us do part' and have seriously underestimated the need to establish a solid friendship first. And yet when I teach dating seminars on school campuses I am confronted by zillions of young people aged 13 and up who lay claim to Stage 5 dating! They are new to the school; it is early in the school year; yet when asked, the vast majority say they are engaged-to-be-engaged. There is nothing wrong with Stage 5. It is a positive stage through which all young adults should pass (when the time is right); but if you are only 13, 14, 15, 16, 17 or 18 years of age and you are already at Stage 5, how far from marriage are you? Two short steps! At 13, 14, 15, 16, 17 or 18 years of age, are you ready for the responsibilities that come with marriage? Hardly.

Every couple, regardless of their ages, circumstances or experience, need to take two full

years
to
evaluate
their
compatibility
and readiness for
marriage. When they
do, they have a
significantly higher likelihood
of making a good choice. The
most important advice I give in
this book can be summed up in
three words: TAKE YOUR TIME!

Pushing, Rushing and Other Foul Play

Rushing too fast through the stages of dating causes two problems for a couple. First, there is a strong possibility that they will never learn how to settle conflicts or handle power struggles. Immature couples tend to resolve their conflicts in bed. Their relationship lacks depth, and the first hint of difficulty signals a serious threat – so they head for bed, which makes things better (temporarily). The second problem is that there isn't time for infatuation or the romantic glow to fade and reality to set in.

Developing a relationship with someone of the opposite sex is so electrifying it becomes difficult to spread relationship building over enough time for real depth to develop. A compelling desire to spend as much time together as possible immediately propels the couple towards physical intimacies and intercourse.

Because of the intense attraction between the sexes, it seems more exciting to be 'in love' and all that goes with it than to exercise self-discipline, slow things down, think things through, and pace the relationship properly. It is more thrilling to be going steady, be in love or about to be married than to be 'only friends'. There is a sense of security in 'belonging' to someone.

Both sexes are guilty of pushing the stages forward, but they do so for different reasons. Girls do it for the security it brings. A guy may take her out once and she tells all her friends that he asked her to go steady. He said nothing about going steady! Why does she do this? Most girls long for security, love, and eventually marriage and children. She'll never fulfil that longing at Stages 1, 2 and 3, so she pushes for 4 or higher.

Boys do it as well, but for an entirely different reason. Depending on his morals, he'll probably push a girl sexually as far as she will let him go. If she's a girl with high moral principles, he's not going to get far with her if they are only in a 'casual relationship' (Stage 2). So he tells her he loves her and asks her to go steady because he knows (or hopes) that if they are going steady and claim to be 'in love' she'll let him go further. Once a guy and a girl get into a relationship, there is a lot of 'game playing' that goes on. Each, with a hidden agenda, attempts, in a backwards way, to know the other. They become sexually involved and later attempt to build a friendship. Be smarter than such people. Go *forwards* through the stages of dating, not backwards. And take it slowly!

Part 5: Great Dates – Where to Go and What to Do

Peter: My first date with Pat. A spaghetti dinner and a Christian music concert. I can't wait. Pat is some girl. What a night!

At dinner:

Pat: (to herself) Boy, he has lousy table manners. And he isn't much of a conversationalist, either.

Peter: (to himself) Pat isn't nearly as much fun as I thought she'd be. She ordered a lot of food, and at these prices she'd better finish every bite. (Out loud) Pass the bread.

Pat: Here.

At the concert:

Peter: Good music, isn't it?

Pat: Yeah, really good.

On the drive home:

Peter: I really enjoyed that music tonight.

Pat: Me, too.

Peter: G'night.

Pat: G'night.

Later:

Peter: (to himself) That will be the last time I take Pat out. She's a bore.

Pat: (to herself) I wouldn't go out with Peter again if he begged me.

Maybe you have had a date similar to that of Peter and Pat. You looked forward to it, spent a good deal of money getting ready for it, and had a rotten time. Afterwards you couldn't work out why. The combination of personalities has a lot to do with it, but so does where you go and what you do.

Basically, there are two kinds of dates – and I don't mean good ones and bad ones: (1) the spectator date, during which you sit while being entertained, and (2) participation dates, in which you are actively involved in recreation that is provided for you or you create yourselves.

Spectator Dates

Spectator dates include going to movies, plays, concerts, and sports events, watching TV or DVDs and listening to music. Spectator dates are popular because most people enjoy spectator entertainment and on first dates there is less stress involved in trying to keep the conversation going. Furthermore, literally everyone already knows how to be a spectator – sit and watch. That's another plus.

On the down side, spectator dates can be expensive. And the main purpose of dating – getting to know one another – is defeated, since watching someone else perform allows for little interaction between the two persons on the date. Furthermore, we all do too much sitting and watching already. Spectating does very little to raise feelings of self-worth, requires very little creativity, and will probably make you tire of each other faster than during other kinds of activity. I can almost guarantee that if your dates are mostly spectator ones, you'll be so bored with one another that within six months you'll break up.

Watching TV or DVDs or listening to music is particularly dangerous because they involve being alone, usually with the lights low. Hours spent alone like this weaken resistance to sexual temptation and rapidly hurl a couple towards premature expressions of physical intimacy. Several short spectator dates are safer than long or all-day dates.

Participation Dates

The second type, the participation date, is totally different and includes such activities as playing miniature golf or tennis, canoeing, sailing, hiking, visiting a museum or a zoo, craft projects, or planning and cooking a meal together. Such dates are seldom boring. Instead, participating together in an activity encourages the expression of creative abilities, reaffirms feelings of worth, usually costs less, and allows the couple to explore likes and dislikes. Each can develop new skills and abilities as well as gain insights into the other. Participation dates also

provide fewer opportunities for petting or sexual temptation.

Participation dates call for an investment from both parties. Too many young people are lazy and uncreative and would take the easy way out – they would sit and watch something rather than plan an activity. Would you prefer a picnic or a walk to sitting at home and watching TV? Of course, some people are too self-conscious for participation dates. They don't think their skills are good enough. With a little ingenuity, however, everyone can come up with activities they can enjoy.

Here are some ideas. Some require athletic ability but many don't. Sports such as tennis, golf, swimming, ping-pong, croquet, rollerblading, jogging and hiking. Do-at-home activities such as craft projects; making ice-cream, bread, or a gourmet dinner; board games. Or explore a housing development, go picture taking, ride bikes, throw Frisbees, collect shells from the beach, hand out Christian literature, or visit a nursing home.

You can spend money to make a date unforgettable, but it isn't necessary. Designing a creative date with a personal touch is the secret.

Smart Love

chapter two

Cheap Dates for Cheapskates

Here are some creative ideas in order to spark some of your own:

Purchase outlandish outfits at a bargain store and take a stroll through the park, stopping to eat a picnic lunch.

Rent a bicycle built for two, decorate it, and ride it through a local park or scenic area. Invent some games to play while riding.

Make your own kites and fly them.

Produce your own DVD. Invite friends over for a première showing. Serve popcorn.

Purchase a bag of balloons. Go to the park and blow them up. Tie ribbons to them and give them to passers-by.

Walk through a cemetery and read inscriptions together for a surprising glimpse into your town's history.

Take a bus trip round your town and see how much you can discover.

Spend an evening going through one another's family albums, guessing who's who.

Our son Rodney was always able to think of creative ways to date. Once he invited a girlfriend for a motorcycle ride and a picnic in the woods. It rained that day, but they went anyway, built themselves a small fire in an enclosure, and ate as they huddled by the fire under a tarpaulin he rigged up. They had a good time and got to know one another better, despite the adverse circumstances.

Participation dates are not only more fun but they also stimulate creativity, are educational, tend to be more helpful to others, are more relaxing, are less selfish in nature, and provide unique and unhurried ways for a couple to get to know one another better. Look at a couple who chooses to cook a meal together rather than going to the movies. As they discuss their menu, they learn about one another's food preferences. By shopping together for food items, they can learn a lot about the other's spending habits and how money is valued. While preparing the meal they learn how they work together and whether they complement each other's abilities. After the meal, clearing up provides extended time for fun as well as determining whether they are a good match as a couple.

Most participation dates are inexpensive or free. Some may be too inhibited to try a participation date, and for such people participation activities may not be ideal on a first date. But many people welcome the change of pace, and this type of involvement and interaction with another person will certainly perk up a relationship between a couple who date regularly.

Since participation dates offer more advantages than spectator dates, they should make up a larger portion of your dating activities. You may not always be able to handle one on a first date, but if you can – go for it!

A couple can control the progression of their relationship when they choose their dating activities wisely by frequently including participation dates and by limiting their time alone together.

Part 6: **Who's Going to Make the First Move?**

Girls have their own ideas about how they would like to be approached for a date. Most girls would rather not have you move in without advance warning and – boom – ask them out. In most cases a girl would prefer that you paid her a little attention first. Call her several times, and make small talk. In other words, a girl would rather have you be friendly first and work up to asking her out.

Many girls nowadays think it is all right to call a boy and ask for a date, but most boys still prefer to do most of the asking. Girls who become too aggressive in dealing with guys scare them off. (Guys are already a little scared of girls as it is! Remember, until guys are in their early twenties they remain emotionally about two years behind girls. This is the reason some boys don't date at all. Girls often forget that every time a guy asks a girl out he puts his ego on the line

and risks being rejected. It hurts to be rejected, and, consequently, many guys will not take the risk unless they have good reason to believe that the girl will accept.)

But times are changing, and a girl has many options today that she didn't have a few years ago. Some schools initiate a 'reverse date' in which the girls invite the guys. This can be a lot of fun and a real opportunity for a girl to date a fellow she's had her eye on.

Usually, however, when a girl makes the first move, she has to be very subtle or find a way to make the guy think it was all his idea.

A girl can use some subtle ways to show a boy she is interested in him. She can arrange to sit near or across from him, try to catch his eye and smile. Eyes can convey a lot – but don't overdo it! He can get the message from gentle hints. If you are having a conversation with a guy, pay close attention when he speaks. Act interested in what he says. This impresses a man. Sometimes a friend can pass on information in the right manner. Make sure this person drops hints tactfully, or you might be worse off than when you started!

Join the same club or take up the same activities he participates in. Ask for help with homework or a project you are working on.

Plan a party. Participate in group dates, and go where young people meet each other – parties, sporting events or church activities. Get together with a couple of friends and plan an afternoon picnic. Invite four or five others to join you. (Hint: keep the numbers uneven to avoid the tension of having to pair up.)

Whether you are a guy or a girl, choose someone who is about the same age and stage of dating as you. During the teen years you should not be dating anyone more than two years older or younger than you. When you choose someone approximately where you are along the dating road, both of you can learn and grow together with as little pain and embarrassment as possible.

What Do Guys Like?

What do guys really want from girls? What goes on in their heads about girls, and what do they expect from girls?

Good questions. Young women understand very little about young men and vice versa. Before I answer these questions directly, let's consider some of the social and psychological feelings of a boy between the ages of 13 and 18. A boy reaches puberty between the ages of 13 and 14. At this time his reproductive system begins to produce sperm cells. Typically, his height will spurt up and his attitudes will change. Cars become very important to him, and yet he cannot drive. He cannot vote or drink until he turns 18. He can't marry, enlist, borrow money, drink, or make his own decisions, but he must continue in school, whether he wants to or not. He often feels suspended in time and space. And he remains in this state as long as he is financially dependent upon his parents. During this time he has neither the privileges of childhood nor the freedom of adulthood.

Uncertain about himself, he lacks self-confidence – although he would never admit this and may work hard to cover up his true feelings. Nevertheless, they are there. In addition, he feels unsure of himself, of his sexual desires, and about girls. He is also unsure of life and is searching for identity and purpose.

Boys should not be ashamed of puberty. Instead they should be happy, proud and challenged with the fact that they stand at the entrance to manhood. What they are experiencing is normal and natural. Girls and parents should try to understand boys when they are going through this period of uncertainty.

Now that we understand this

much, let's look at what guys like and want from girls. Let's establish one thing: Boys do like girls! During the early-teen years they enjoy boy-girl gatherings, but they tend to stay together in groups because of their inexperience with the opposite sex. For the most part, they hesitate to show their interest in boy-girl relationships. Around the age of 14 boys tend to lose interest in girls for a while. Some do not show interest again until they are 17 or 18 years of age. Others date a series of girls that change with the seasons. Break-ups appear to bother them little, if at all.

Other boys at ages 15 and 16 like group gatherings. They feel more secure when they do not have to depend entirely on their own abilities for conversation and social skills. Still others feel most comfortable in 'brother-sister' relationships. Our son Mark had several of these during his mid-teen years, and they were good for him. He learned about girls and formed true friendships with no commitment. Boys enjoy such companionship but will drop the 'sister' immediately if she begins to move out of the sister role.

A few boys will rush into going steady and heavy relationships. In most cases those who do are insecure. They lack confidence in their ability to meet others, carry on a conversation, and interact, so they choose a steady relationship, thereby sheltering themselves from new circumstances that might underscore their feelings of inadequacy and self-

consciousness.

Although most mid-teen boys enjoy being with girls, the majority are not ready for serious relationships as girls often wish they were. At 18 Mark began going with a girl of the same age who really pushed him for marriage. He staved her off well, and they continued their rocky relationship for two more years. Once I asked him if she pushed him as hard for marriage at 20 as she had done when she was 18. 'Oh, no,' Mark responded. 'She hardly even mentions it now.' How much their interests had changed in two years! They were both beginning to find themselves and no longer needed to look to marriage as the solution to all their problems.

What Do Girls Like?

Just as young ladies want to know what boys like, so young men want to know what girls look for in them. Let's consider the development of a girl during puberty, which she reaches at about 12.6 years of age. Her monthly menstrual cycle begins, and she undergoes a major change in height and attitudes. Life means something different to her since she can produce children. She now becomes openly interested in boys.

Some girls reach puberty at age 11 or even earlier. These girls become interested in boys two years before the boys show any interest in them. This often places a girl in an uncomfortable and embarrassing social and emotional position. Her parents and peers may call her 'boy mad' when she is merely responding to the changes taking place inside her. She is leaving the little girl behind and entering young womanhood.

Girls do like boys, and they will make it known in a multitude of subtle and not so subtle ways. But basically girls like boys who are neat, clean and well-groomed. They like young men who are honest and do what they say they plan to do. They want a guy who comes at the time he says he will and not an hour early or late. They like guys who contribute to interesting conversations, not leaving it entirely to them. They do not enjoy young men who only talk or brag about themselves or who get jealous or possessive when the girl talks to other boys.

They also like decent, mannerly guys who respect them as a person. They prefer boys who respect their moral decisions and do not persistently push for more. They like fun-loving guys who can tease but know when to stop. They like guys who can give honest compliments, who appreciate their attractiveness but who also appreciate their inner qualities. They want to date courteous guys who know their manners. They prefer guys who don't drink, smoke or use drugs. They very much dislike guys who swear, are crude and brash, or who tell dirty jokes in their presence to prove how 'cool' they are.

All Grown Up and Ready to Date?

There are two kinds of age: physical and emotional. Your emotional age reveals how mature you are and is far more important than your physical age. Differences in emotional age vary greatly. Some 13 year olds are as emotionally stable as some 18 year olds. Some 18 year olds act more like 13 year olds.

The trend today is for young people to date at earlier and earlier ages. Many young people say they have already dated by the age of 13 to 14. When you take into consideration that the average girl reaches puberty at 12.6 and the average boy at 13.5,

a considerable number are dating and going steady before they reach puberty! This is ridiculous.

Girls between the ages of 12 and 14 often become over-anxious to begin dating. Most 13-year-old girls feel they are more mature than the average and therefore should have dating privileges. If this description fits you, and your parents are holding back, it isn't that they wish to deprive you of pleasure or are old fogies, but because they know what lies ahead. Data indicates that *the earlier you begin dating, the earlier you will marry; the earlier you marry, the greater your chances of becoming a divorce statistic.*

Furthermore, your parents have the right to set up rules regarding dating. The privilege of dating should be granted only after such factors as age, dependability, willingness to accept responsibility, and mature behaviour have been examined. Did you notice the word 'privilege'? Dating is a *privilege* granted when you show responsible behaviour. Resist demanding dating as your *right*.

The younger a girl begins to date, the more likely she is to have sex before leaving school. The following chart will help you visualise the impact of early dating on your life.

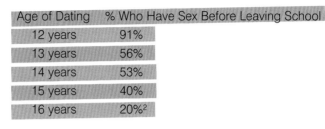

Age of Dating	% Who Have Sex Before Leaving School
12 years	91%
13 years	56%
14 years	53%
15 years	40%
16 years	20%[2]

Moreover, girls who first have intercourse at age 15 or younger are almost twice as likely to become pregnant within the first six months of sexual activity as are those who wait until they are 18 or 19. This is related to their ignorance about birth control and to the level of maturity. These girls do not understand, or refuse to believe, that they could ever get pregnant. Their bodies are mature; but their emotions are not. They are totally unprepared to handle the pressures of their sexual hormones. When asked how or why this happened, the majority will tell you they felt pressured into sexual contact because they didn't know how to say NO. That's what *Smart Love* is all about.

A large majority of teen pregnancies are caused by males over 20 years of age.[3] And there is a greater age gap between the girl and the boy than most people think. For example, when the mother is only 12 years old or younger, the father averages 22 years of age. By the time a girl reaches 13-15 the father is usually five years older. The father of girls who bear children during later school years averages nearly four years older.

This epidemic of older fathers can account for the high rate of STDs and AIDS in teen females, where rates are 2.5 times higher among girls than in teen males. This points to transmission from older men. This also suggests predatory behaviour of older guys and is why many countries have an age of consent.

When girls are asked whether they had sex voluntarily, as many as 69% said it was. But young girls may not be equipped to recognise manipulation by an older guy whom they see as wiser and most desirable.[4]

It is normal, natural and healthy for boys and girls

during their teen years to show an interest in the opposite sex. But if early dating isn't the answer, what is? The solution is simple. Every church should provide regular recreational activities for young adults to enjoy to accommodate their desire to be with the opposite sex. These gatherings can allow for some pairing off, but there should be no dating during the early teen years. The emphasis should be on being together in a relaxed and healthy atmosphere that adults can properly supervise. This leaves couple dating where it belongs – with those 16 and older.

Parents can easily get around early single dating by making their home a warm and welcome place for teenagers' friends to gather. Families with teens can engage in activities together, thus providing opportunity for teens and their friends to be together without moving into real 'dating'. Families can get together at one another's homes, go on a picnic, go skating together, or foster any number of activities that allow mixing under controlled circumstances. Church and school activities can supplement the activities planned by parents.

Rules for First-time Players (for guys)

The next most important thing to know is how to ask a girl out. A sequence of events should take place.

Step 1: Decide on the girl.

She will probably be someone you find attractive – someone you know but not well enough. Hopefully you will take into consideration more than just her looks and personality. Think also of her morals and her relationship with God. If she is lacking in both, question your motives for dating her.

Step 2: What would you like to do on your first date?

A first date should be an activity that is easily acceptable to someone with whose likes and dislikes you may not be very familiar – an activity that will allow you to talk and become better acquainted. The easiest date in the world is to attend a movie, but watching a movie allows little time to talk and get to know one another. Think more of an activity you would both enjoy – miniature golf or going to the zoo.

Step 3: Where will the date take place?

If food is involved, you will have to choose the place as well as the time. If you attend a sporting event, the location and time have already been selected for you.

Step 4: Get the facts.

Get the time, date and place down pat so there will be no misunderstandings. Now devise Plan B. In other words, should she turn you down, choose another girl, activity or place. Be prepared in advance. If the activity requires booking, now is the time to organise that. If you do not have your own car, you must also arrange for transportation.

Step 5: Ask her.

This is the trickiest part, due to fear of rejection. Look for an opportunity to find her alone and when there will be no interruptions. Many guys find it easier to ask over the phone.

When asking her, avoid such questions as, 'What are your plans for Saturday night?' Her personal schedule and habits are none of your business at this point. Don't be negative by saying, 'I don't suppose you would be interested in going out with me?' (This reeks of low self-esteem.)

Perhaps the best way to ask would go something like this: 'I'd really like to get better acquainted with you. There's a championship tennis play-off on Sunday afternoon at the Racquet Club. If you like tennis I'd love to have you join me and we can go out for something to eat afterwards. I know a good Mexican restaurant that serves great enchiladas.' Act and sound as though you expect her to accept the invitation and she will be more likely to do so.

And don't be afraid of her. She is just another human like you. The big difference is that she's female and you are male. Avoid talking too fast or being too pushy. Otherwise she might back off. If you mumble and act as though you don't know what you are doing, you might well put her off. Ask for the date several days in advance of the event. If it is an annual banquet that occurs on Sunday night, better not wait until Saturday to ask someone. If you plan to drive through Christmas Tree Lane, there would be no need to invite her three weeks in advance. The more formal the occasion, the earlier you should ask. You can set up more casual dates only one to five days prior to the occasion.

Step 6: If she says Yes, you have made it

But avoid acting overly grateful so she doesn't wonder why you are so overjoyed. It will make her think you never had a date before! After she has accepted, gather your wits together and make sure you give the necessary details she needs to know. The dress required for a fancy dinner out differs from what she would wear for miniature golf.

Should she turn you down, try not to fall apart. Analyse what kind of No she gave.

Did her tone and words say, 'No, and that's final' or did she say, 'Due to circumstances beyond my control, I can't go with you this time, but please ask me again'?

'No, and that's final' sounds something like this: 'Sorry about that, but I'm busy,' or 'I just can't work it into my schedule.' These responses mean that she doesn't have time and isn't interested in making the time.

Examples of 'Due to circumstances beyond my control . . .' include: 'I'm busy on Sunday afternoon, but I'd enjoy getting together with you another time,' or 'I'd love to see a tennis match some time but I'm committed to something else that day. How about another time?' Should she suggest an alternative date, you know she wants to go out with you.

If a girl turns you down with no explanation, forget about asking why. You have no right to that information just because you asked her for a date, and she does not have to respond. It would be out of place.

Step 7: If your self-esteem is still intact and you would enjoy going out with someone, ask another girl. But never let the word slip that she is a second choice! Openness and honesty are good up to a point, but this would hurt her feelings and most probably leave you dateless again!

The Game Plan for Accepting Dates

First dates are just as nerve-wracking for girls as they are for guys. One young lady, on the day of her first date, made everyone in her family cater to her wishes, refused to help around the house because she had to get ready, shouted at everyone to leave her alone so she could have peace, and tied up the bathroom for hours. This is overdoing it!

Picture the scene:

1. The phone rings. Your mum answers it. 'It's a b-o-y.' She spells it out.

2. Your mind races, your heart gets stuck in your throat, and your pulse pounds. In spite of all this activity, you listen closely because you have to know who it is and what he wants.

3. You hear his voice, and instantly you know who it is. While he is still asking, you have a few split seconds to decide whether you want to date him. The best way to handle this is to make an agreement with your parents that you will never accept a date without checking with them first. This might sound a bit childish, but it could get you out of some tough spots. It would also give you time to investigate the boy if you don't know him that well – reputation, character and morals.

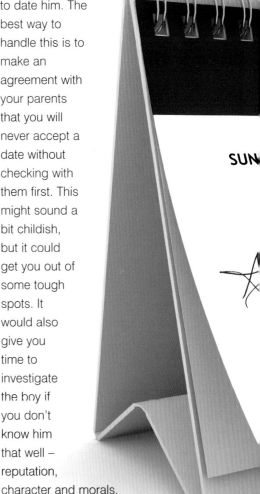

SUN

4. Evaluate the activity before you give him an answer. Is it something you wish to participate in? If he suggests going to a rock music concert and you have chosen not to attend such entertainment, you will need to respond in such a way that he understands that it is rock music you oppose and not him. If it is a healthy, fun-filled activity, let him know how much you would enjoy going out with him.

5. Check your calendar for conflicting events. If you can't go at the suggested time, it is perfectly all right for

you to let him know you would enjoy going with him another time if it could be worked out.

6. If you have no objections to the boy, his character, or the activity, then accept it. And accept with enthusiasm (without overdoing it).

Now picture another scene. The phone rings. You answer. This time you do not recognise the voice. After he introduces himself, you remember him. Big problem. He is not someone you want to date.

When turning down a date, honesty is always the best policy even if it hurts the guy a little. Avoid making excuses in order to put him off. It rarely solves the problem. One fellow kept calling a girl, trying to get a date. She invented one excuse after another. One night he called her again, and she said she had to wash her hair. 'You told me that a couple of days ago,' he countered. 'Well,' she continued, 'I decided to wash it again tonight since you called.' He got the message. Avoid saying, 'My parents won't let me go,' unless they won't. He might see you going to the same event with someone else. Or don't say, 'I'm busy that night,' as he might ask again. Don't reply, 'I'm going steady with Charlie Brown,' unless you really are. Don't respond with, 'Let's make it another time,' unless you want him to take you literally. Avoid any sarcastic remarks that would put him down: 'What? Go out with you!' or 'You must be kidding!' Just because you do not care to date him does not make him an unworthy person. He thought enough of you to ask you out. You can think enough of him to leave his self-respect intact.

Keep your response simple, and as courteously as possible tell him why you choose not to go out with him. It might go something like this: 'Thanks for asking me, Ron, but at the present time I'm not ready for a dating relationship with you.' Or if it is someone you have known fairly well you might even say, 'We've been good friends and I've appreciated our friendship. I hope you won't take this the wrong way, but I'm not ready for anything more right now. My decision has nothing to do with liking you as a person.'

Regardless of how tactful you attempt to be, your refusal may hurt his feelings. It may be uncomfortable for a while if you have to be around him, but it is kinder to turn him down than to string him along. Rejection is never fun; it always hurts. But it is harder on both of you to tell 'little

white lies', make up excuses or give insincere answers filled with uncertainty. A simple, courteous response with the reason why is the best way to handle it.

If someone asks you out who doesn't share your religious convictions you should not say, 'I'm sorry, but I'm a Christian, and I can't date you because you aren't one.' Such an attitude implies that you feel superior. You don't want to give the impression that you feel self-righteous or sanctimonious. If appropriate, you can tell this person that you have decided not to date anyone who is not a member of your own faith. Or you might say that you have made a pact with your parents that you won't date those who hold different spiritual values. If you don't know the person well enough to know what his spiritual inclinations are, say so. 'I don't know where you stand on this, but if you would like to discuss it with me sometime I'd be happy to get together with you.' This could set

the stage for you to share your faith in a positive way. If the person is someone you would never care to date, then you need not bring religion into the picture at all.

One more thing. When dating, both sexes try to date the most desirable persons – obviously! This is only natural. But many people make really fine dates in spite of the fact that they wear glasses, are short, underweight, overweight, have acne, are shy, not part of the 'in' crowd, or are not a star athlete or a beauty queen. Sometimes the best 'finds' just haven't blossomed yet. You might overlook someone with great potential just because you want to date some good-looking, popular person you've had your eye on. Avoid such shallowness. Some very interesting people come wrapped in plain packages.

Curfews

Dear Mrs Van Pelt: My parents are impossible! They never allow me to stay out past midnight. This is ridiculous nowadays. Often I have to leave a party just as things get going. It is so embarrassing. My dad says he doesn't want me to get into trouble. I can do that just as easily before midnight as after. I know I'm supposed to obey my parents, but do I have to when they are so unreasonable?

How should young people react when they feel their parents take an unrealistic position on curfews? When your parents made the rules regarding curfews they were probably thinking back to their own dating days and what they did after midnight! Those thoughts haunt them, and they wish

to protect you from some of the mistakes they made – whether or not you want such protection.

Sometimes a simple rule like: 'You must be in by midnight' can save you a lot of grief. Parties that just get going by midnight bother me. What goes on at a party that just begins at midnight? Whatever the activity, couldn't it begin earlier? And many 'Touchy Situations' and 'Close Encounters' get started after midnight. Obviously, if you are alone with a member of the opposite sex for long periods of time after midnight, all the resolves about how far to go could easily get lost in the heat of the night.

Undeniably there is more to do after midnight than just 'making out'. If you really feel your parents are being unfair, ask them to discuss the rule with you. Explain to them exactly what you would like to do after midnight, why you can't return home before that time, how it makes you feel when you must leave before others, and exactly what time you could be home.

If you haven't proved yourself trustworthy in the past – if you have come in after curfew and gone to places you said you wouldn't go to and done things you said you wouldn't do – don't expect your pleas for leniency to impress your parents. If you want to prove you are trustworthy, then you have to *be* trustworthy. Remember, the parents who gave birth to you and raised you might know you better than you know yourself.

Part 7: Tactics for Playing a Really Good Game

First dates can be quite traumatic. You may be frantic over what to wear and how to be appealing. You may worry that the evening could be a total disaster. With all this going on, you'll probably be anxious, tongue-tied and possibly even clumsy. Here are some success secrets to ease first-date jitters:

Daytime is better for first dates than evening. A first date should be informal and non-threatening. A picnic in the park with a Frisbee or lunch at an outdoor café with a walk in the park would be perfect. This type of date offers more opportunity to chat and get to know one another than watching a movie. This way you can find out if you have anything in common. Get outdoors into a daylight activity. Go for a walk or a swim, ride bikes or play tennis.

Set a time limit on your date. The tendency is to make first dates long. People think that spending longer periods of time together will make the relationship special more quickly. But dates, especially when you are getting to know one another, should have a beginning and an ending time set in advance. Then if the date is a disaster you can more easily change your plans.

Be on time. If you say you'll be ready at a certain time and you aren't, you are being rude. It is no longer considered acceptable to keep a guy waiting. It is just as improper for a guy to be late. If you are going to be late due to some emergency, call your date and inform her. Being late for a date conveys a message: This event is not important enough for me to arrange my time accordingly. First impressions come from (1) being on time and (2) by complimenting your date's appearance or personality.

Be mature. Regardless of your age, be mature. Have respect for the other person and yourself. One thing this means is No Sex. There is no place for sexual intimacy before you and your date have achieved emotional intimacy. This is backwards again.

Relax. Concentrate on putting your date at ease. Think of your date as a friend rather than a romantic partner. Then you'll be able to relax. Joanna was terribly nervous over her first date with Tom. Even though she knew him from school, a date took their relationship to a new level. He was an excellent conversationalist and encouraged her to talk. This first date was followed by many more. Much later Tom told Joanna he was a nervous wreck on their first date, yet Joanna knew nothing about it, because Tom had helped *her* feel at ease.

Be fun to be with. Contribute to the date by being fun. Don't expect to sit back and be entertained without contributing something to the evening to make it memorable. Allow yourself to act a little silly as long as it is in good taste. Join in with what your date has planned even if you feel a little self-conscious.

Participate in the activities as long as they don't conflict with your principles. If they do,

bow out gracefully, offering an acceptable alternative. And don't complain when something doesn't go as planned.

If you did your best and things didn't go well, it doesn't mean you were a failure. First dates can be tense. With more experience you'll do better.

Let's Talk

If you want to survive in the world of dating, you must learn how to talk to those of the opposite sex. Two main problems crop up here. First, when guys talk to each other, their conversations centre on cars, sports, work and girls. Their manner often tends to be coarse, if not crude. When females talk to each other, they tend to discuss clothes, other people, their relationships with the guys, and 'girlie' stuff. They are often cliquish. Obviously, if the sexes attempt to talk to one another about such things, each would bore the other. Second, nervousness and self-consciousness sometimes produce foolish behaviour.

Your attitude towards the opposite sex is actually more important than tips on what to say, because your attitude determines your behaviour. If a fellow is concerned about a girl's feelings, he won't talk or joke with her in a coarse manner. He will ask questions to find out what she is like and what her interests are. A guy who rambles on about all the medals he won in track and field or his computer's processing power would hardly interest his date. He would not be considered a good conversationalist. Likewise, a girl who is preoccupied with her hair, dress, and making catty remarks about other girls would bore her date. She, too, must put away some of her interests in order to sound him out.

chapter two

To Kiss or Not to Kiss

Sam walked Ashley to the door after their first date. He had enjoyed going out with her and reached for her hand. 'She's a nice girl,' he thought. *'We had a good time together. I think I'll kiss her goodnight.'*

Ashley's heart skipped a few beats when Sam took her hand. She anticipated what was coming next and let him kiss her. After she was inside she threw herself on her bed, her mind racing. L-O-V-E! At long last she was really in love, and he loved her too!

On the way home Sam thought, 'I enjoyed being with Ashley. Maybe I'll take her out again sometime, but I don't want to get tied down to anybody.'

Demonstrations of affection mean different things to different people – and particularly to girls! The significance of holding hands and kissing varies from person to person, but, overall, girls tend to place more meaning on kissing than do boys. In this case, Ashley had kissed only one other boy in her whole life. Sam, on the other hand, had dated quite a few girls, and a first-date peck meant little more to him than affectionate friendship.

Imagine what might happen next. If Ashley thinks she has found true love, Sam will withdraw when she tries to latch on to him. Then she will think he didn't like her at all and might conclude that all guys want from girls is the physical stuff.

In fact, neither perception would be accurate. Generally speaking, boys seek demonstrations of affection because they consider it fun and challenging. Girls, however, interpret affection as love. Both sexes need to recognise the other's perspective and not attach more significance to certain acts than was intended.

If a couple has just begun dating and they begin 'making out' too soon, several problems will surface immediately. One of the main purposes of dating is to get to know one another better. Obviously, if you spend a good deal of your time necking and petting, you can hardly engage in much verbal communication (although a lot of non-verbal communication is going on). Your relationship will tend to remain at a very shallow level as it explores the physical too soon. I am not implying that a couple should never hold hands or kiss but holding off will help a couple develop a more balanced relationship. Many a perfectly good dating relationship has been ruined prematurely because the couple was preoccupied with 'making out'. More on this topic in 'Touchy Situations'.

The Dating Game

Going Steady – Security for Teens!

We all have favourites – favourite foods, favourite friends, favourite teachers, favourite clothes. After dating around for a while, some realise that one person stands out above all others and they begin 'going steady'.

The rules of the dating game change when you are going steady. In casual dating you like each other but are not in love, and both are free to date others. In steady dating you have exclusive rights to one another's time and attention. Neither partner is free to accept or initiate a date with someone else. The exchange of gifts on special days such as birthdays, Valentine's Day and Christmas is usually expected.

Steady dating offers several advantages. Neither person wonders who will go with him or her to a party or function. It is a foregone conclusion – and without any formal invitation – that they will attend together as a couple. Going steady offers security, since it protects both of them from being dateless or stuck with an undesirable date.

It also offers emotional security. The teen years provide many crises when it seems that parents, teachers, friends and even the church stand in the way of everything you want to do. Sometimes it seems that the whole world is crashing down on your head and that no one understands what you are going through. A steady partner, one who knows how to listen and understands how you feel, can be a great emotional asset.

In a steady relationship, it is meaningful to receive someone's special attention and affection. It symbolises trust, attraction, and a degree of commitment that makes you feel cared about in a special way. This in turn builds up your feelings of self-worth. Perhaps you never had the opportunity of counting on anyone in a special way before. But when going steady you find that your confidence in other areas of your life increases. You feel more likeable and worthwhile. You begin reaching out to others and speaking up in groups – something you would never have dared to do previously. Feeling loved and cared for works wonders for self-worth.

Going steady also saves money. The longer a couple dates steadily, the more casual the dates become. You no longer have to go out on a 'date'. Now you plan times of just being together – watching television at one another's home, shopping, studying together or just 'hanging out'. No longer do you try so hard to impress one another.

Lastly, a steady relationship can teach you a lot about how relationships function. The closer you get to someone, the better you know and understand that person. This closeness will demand that you become less selfish and more giving. As a result, you will learn how to get along with someone of the opposite sex.

On the other hand, going steady is not all roses. Too much togetherness can be a burden, especially if you move too quickly or too soon. Going steady at a young age or too soon in the development of a relationship presents certain temptations that damage personal and spiritual growth. The greatest drawback to a premature steady relationship arises from the arrest of personal, emotional and social growth.

Going steady also causes identity problems for some young people. Penny likes classical music, onion rings and antique cars

because her boyfriend loves these things. She becomes a carbon copy of his likes and dislikes. In chameleon-like fashion she changes personality and likes along with her boyfriend. Her own personality never has the opportunity to develop, and some day she will probably wake up and find that she is bored and frustrated. She'll never know who she is or what she likes.

Another disadvantage to going steady is the increased opportunity for 'touchy situations'. It is difficult to pace a steady relationship when you are years away from marriage. Even young persons with high ideals fall into premarital sex as a result of going steady. Such young people often get caught by pregnancy, because they think of themselves as 'nice kids' who would never go too far. Caught by the emotions of the moment, they take no precautions, and the girl ends up pregnant because to take precautions beforehand would mean they *planned* to disobey God.

Each year in the US more than 1,100,000 teen girls become pregnant. Sixty percent of these girls will be pregnant again within two years and be forced to make gut-wrenching decisions about their unwanted pregnancies. Of these girls who become pregnant, 30,000 are under 14 years of age and 80% will drop out of school. Even when the end result is not pregnancy teens risk sexually-transmitted diseases. There is now an unprecedented outbreak of sexually-transmitted diseases among teenagers. The statistics are staggering. Gonorrhoea among teen girls has increased 400% in the last thirty years and is the highest of any age group.[5] And Christian young people are not immune from either pregnancy or STDs.

Another major hazard of going steady is

SLOW

that it gets to be a habit. Many couples continue to go together long after a good thing is over because neither knows how or has the courage to end it. One fellow put it like this: 'At first I liked Connie a lot. I eventually talked her into doing things I'm not too proud of now. Now I've lost interest in her. I feel like a rat but don't know how to ditch her without hurting her.'

What happens after you go steady? Do you assume that someday you will break up? Get married? How can you build a relationship with someone without thought of marriage?

A couple who are years away from marriage must face many problems. They don't want to break up. They are not ready for marriage. And they don't want to wait for sex. This offers a relationship with no purpose or direction. A dangerous state!

Going steady itself is neither right nor wrong. It is an important and essential stage of dating. It is a serious trial period during which a couple thoroughly studies one another's emotional, moral, spiritual and social characteristics while analysing whether they will make a safe marriage risk.

But the longer you go together, the more is demanded of you romantically. As you

went into Stage 4 you may only have been holding hands and doing some light or dry kissing. A long-term steady, relationship demands increased demonstrations of affection. The kisses will most likely become longer and more passionate. As passion rises, the hands may begin to explore one another's bodies. All sexual motors are racing and accelerated. This places you on dangerous ground. The relationship must be slowed down – and now!

Two things can help at this point: (1) seeing each other only when others are around, and (2) engaging only in participation dates where you are around others and physically active. Promising each other that you will never engage in petting again are promises made from ropes of sand.

I Need Someone Now!

Charlie Brown of the *Peanuts* comic strip puts his finger on so many basic issues in life. One of the Charlie Brown Valentine specials depicted an episode where all the students in Charlie's class brought Valentine cards to school and put them in a brightly decorated box. When the time for the party came, the box was shaken and then 'teacher's pet' passed out the Valentines. Everyone in the room began to receive Valentines – everyone, that is, except Charlie Brown. There he sat with all his friends, but entirely forgotten. In *Peanuts* series books he parks himself outside his mailbox on Valentine's Day and the caption reads: 'I'm going to stay right here until someone sends me a Valentine.' He never gets one. He's the loneliest guy in town. Many of you probably identify with the episodes from his life.

How hard it is to sit on the sidelines and watch others having a good time in a round of dates with friends! A young person left dateless can cry out in loneliness to God, 'Please, God, if you are there, why can't you provide a special friend for me now?'

It hurts to be left out. Some surveys state that loneliness is the biggest problem confronting teenagers today.

But sitting on the sidelines of life and begging God to 'send somebody – anybody' is hardly the right way to respond to loneliness. If you are not dating yet, relax. Remember that in six months you may be seeing someone on a regular basis, and the popular person you envy so much now may be sitting on the sidelines. And just because the popular kids are dating does not mean that you have to. Each group has many different subgroups. If the 'in group' isn't to your liking, then seek out a subgroup you can relate to more informally. Share something of yourself with the group – a common interest, time or activity.

One of the worst things you can do is to act as if you are in limbo waiting to come to life when Mr Right or Miss Perfect enters the scene. Without goals and a sense of direction, you will be a poor specimen of humanity, and no one will want to date you. And if you finally do get into the swing of dating, you will find that you still have not discovered the key to happiness. You have never developed the abilities needed to make a success of your life. Chances are you will still feel lonely and frustrated.

Learn to accept loneliness for what it is – an emotion. Emotions are not permanent but change according to our moods. In the meantime, form some solid friendships with both sexes so you will be ready for a one-to-one relationship when it comes. Join a group, take up a hobby, and stay active. The loneliness you are experiencing can develop attributes of caring for others that you might not develop otherwise. Perhaps God wants you to search out other lonely persons and minister to their needs. Forget your own misery and be a real blessing to others. God may also be allowing you to experience loneliness so he can have your full attention and allegiance.

Endless Possibilities

The teen years are precious, so use them to your full advantage. They are carefree years with few obligations and endless possibilities. It is the time for developing honourable values, worthwhile goals and standards of behaviour. Get involved. Meet new people. Develop many friendships without heavy commitments. You short-change yourself if you limit your opportunities during the early years.

Everyone who comes in contact with your life will leave a part of himself with you. You can learn lessons even from a complete bore, braggart or gossip – lessons like tolerance! Give yourself a real basis for comparison. Don't be like the fly in the bottle of vinegar who thinks it is the sweetest place in the world because it is the only place he has ever been!

Smart Love

chapter three

used to be. He doesn't laugh and joke and share as much as he once did. When you ask him if there is anything wrong, he always says 'No' and changes the subject. Nagging doubts plague you. Then panic begins to rise. You don't hear from him for several days, and you don't call him either. When you finally see him again, you ask in a whisper, 'What's the matter between us?'

He's been treating you differently. You can't quite put your finger on what it is, but things just aren't the same. Last night after the game he dropped you off at the house and didn't even come inside. Said he had to get right home. You heard from a friend that he spent time with his mates after that. The last time he kissed you goodnight you got the impression that he did it because you expected him to. Lately you phone him more than he calls you.

He doesn't seem to be as happy as he

You're afraid to hear the answer. He looks away. His shoulders droop. You know what he will say before he speaks: 'I guess it's time for us to break up.'

It's over. The one you care about wants out. It hurts. Sometimes you think it's the worst thing that could happen. You can't believe it's true. You play the past over and over again, like an old video. You try to remember every minute of your time together, trying to figure out what went wrong.

Breaking Up Is Hard To Do

Then you play the 'if only' game. . . . *If only* I hadn't complained about his wanting to spend more time with his friends. . . . *If only* I hadn't been so possessive. . . . *If only* I had done this. . . . *If only* . . .

What happens now? Dating forms a cycle – dating around, going steady, breaking up; dating around, going steady, breaking up, and so on. With the exception of the person you eventually marry, you will break up every time you go steady. But how you handle it when the time comes is crucial. Let's learn to do it right.

Part 8: Danger! Trouble Ahead!

Sometimes breaking a relationship is healthier than keeping it going. But some couples get so wrapped up in each other that they fail to see the danger or close their eyes to it. When a couple becomes emotionally involved, they often lose perspective. Temporary insanity takes over! Let's focus on some circumstances that indicate trouble. This list, although not exhaustive, will act as a starter for sluggish hearts who are slow to face reality.

Danger Signal 1: Arguing and Fighting.
Some arguing and fighting during a steady or ongoing relationship is normal. If a couple never disagrees or argues, they are 'masking' or not being themselves. But there is such a thing as too many disagreements,

and there is a danger when they become loud, long or continuous.

If a couple does not learn how to manage conflict, their relationship will become a rubbish dump for unresolved disagreements. *The ability to manage conflict is more important than how much in love they are, how compatible they are, or any other factor.*

Our son, Mark, was in a long-distance relationship with Angela when he was 19. To maintain the relationship they spent hours on the phone – mostly arguing. Their relationship was one constant argument. 'If you argue this much while dating, think what will happen should you marry,' I chided – advice that went unheeded. On one occasion Angela spent the weekend with our family. Mark prepared to take her out for dinner. I watched and waved from the front porch as they drove away. Before my arm came down, the car had been thrust into reverse. Within seconds a tearful Angela collapsed in my arms while Mark roared off in his car – alone. When questioned, Angela explained that Mark didn't like what she was wearing, and it escalated from there.

Even well-matched couples may have a series of misunderstandings; but, overall, if misunderstandings, arguments and fights outnumber your periods of peace, it's a danger signal.

Watch also the respect shown for each

other during your disagreements. Some people resort to fits of temper to try to control others. When angry, such a person will say or do anything, regardless of how hurtful to the other. Often the words used are hostile, bitter and nasty. People who react this way suffer from more emotional problems than you are equipped to handle. Also watch who wins and who loses when you do fight. Does one always win and the other always lose? Most of us don't mind losing once in a while, but none of us enjoys losing *all* the time. Do yourself a favour. Do not walk, but run from such relationships.

Danger Signal 2: Extreme Physical Involvement. Fred and Claudia can hardly wait to be alone together so they can 'make out'. Their relationship revolves around the physical thrills they receive from each other. They participate in few activities and engage in so much hugging, kissing and petting that they have very little time to talk or continue to get to know one another. Claudia wishes there were more depth to their relationship but she is afraid of losing Fred. When a couple gets this involved physically, other areas of their relationship fail to grow.

A good question to ask yourself is: If you took sex out of the relationship, would your girl or boyfriend stick around? If not, you know what he or she wants. And if you said NO would your partner respect and support your request? Remember, it is possible for two total strangers to become sexually intimate within a matter of minutes. Sexual intimacy is easier to attain than emotional intimacy. When heavy physical intimacies or sexual involvement are engaged in, it is time to break up and make a new start with someone who will respect and honour your commitment to sexual purity prior to marriage.

Danger Signal 3: Conflicting Goals and Values. Phil and Jenny think they are compatible. They both enjoy skiing, country music, bird watching and pizza. But this only tells what they like to do in their spare time. Their goals and values are very different. Goals and values make up what you are, who you are, and what you will be in the years to come. If one of you drops out of school while the other pursues a PhD in chemistry, your goals in life will differ so drastically that no amount of compromise will solve the problems you encounter. After you marry and realise you have nothing in common, you can utilise sophisticated communication and negotiation skills, try counselling and agonise in prayer and still not solve your problems.

If one of you values home and family along with a simple life in the country while the other prefers a fast city life, if one is deeply committed to God and the other is not, if one desires to serve in a mission field and the other wants to make a fortune in business, your values and goals are so different that no amount of compromise or prayer can help you solve the multiplicity of problems that will follow.

It is very important to discuss and understand each other's current and long-term goals and values. Some couples attempt to gloss over conflicting ideals, saying they aren't important or 'We can work this out.' But different goals and values can drive a couple apart. In a survey I conducted, college students indicated that disagreements over values and philosophy of life were the main sources of most conflicts in their love lives.

Danger Signal 4: Abuse. A 14-year-old girl began dating a guy from school she had known a short time. He was friendly and strikingly handsome. After a week of dating, he began telling her that he loved her. But the deeper they got into their relationship,

the more controlling he became. 'You can't be more than an arm's length away from me at any time,' he demanded. When in the car with him, she had to be right next to him or on his lap. Then he began to isolate her from her friends. Her only friends were his friends.

One night after he'd been drinking, he grabbed her roughly and threatened to kill her if she didn't spend more time with him. She survived this traumatic experience and broke up with him. The next day she was still hurting and had welts and bruises on her body. She hid the evidence from her parents by wearing clothing that covered her bruises, and never told them.

One in ten teens now experiences physical violence in a dating relationship (slapping, hitting or punching). US national statistics show that about 12% of high school students experience violence in dating before graduating. The likelihood of violence increases to 20-25% by the time they are in college. A St Louis study of 885 teenagers showed that 33% had been threatened by physical violence when dating.[1] A mere 4% ever told their parents or an authority figure about it.

Others play mind games that relegate a boy or girlfriend to the land of Nerds. A St Louis study showed that 52% of the subjects had experienced one or more of the following forms of emotional abuse while dating: constant criticism, blame for all problems, threats of physical harm, isolation, repeated insults, destruction of possessions, and being completely ignored.[2] Intentional public humiliation that makes one look and feel like a fool in front of others is also a form of emotional abuse.

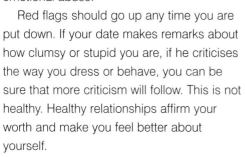

Red flags should go up any time you are put down. If your date makes remarks about how clumsy or stupid you are, if he criticises the way you dress or behave, you can be sure that more criticism will follow. This is not healthy. Healthy relationships affirm your worth and make you feel better about yourself.

Make it clear early in a relationship that you will not tolerate put-downs or negative remarks. If your partner refuses to stop, get out of the relationship before your self-worth is destroyed.

To tolerate emotional or physical abuse while suffering in silence, hoping the other person will change his behaviour, only encourages such behaviour and degrades your self-worth. Any time a relationship includes any type of abuse, get out! Things won't improve. To continue in a relationship of this nature shows gross insecurity and a lack of self-esteem. Anyone with positive feelings of worth would not allow herself to be used as a punch-bag or the butt of jokes. There is never a good excuse for causing physical or emotional pain. End it!

Danger Signal 5: Withdrawal. Chris spends so much time with Dave that her friends hardly see her anymore. She doesn't have time for them. Her grades have dropped, and she seems to have lost interest in sports, school, friends and church activities. Love should expand Chris's interests, not close her off. Love is a constructive force that helps you develop into the best kind of person you can be. It releases energies within you that should help you produce your best, not drop out from life. Relationships that crowd out friends, school, sports and church should be terminated.

Danger Signal 6: Separation. Ryan and Kaylene met at a teen Bible camp. Their friendship blossomed during the week together. At the close of camp they promised to stay in touch via email, phone calls, and visits to each other's homes. Even though 700 miles separated them, they kept their relationship alive. Following a two-year courtship, they married. Four years later they divorced. I learned that during their two years of dating they had seen each other only every other month, or a total of twelve times before marrying!

Even though Ryan and Kaylene thought

they knew one another and had waited two years before marrying, their relationship failed. Why? This couple did not really know one another because they had not had enough face-to-face interaction. Fifty-five percent of communication is delivered through posture, facial expressions and gestures. When talking to someone on the phone, you have 38% (tone of voice) and 7% (the verbal message) that you can tap to get to know someone. But a whopping 55% of the message (the non-verbals) isn't there. In emailed messages, where only 7% of the message comes through, 93% is missing. People say one thing with their mouths but lie with other parts of their bodies. You must be able to see and hear and evaluate the total message in order to make a definitive judgement.

long-distance phone calls, love letters, emails and promises won't stall the mortality rate. Young love can survive only in a here-and-now environment.

Danger Signal 7: A BTN. Any relationship that's OK but not great is BTN (Better Than Nothing). A BTN is a comfortable relationship with the wrong person. BTNs include all those people you cared about but who never cared about you, or relationships that were never any good in the first place. BTNs are OK if you recognise that they are only better than nothing and that's all you want.

BTNs waste time, and yet people stay in them because they offer security. They are safe, even if they aren't wonderful. They also mean you have a special friend for the time being. Often BTN relationships are hard to

When one leaves school and goes to college or university, or when distance separates a couple, two factors should be considered as to whether they should break up – their age and the distance between them. If a couple is 14 or 15 years of age, ten miles might cool their heels once school is out and they can't see each other daily. If you are in your mid-teens and your special friend moves away or graduates, don't try to prolong the agony by swearing faithfulness to one another 'forever and ever'. All the

get out of because they have been going on so long. Some stay in BTNs long after they should because they didn't have what it takes to get out when it would have been easier.

People stay in BTNs because they appear better than nothing, but in reality they are worse because they chip away at your self-esteem. Your date life should reinforce your self-esteem. When you spend time with someone who does not contribute to your self-esteem, you will have difficulty feeling good about yourself. When you stay in a BTN you indicate that your self-esteem is already in trouble.

Do yourself a favour. Squarely face and carefully evaluate all the danger signals in your relationship. If the obstacles are too big, rather than blinding yourself to the truth while pressing full steam ahead, end the relationship. If you are too insecure to let go or too emotionally dependent to evaluate it truthfully, get help. If you can't end it alone, enlist the help of a parent, an adult, a teacher or youth pastor. Whenever a relationship

becomes destructive or leads you astray, or comes to a dead end, it's time to call it quits – and the sooner the better.

If a relationship isn't working (even when parts of it may be great), get out when you first sense the problem. That moment may come on your first date or five months later. Some cases are more clear-cut than others. If you learn someone is married, homosexual, on drugs or alcohol, or is violent, don't hang around to see if you can 'fix' him. If you want to have a forever relationship and the one you are going with isn't going in the same direction, the earlier you end it the better it will be for both of you.

Saying Goodbye Like A Fool!

Breaking up is painful, so we refuse to think much about it and consequently never learn the procedures for handling this aspect of dating in the right way. But much of the pain associated with breaking up could be avoided if a little tact were used. Following are some hurtful and unchristian ways of ending it that should be avoided like the plague.

Avoid telling your partner off. Fran was bored with Larry and found someone else she was attracted to. Fran magnified Larry's faults in her mind so she could justify 'telling him off'. The next time she saw him she really let him have it. Now Larry hurts. Not only has Fran told him off, but she also made him feel unworthy and unlikeable. This is devastating to another person's self-esteem.

Avoid appearing in public with a new love. If you become interested in someone else and don't know how to break the news to your current steady, the most unfeeling way to do it is to appear in public with a new love on your arm. Especially ditch the idea of expressing affection in front of your old flame in order to help that person get the message.

To give your date the silent treatment or to avoid showing up when and where you usually do is not the way either. Such treatment transmits varying questions to the other person's mind: 'What did I do wrong? Did I say something to hurt his/her feelings last night? Maybe he/she has been trying to ditch me for weeks and I've been too stupid to realise it. I never catch on!'

Avoid the hot-and-cold treatment. Bruce is seriously thinking about breaking up with Louise. He's tired of her, yet he needs the security of their relationship. Besides, Louise is good-looking and the guys envy his relationship with her. He vacillates in his treatment of her according to his mood – sometimes he is attentive; at other times he treats her coldly. By treating her attentively, he tries to convince himself they can make a go of it. By ignoring her he signals it is over. Such treatment is confusing to the other person. Forget the hot-and-cold treatment while making up your mind.

Avoid breaking up at the wrong place or time. Don't drop the bombshell during the holidays, the night before a major exam, or just before the major social event of the

year. This makes a difficult situation even harder. Never break up in front of others or in a public place. A break-up is personal, not public, business. Go to a private place where you can be alone, rather than a romantic spot or where you first met.

Avoid sending a message that could be misunderstood. If the time has come to break up, examine your reasons carefully and then state them openly, clearly and honestly. Be careful to say what you mean. You may want to soften the blow of the break-up. But you must do it in such a way that your message won't be misunderstood. Don't leave the other person hanging or with hope that you may change your mind. Be definite.

Should you be separated by distance, you may have to resort to a Dear John or Jane letter. This type of letter has become the butt of many jokes, but in reality writing your message out clarifies your thinking and will help you express yourself clearly. It is always better, however, to end a relationship face to face. Afterwards always allow time to talk it over. Don't just break up and run. If you have been special friends you owe it to the other to stick around long enough to answer questions and ease the pain. Treat the other person the way you would like to be treated.

A mature individual does all he or she

can to make a relationship work. If that's impossible, the mature person ends it in a caring way so that bitterness does not develop between them. This is possible when the couple concentrate on the positive: the good things the two have shared, the pleasant memories of good times, and the personal growth that resulted from the friendship.

Part 9: Saying Goodbye with Class

Before Breaking Up. For a couple who have cared about each other, there is no easy way to break up. There is a high probability of hurt feelings, disappointment, anger and pain. But it is possible to soften the blow and prevent further complications. Here are some suggestions.

Pray About It. Ask the Lord to make it clear that you have chosen the right course of action. Request divine guidance as you carry out your decision with kindness. The Bible says: ' "For I know the plans I have for you," declares the Lord, "plans to prosper you and not to harm you, plans to give you hope and a future. Then you will call upon me and come and pray to me, and I will listen to you. You will seek me and find me when you seek me with all your heart. I will be found by you," ' Jeremiah 29:11-14.

He will not only guide you but also give you strength to do what is right. Ask God to give you the right words to say and help you deliver them as kindly as possible under the circumstances. Pray that the person you are breaking off with will heal without unnecessary hurt.

Seek Advice. Should you have doubts about your decision to call it quits, seek advice from someone you trust and respect. When emotionally upset, we often say and do things we regret later. Many couples who have broken up during the heat of an argument later wish they hadn't. Unburden yourself, if necessary, to a trusted friend, a minister or a counsellor. Explaining the whole situation in detail will help clear your mind, and the objective opinion of someone not emotionally involved often proves helpful.

A Winning Plan

Beth thinks Matt is too involved with sports, and she resents all the practice sessions and games he attends during baseball, basketball and football seasons. Matt says that sports are very important to him and Beth had better get used to it. Beth's feelings get hurt. Matt loses his temper and Beth cries. Each says a few more hurtful things, and they go their separate ways. Their last memory of one another is bitter. Each has his or her pride at stake and they protect themselves by remaining enemies. The hurt lingers for months, which keeps them from freely moving into new relationships. And their friendship is lost forever.

It doesn't have to be this way. Even though breaking up will always hurt, there are less painful ways to handle it. This three-step plan is a winner:

1. **Point out something good about the other person.** When you break up with your partner, he or she feels unloved and rejected and it is a major loss to self-esteem. So avoid dragging up all the negatives which can only make them feel worse than they already do. Instead, emphasise all the good times you have had together. Mention at least one way in which he or she has contributed to the relationship and spell out at least one thing you admire. Instead of letting the relationship end in bitterness, Beth could have said, 'Matt, we've had some great times together. You've taught me a lot about life, guys and relationships. I'll always remember the fun we had.'

2. **Admit your own failures.** Admitting mistakes will help you learn to accept responsibility for your own actions and prove your maturity. Sort out why things went wrong and the part you played in it. In Beth and Matt's relationship, Beth is partly to blame for the failure. Admitting this takes maturity but will provide insight for Beth and soften the blow for Matt. 'I can see now that I've been failing you by not enjoying sports as much as you do. I pretended to enjoy them, at least at first. But I wasn't being honest. I never meant to hurt you. I'm sorry for this.'

3. Give an honest reason for the break-up. You have a responsibility to tell the other person why you want to break up. Everyone I've ever talked to wants to know the reason, even though it may hurt to find out. In the long run it will prove beneficial. Mature persons want to learn from their mistakes. So honestly and openly state the problem without being brutally frank. Do not deliver negative information unless you do it kindly.

'Matt, I need more from this relationship than I'm getting. Sports bore me and I need someone who shares my interest in music and art. I think it better that we build a relationship with someone who shares our passion for the things we love. I will always remember the good times we shared and I want to consider you a friend for life.'

It still hurts. It is worse for Matt than for Beth, since he is the one being rejected. But this is better than angry words and bitter feelings that can linger for months, even years.

4. End the relationship as soon as it's clear you should. Rather than leading the other person on, take steps to end things after you have cleared reasonable doubt. Don't pretend to care about someone in whom you have lost interest. Once you have made the decision, stick with it. Don't be conned by promises to change, compromise, or do things differently.

5. Spare the other person's feelings of self-worth. It is a major loss to the self-image when the person you love rejects you. Avoid dragging up all the negatives about the other person. Instead, emphasise all the good times you have had. Talk about what the other person contributed to your friendship during your time together. Spell out appreciation for at least one fine quality you admire.

6. Let your emotions heal a little before trying to see the other person again. When you do see each other, keep your conversation light and short. Don't try to sound overly friendly too soon, lest the other person misconstrue it as an attempt to get back together.

Keep to yourself any personal information the two of you shared. Avoid the desire to broadcast dirt and gossip to your friends. The nicest thing you can say (for yourself and the other person) is: 'We used to go out together, and he is a fine person. We'll always be friends.' If you circulate damaging information, you do yourself a disservice. If the other person was such an anorak or bimbo, why did you go out with him or her anyway? Don't advertise your own poor judgement!

Sometimes, when the emotional dependence on the relationship has been great and self-esteem is low, the one who wants the relationship to continue may use threats, blackmail or even violence to get his way. There may be threats to tell personal secrets, get high or drunk, or commit suicide. Wild threats are usually just that – desperate attempts to hold on to someone. But don't count on it.

On a steamy June day in North Salem, New York, a 17-year-old student hanged himself with his own belt in the bathroom of his home. It was three weeks after his girlfriend, last year's homecoming queen, took her life in a similar manner following a quarrel between the two.[3] Suicide threats should be taken seriously, since the suicide rate for the 15 to 25 age group has risen 300% in the past twenty years. One of the leading causes of suicide in this age group is the pain and rejection from break-ups. Immediately report such threats to a school counsellor or your pastor. This is proof that the person is not emotionally stable. Under no circumstances should you stay in a relationship to pacify threats of suicide, violence or blackmail.

Part 10: *Letting Go: Facing Life Without You*

It's over. Your steady wants to date someone else. What will you do? Tick one of the following:

☐ Beg him or her to take you back.

☐ Make wild promises to become exactly what he or she wants you to be. You promise to change.

☐ Cry uncontrollably so he or she will feel sorry for you. If that doesn't work, fall on your knees, allowing deep sobs to rack your body.

☐ Threaten to commit suicide.

☐ Thank him or her for the good times you have shared and leave with your head high and your self-worth intact. (Then fall apart privately, if you must.)

You may be so hurt that you want to lash out angrily at the one who has hurt you. The temptation to do so is usually an attempt to justify the hurt. You may also be tempted to rant and rave about how stupid he is anyway and how you should have broken it off ages ago. But refuse to mend your broken ego by slandering the other person. Try not to defend yourself by intimating, 'You're the bad guy. I'm the good guy,' or 'When word gets around what you're really like, no one else will want you either. I'll see to it that you get what's coming to you!' Forget about saying, 'If I can't have you, I will personally see to it that no one else will want you either!' You may have these thoughts, but don't verbalise them.

Other times revenge takes the form of a more direct attack. When Dennis breaks off with Emily, she lashes out at him, 'I knew you would do this to me. I should never have gone out with you in the first place! You've hurt me so many times I've lost count. I've given you everything, done everything for you, and look at the way you treat me. I should have known better. You were never good enough for me in the first place!' Emily wants to make Dennis feel as terrible for dumping her as she does for getting dumped.

Avoid rebound romance. It's OK to cry on Jacob's shoulder because you and Mark broke up, but don't get carried away. Remember, you are vulnerable to any attention right now and will probably leap at any chance to fill the emptiness and hurt inside.

Rebound romances are phoney to the core. Time and healing are needed before you will be ready to build a love relationship with anyone. At any cost, avoid marriage on the rebound. Such marriages have little chance of succeeding because they are not usually based on long acquaintance, matched backgrounds, shared values and maturity. Your pride may hit rock bottom following a break-up but marrying someone on the rebound will only intensify an already traumatic situation.

Drowning In Misery

Surviving a break-up can be difficult if you still care for the person. But how much better to leave the other person wondering if a terrible mistake has been made rather than creating a scene and removing all doubt. Try to leave the other person thinking, 'She is really something,' rather than, 'Phew! Am I ever glad to be rid of that one!'

Tips to lessen the pain:

1. **Talk it over.** The break-up may have come as a surprise or shock. You may not understand why it is over. You have every right to ask if you have not been told. You may also say that it will be difficult to stop loving him or her. Talk it over as much as you need to and the other person is willing to. But when all is said and done, accept the situation and use it to your advantage rather than detriment. Instead of looking and acting as if your world has fallen apart, bow out with class. Carry your self-respect away with you. Remember, you are not unworthy just because you have been dumped – even though you may feel like it. This remains only temporary.

2. **Go ahead and cry about it if you need to.** Tears are a normal reaction during a time of hurt. If you feel like crying about it, go ahead – and this goes for males as well as females. Crying is a natural release for stressful situations and a healthy release for pressures that build up. Just do your weeping privately.

Where Do You Go from Here?

OK. The relationship has ended. Your entire life seems empty, off kilter and out of whack. You feel like getting drunk, running away, leaving school, jumping off a cliff or dropping out of the human race. What now? Even if you do get over a break-up with a minimum amount of pain, there are still some questions to answer. 'What do I do now?' comes first. Getting back into circulation takes time and effort.

Give yourself a chance to heal. Although some people take longer to recuperate than others, time is a wonderful healer. The time involved in bouncing back from heartbreak will usually be in direct proportion to the length of time you went together. If you only went together for a few weeks, you should bounce back within a few days. If you've gone together for a year or longer – which is a really long time in your teen years – it will be as if a part of you has been cut off.

Eventually you will notice that you begin to feel a little better. You no longer feel the intense pain. You begin to get your life back on track and become interested once again in the opposite sex. You'll feel normal on a daily basis. The wounds have healed and you have survived. Although you may never totally forget this person, the fresh pain of the break-up is behind you and you can surround yourself with new friends, new activities, and new interests. You are emotionally healthy now and ready to risk loving again.

Put reminders of the past away. Give back pictures and mementos collected during the time you went out together. If your boyfriend gave you a teddy bear for your birthday and you dissolve into tears every time you see that teddy bear perched on your bed, send your teddy to Russia with love. Getting rid of constant reminders helps put the pain out of your mind.

Keep yourself busy. Hibernating in your room and brooding over the break-up is a definite no-no. Enter group activities that will help distract your mind from your problems. Get involved with helping others. This way you will be more inclined to forget your own troubles as you think of others who just might have bigger problems than you. Get involved, but not with a person of the opposite sex (not yet). Helping others will take your mind off your problems and allow less time for crying, brooding and playing the 'if only' game.

Attempt to be friends again. Hopefully the two of you can be friends again. It's difficult to break up with someone who attends the same school or church as you, but continue to bump into him or her at gatherings or in the hallways. Or worse yet, be seated next to this person in class! Trying to avoid the other person is difficult, uncomfortable, and sometimes impossible.

A youth pastor invited me to speak at a teen youth retreat and confided an interesting story. As a teenager he had gone with a girl he cared for a lot. Later he broke up with her in an unkind manner. Each went his own way and married someone else. Fifteen years later he was pastoring a church and while speaking during the worship service he spotted this girl as part of his congregation. He knew he had to make it right with her. Fifteen years later he had to go back and right old wrongs. Break-ups from the past have a way of following us into the future.

Christopher and Lisa dated for a year before their romance died. Since both attended the same school and church, they were often inadvertently thrown together. At first they avoided one another. But eventually, when the initial hurt died, they became friends again. One day Lisa bought a new car right off the showroom floor and wanted to share her joy with a friend. The first person who got a ride in her new car was Christopher. After all, he was one of her best friends!

Immediately following a break-up, an effort on your part to be friends again might be misconstrued by the other person. So you may have to wait a bit. But it's worth the effort. As Charlie Brown says, 'I need all the friends I can get.' We all do.

And pray about it. God knows and cares about what has happened to you. Tell him how you hurt and ask him to help you heal. Claim the promise that 'in all things God works for the good of those who love him,' (Romans 8:28). God has a purpose in allowing hurt to touch our lives. It teaches us to respond by seeking a closer walk with God. For whatever reason hurt enters your life, you must trust God.

Andre Crouch, the gospel singer, loved a woman ardently. Then one day they broke up. Andre Crouch hurt deeply but he turned his thoughts to God, and out of the depth of his grief he wrote the beautiful gospel song 'Through It All'. You may never have thought of the song as a break-up song, but it is. Through it all Andre Crouch came to depend on God's Word. Through it all he learned that God could indeed solve his problems.

It Hurts Too Much

If you've tried all this and it just isn't working for you – the pain continues to hurt you more than it should or longer than it

should – you might try some other tactics.

Play 'your song' over and over and over again until you can't stand to hear it one more time. With a friend, go to the restaurant or place where you spent a lot of time together. Have a drink. Leave. Go in again. Do this again and again until it doesn't bother you to go there any longer.

Take a photo of your ex. Describe to a friend what you feel when you look at it. Repeat this over and over again until you get tired of looking at that photo. Visit places that are charged with memories. Talk about your memories with a friend. Get it all out.

Take a note out of your wallet or purse and put today's date on it. Then tuck it away in a safe place. Pull it out in six months and see if you can even remember his name!

If, after all this, you still feel as bad as the day your ex broke up with you, you need professional help.

Making A Comeback

The natural inclination after hurt is to insulate yourself so no one can ever hurt you again. Some protection may be necessary during the healing process, but a time comes when it is necessary to risk a new relationship. Withdrawing into a shell cuts you off from loving again.

The greatest hazard in life is to risk nothing. In risking nothing you may avoid hurt, but you cannot grow, change, learn to live, or relate better to others. No one is chained to the heartbreak of a broken romance. Peace comes as you let go of the hurt and risk loving again.

You are attending a football match with a friend, and suddenly you see him enter the stadium. A redhead clings to his arm. You don't know her, but you've seen her around. You wait for the inevitable hurt to engulf you, but only a twinge of pain comes and goes. It surprises you. Then you take another look at the redhead and wonder what she's got that you don't have. Naturally you wonder if he already feels the same towards her as he once said he felt towards you. You reflect for just a moment. Your home team scores a goal. You cheer along with the others and heave a big sigh of relief. It doesn't hurt the way it used to. 'At last,' you whisper under your breath, 'I've finally put myself back together again!'

Smart Love

chapter four

Falling in love is one of the most exciting events in life. Everyone wants to find True Love and when it happens life takes on a new meaning. Sudden energy surges through the system. New enthusiasm provides zest for the most boring tasks. A special chemistry works overtime. Time is too short when a couple in love are together and too long when they are apart.

In the early stages of love, time together is filled with exciting adventures and affectionate interludes. Each look and touch, every conversation and kiss take on monumental significance. Everything is so right, so good, so perfect. Suddenly, everyone faces the same challenging question, 'How do I know if this is the real thing?'

Part 11: Help! I think I'm in love!

• I'm going with someone I really like. Everything between us is good. No problems. But how do I know if this is True Love?
• I'm just out of a painful break-up. I never want to go through again what I'm going through now. How can I tell in advance if I have the real thing before it ends in disaster?
• I've been in one relationship after another and thought I'd found True Love each time. Yet each relationship ended when I thought it would last forever. How can you tell True Love when you find it? I know I can't!

None of us deliberately sets out to make wrong choices in our love life. We want our relationships to work. At the time we make our decision about who is right for us, we believe with all our heart that we are making the right choice. But more often than we like to admit, that choice is wrong.

Love is so exhilarating that some people close their eyes to anything that might spoil the fantasy. Telling the difference between True Love and infatuation is tricky, but not impossible. Applying the 'test of time' – two full years of dating before marriage – will help.

To clarify what you really know about True Love, take the What's-This-Thing-Called-Love test on page 94. Then read the chapter to clarify issues where you disagree or are confused.

True Love Conquers All

Many couples are doomed before they begin their relationship because they have bought into the theory that true love conquers all: 'Regardless of what the problem is, we can beat it.' 'We love each other so much we can make our relationship work.' 'No problem is too big for our love.'

Anyone who buys into this theory is not facing reality. Couples with one or more of the following problems hold to the 'love-conquers-all' theory when insisting that the following don't matter:
age differences
racial or cultural differences
religious differences
completing an education
not having enough money to live on
a current or previous marriage
parental disapproval
not wanting children
a drinking, drug, gambling or other compulsive habit

Tina and Max dated for a year. Tina was brought up in a strict religious home and

Max was raised in a home with no religion at all. Before meeting Tina, he had never even been to church. While dating they discussed their religious differences from time to time, but not in depth. Max went to church with Tina to make her happy but never made a commitment to the Lord. Because he attended church with her most of the time, Tina thought Max was accepting her faith, even though Max never said anything to lead her to think this. They got along so well in every other way that both skirted the issue of religion, hoping it would all work out. Neither wanted to rock the boat. Inwardly Tina knew she could never give up her faith, and Max knew he could never be religious like Tina. Both thought their love for each other could beat all obstacles.

Tina and Max married but parted ways over issues of faith, church and spirituality. By avoiding the issue of religious differences prior to marriage they were really saying, 'If we love each other enough, we can overcome this problem. True love can conquer our different religious values.' After they were married they found it wasn't that easy. Max no longer tried to accommodate her wishes by going to church. Tina tried to love him anyway, but she didn't have the spiritual leader in the home she really wanted. She wanted a man who would pray with her about problems, provide spiritual guidance, and be a godly model for their children.

As much in love as you are now, as much as you vow never to allow some of the issues mentioned to separate you, dealing with any of these issues over time will eventually wear out your love and devotion for one another. You can count on it, even if you think you can beat it now.

What's-This-Thing-Called-Love Test

Circle the letter that identifies what you believe to be true. (Answers are given on page 115.)

T F 1. Girls fall in love more rapidly than guys.

T F 2. When you find true love, you will know if it's the real thing.

T F 3. Infatuation and true love are so different that it is easy to tell one from the other.

T F 4. Sexual attraction can be as urgent in infatuation as in love.

T F 5. Once a girl thinks she is in love, she is more emotional and romantic than a guy.

T F 6. One of the best ways to find true love is to be friends with someone for a long time first.

T F 7. If you and your partner have found true love, you will never argue.

T F 8. It is possible to be in love with more than one person at a time.

T F 9. A strong sexual attraction is an indication of true love.

T F 10. Having the approval of family and friends for your marriage is one of the most important factors in determining future happiness.

T F 11. The desire to be together constantly means you have found true love.

T F 12. Love at first sight is the most enduring type of love.

T F 13. It is possible for a couple to determine true love after going out together for six months.

T F 14. It is permissible for a couple to have sex before marriage if they are certain they have found true love at last.

T F 15. Love at first sight is possible when you are mature for your age.

T F 16. Those who go together for two years or longer don't need premarital guidance.

T F 17. When a couple find true love rather than infatuation, they will be able to overcome all obstacles that stand in the way of their happiness.

T F 18. With careful observation, it is possible early in a relationship to tell if the one you are dating is being totally honest with you.

T F 19. If you have found true love, it doesn't matter whether your parents approve of your dating partner or not.

T F 20. God has created one special person for each of us, and through prayer and searching I will be guided to this person.

The Young Adult's Number One Dilemma
– How to tell if you are really in love

Love Lessons

While growing up, we are all conditioned or programmed to fall in love. How does such conditioning occur? First, a person must be raised in a family that believes in the concept of true love, teaches it, and lives by it. Second, the concept is reinforced by a culture that does likewise. All western cultures teach this concept to their youth through romantic adventure movies, television, DVDs, music and books. Both elements, home and society, then, have taught young adults to expect to fall in love, desire love and seek love. This creates a mindset that makes falling in love a sought-after state of being. Thus, by the time youngsters reach their teens, they not only want to fall in love but are expected to do so.

By the time young people are 18 or 19 years of age, most teenagers will already have been 'in love' two or three times. Our society has created the illusion that one can fall in and out of love as naturally as breathing. But if it is so natural, why do so many people make such a mess of it? The reason is that we never learn to love properly.

Learn to love? Yes. The ability to love is a learned experience that begins at birth. As infants our love lessons are completely one-sided. Our parents fill our needs for survival. We eventually begin reaching out, responding to and smiling at those special

people who satisfy our needs. Bonds of attachment are formed long before the words 'I love you' are understood.

The tender touching, kind words, kissing, caressing and nurturing we receive during our growing-up years prepare us for adult relationships where lovers caress, kiss and express their feelings of love for one another. Those who grow up in a physically or emotionally abusive home or in cold, uncaring homes where love is rarely expressed, find it difficult if not impossible to establish a warm, supportive love relationship as adults.

We learn to love by observing the love our parents express to each other. When Mum and Dad are affectionate with one another, we learn that this is how adults who care about each other respond. When patterns of hostility, silence, anger and withdrawal are noted, we learn that this is the way adults relate. The homes we grow up in, then, really are a 'school' for marriage.

Love, then, is a learned response to a pattern of actions and reactions observed early in life. Some of you are fortunate enough to be raised in emotionally healthy homes that foster self-worth and emotional security. Eventually a combination of attitudes and sensations develops that gives you the ability to love and be loved in return. When a couple are from similar backgrounds and have developed similar love patterns, their chance of a happy future far exceeds the chance of a couple from totally dissimilar or dysfunctional backgrounds who have developed different ideas about how to love.

Love is Strange

During the early stages of falling in love, you will probably experience a wide range of feelings and responses, including intense passion and idealisation of your partner – thinking he or she is absolutely 'perfect'. This romantic phase, which is also called *infatuation*, includes curious emotional and physiological changes – changes that have been laboratory tested and are 100% real. For instance, the sense of being in love makes a female appear more beautiful. Research explains that 'men and women who are in love walk more erectly and appear to have grown taller because the

spinal column is stretched.' All motor responses are intensely activated, making those in love extremely aware of and emotionally receptive to their partners.[1]

Eyes appear shinier when you are in love because the production of tears increases. This explains why eyes actually appear to sparkle and why you feel that the world is a brighter, shinier, happier place. Hearts also beat faster, which makes people even more susceptible to falling in love. Those in love also have more energy. Being in love spurs the production of epinephrine (adrenaline) and gives energy and strength to surmount problems; hence the feeling that you can conquer anything.[2]

Another study on those who thought they were in love showed that this increased adrenaline actually makes the heart grow fonder. Participants in this project were

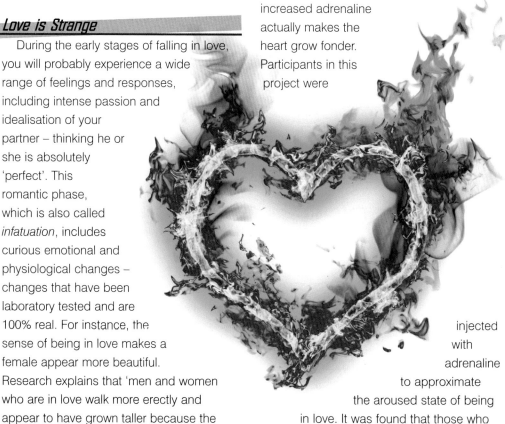

injected with adrenaline to approximate the aroused state of being in love. It was found that those who had been injected demonstrated more affection than those who did not have the extra spurt of adrenaline by injection. In other words, the state of being in love increases the ability to love.[3]

Those in love are more open to and accepting of what life has to offer them. They are ready to enjoy life to its fullest. In contrast, those who are not in love present a more negative or closed attitude to others when hurt or angry. Such responses include holding their arms close to their bodies, taking small steps, pursing their lips, and keeping their heads down. They are more apt to withdraw physically and emotionally from others. In response to their withdrawal, others actually withdraw from them. The result is unhappy persons who think others don't like them and never receive the love and attention they want and need to make them happy.

Some young people puzzle over why they rarely or never have dates and appear to be rejected by everyone they meet. In reality, they send out negative reactions which turn people off to them.[4]

Memory improves when one is in love. The person in love possesses an extraordinary ability to remember everything and anything about their object of affection. He may forget his maths assignment and she may forget to set her alarm, but neither will forget details about the other. When a person is in love, the mind apparently becomes selective about what it remembers.

Those in love want to be physically close to their loved one. If your partner is constantly edging closer, always wanting to be at your side, chances are she is in love with you, or thinks she is.

Love affects brain chemistry. One study concluded that once the emotional state has been defined as 'love', there is an increase in the brain chemical phenylethylamine that maintains the emotional high. Interestingly enough, phenylethylamine is the same chemical compound found in chocolate, a popular gift for those in love.[5]

Love also affects eating habits. Many people experience a loss of appetite in the early stages of love. One teenager laughingly told me that if she could just stay in love forever she would never have to diet again! Others feel as if they are walking on air or being transported to another world where they are barely conscious of their surroundings.

Lovers may have sweaty hands, butterflies in their stomachs, dilated pupils, and so on. Such physiological effects tend to fade in time. Personally, I am glad to hear this or I'd be exhausted after years of going through all that every time Harry walked through the door!

Early in the relationship it is common to think about the loved one constantly. Laura says, dreamily, 'I go to sleep thinking about him and he is the first thought that pops into my mind in the morning. Then I begin another day where he is never out of my thoughts.' This intense focus on the loved one tends to add even more interest and excitement to the relationship. When away from each other it is common for a couple in this early romantic phase to wait anxiously for the moment they will see each other again or intensely desire a phone call.

People in this stage talk endlessly about the object of their affection with anyone who will listen. It is possible that the one in love may become so totally immersed in the love relationship that responsibilities are ignored or forgotten. Kurt says, 'I'm having trouble concentrating in school, and I can't get my homework done. It piles up and I can't even force myself to tackle assignments that are due. I get next to nothing done. The other day I was at a student body officers' meeting. Someone asked a question. I didn't even know someone was talking to me until everyone laughed.'

Idealised Love

A person in love tends to idealise the perfection of the loved one. I distinctly remember this phase when dating my husband, Harry. Harry was extremely considerate and thoughtful, in contrast to other boyfriends I'd had. I thought Harry's interest in my every word was wonderful. He was so well-mannered, and he liked to do everything I liked to do. Harry was absolutely *perfect* for me in every way.

The truth is, I *wanted*

to see only the best in Harry. I chose to concentrate on his positive traits and deliberately ignored any negative ones that surfaced. I saw only what I wanted to see and imagined these positive traits growing under my love and encouragement. If I noticed a negative behaviour, I immediately excused it with a laugh, or the thought that he didn't really mean it, or it really didn't matter, or he'd never do that again. This is normal for people who think they are in love, but brings us back to the 'love-conquers-all' theory.

The Young Adult's Number One Dilemma
– How to tell if you are really in love

Hollywood and the mass media advance this theory through romantic dramas of couples who battle every obstacle and still live 'happily ever after'. We dream of our own storybook romance and put up with problems and disappointments when going out with someone to keep the romantic dream alive – sometimes going far beyond reality.

There is a tendency to overlook differences in likes.

Andrew may notice that Sonia doesn't seem to enjoy going out to places. When he asks her about it, Sonia says she prefers being alone with him. Andrew is adventurous and loves to be on the go. But he tells himself that this is only a phase that Sonia is going through and that she will change over time.

Sarah notices that Sam spends money foolishly. She excuses his behaviour and thinks he'll learn. Once he gets a job, he'll be more responsible. She makes herself believe that in time he could support a wife and children if they married.

Some couples while dating will discuss shortcomings with a partner; others are afraid to or do not know how. Judy thinks that if she talks with Jeff about a problem she sees, he might get upset and break up with her. Her relationship with Jeff is already unpredictable. He is easily hurt by even the hint of criticism. So she puts off discussing an area that troubles her. This is the price she is willing to pay for keeping Jeff as a boyfriend. Someday Judy will pay handsomely for this deception should she and Jeff marry, because neither of them ever learned the communication skills necessary to discuss differences.

While the one in love idealises his partner, friends and family members often clearly recognise problems. Karen's parents don't think Jake is the right one for her because he appears controlling and they tell her so; but Karen doesn't want to see or hear it. She wants to continue living in her dream world, believing only what she wants to about Jake. Jake's best friend notices how moody Karen appears and that

Smart Love
chapter four

Destructive Love Tactics

Some people are so desperate for love they will resort to devious tactics to try to make someone fall in love with them.

Threats of suicide. Suicide is the most desperate of all attempts to attract someone's attention or get sympathy. Such attempts either end up fatal – in which case the victim will never know if he was really loved – or become proof positive that the one who attempted suicide is mentally unbalanced. One girl swallowed a bottle of pills only to wake up a day later in hospital. Her boyfriend still wasn't there, and had no intention of coming back. She had run up a huge medical bill and admitted she never meant to kill herself. She only wanted to make him feel sorry for her and come back.

Threats of pregnancy. 'I wanted to get married so badly I told my boyfriend I was pregnant,' a teen girl admitted. 'He was from an honourable family, and we married immediately. Then I had to make up more lies about a miscarriage. After one child, the marriage ended in divorce anyway, and I always doubted his love for me.' Even if you could get someone to marry you by threatening pregnancy, you would never know if he married you because he really loved you or because of the pregnancy.

Bribes. One girl said she gave her boyfriend money, hoping that he would eventually marry her. 'He charged vast sums of money on a credit card my parents gave me, eventually left me, and quickly married

someone else.' Others bribe loved ones with trips, cars, clothing and other items of monetary value. It may work for a while, but in the long run you can't buy love.

Jealousy. Some people provoke jealousy by pretending there is someone else. They will go out with someone else or invent elaborate stories about another boy or girlfriend to capture the attention of a special person. Such plans invariably fail.

Using relatives. Others try to endear themselves to family members and make themselves indispensable. They send cards, presents and pictures of family events they have attended to all the relatives and fake attention all geared to endear them to their loved one's family.

Some want a boy or girlfriend so badly they will do anything or say anything to get and keep one. But few who are worth having can be fooled long by grovelling, snivelling, lying, bribery or threats. Relationships founded on dishonesty are doomed to failure. Rather than attracting someone by such tactics, one gives evidence of low self-esteem, desperation and insecurity. Resorting to destructive love tactics to attract someone rarely wins true love.

Part 12: True Love or Infatuation? How to Tell the Difference

Studies show that most people tend to rate past relationships as infatuation and present relationships as real love. Undoubtedly, many past romances would have been described as love if the study had been conducted while the romances were in progress. Another survey found that the average person experiences infatuation six or seven times and real love only once or twice. You may already have experienced a portion of your allotted romances. But the Big Question is: How can you tell for sure if it is real love or only infatuation?

A teenager wrote to a newspaper columnist to ask how one can know when one is in love. The columnist replied: 'If you have to ask – you aren't.' The inadequacy of this response is appalling, but many people, when asked how you know when you're in love, say: 'Oh, when it hits, you'll just know!' That's only partially true. You'll know that something has hit you, but you won't know if it is love or infatuation.

Infatuation is a strange mixture of sex and emotions. The dictionary defines the word as 'completely carried away by unreasoning passion or attraction'. The word *infatuation* comes from a Latin word that means 'silly or foolish' which graphically describes some people's behaviour. However foolish, the experience can be wildly exciting. Infatuation feels the same as love and the intensity of feelings is just as strong in both. That's the trouble: infatuation appears real.

Love and infatuation do have one thing in common – strong feelings of affection for someone – which

complicates the matter of sorting out the differences, because many of the symptoms overlap one another. The most passionate and blind infatuation may contain a portion of true love. And true love may include several symptoms found in infatuation. The differences between love and infatuation, then, are often found in *degree* rather than in definition. Therefore, one must examine all evidence with extreme caution.

Love and infatuation share three similar symptoms: passion, a desire to be close, and strange emotions.

Passion: Passion may be present without true love. It is entirely possible, particularly for the male, to feel passionate or to have strong sexual feelings for a girl he has never met.

Necking and petting increase the urgency of erotic feelings until sex dominates the relationship. Passion does not necessarily indicate true love. Sexual attraction can be as urgent in infatuation as it is in true love. Sometimes it is the major part of infatuation. Love, however, is always based on more than sexual attraction or passion.

Infatuation is a stage that is too intense to last. Neither a guy nor a girl can maintain such fierce passion for long, although they vow they will. If all a couple has going for them is passion, the relationship will probably end within three to six months. Should a couple marry based on this initial rush of passion they will learn that when the passion dies there is nothing left to hold them together.

Desire to be close: The desire to be near one another constantly can be just as strong and overwhelming in infatuation as in true love. You may wish to be together all the time, dreading the time when you must part. You may feel empty and lonely when your loved one is not with you, but this does not necessarily mean that it is real love.

Strange emotions: Researchers have confirmed that we experience certain distinct physical symptoms at the onset of infatuation as previously mentioned. You may feel like walking on air when everything is going well and simply ill when things go wrong between you. You may feel icy fingers race up and down your spine, the inability to concentrate, sick to your stomach and unable to eat. But strange emotions can occur just as frequently with infatuation as with real love, although 'funny feelings' and strange emotions are probably more indicative of infatuation. True love encompasses more than a mixture of giggly or sick feelings and will continue long after such strange feelings subside. Certain life experiences can also make you more vulnerable to infatuation. If you are lonely or bored or getting over a broken romance, you are more likely to interpret a new romance as love when it is little more than infatuation. If you are insecure, or have low self-esteem, you must also beware. Although high self-esteem and mature persons can be deceived by infatuation, they are more likely to recognise the condition for what it is.

Don't get the impression that infatuation is all bad. It can be a pleasant and enjoyable

The Young Adult's Number One Dilemma
– How to tell if you are really in love

experience as long as you recognise it for what it is – a brief interlude of romantic fantasy that will not last. Given enough time, it will pass or it will develop into a real relationship that involves more than a rush of emotions. Remember also that some relationships that begin as infatuation will develop into true love over time as they are tested.

True love differs from infatuation in that it provides time and space to recognise the good qualities as well as the shortcomings of your special friend. To commit to, to have sex with, to move in with, or to marry someone on the basis of these early feelings is sheer foolishness and will result in predictable negative consequences.

In the 1820s greenhorn Gold Rush prospectors occasionally mistook pyrite for gold. Pyrite, or fools' gold as it is called, can be detected by popping it into a pan and putting it on a hot stove. While it sizzles and smokes, it sends out a strong stench. But heat will not damage real gold, nor does it smell foul. Unfortunately, you cannot put your love relationship in a pan on a hot stove to see if it produces a stench; but you can test it against the following twelve factors. They are not listed in order of importance. Consider each factor as objectively as you can.

1. **Love develops slowly; infatuation rapidly.** Most people think that falling in love happens suddenly and intensely. When questioned about it, many people report

falling in love at least once in their lives.

When asked about this, James said, 'I fell hard the minute I saw her. She looked just as I always pictured she would. On our first date we talked half the night and I felt as if I'd known her all my life. I felt as though she was my best friend. Dreams really do come true!'

James thinks that dreams come true, but his evaluation of his dream girl won't be valid until after a year of dating. Why? Because love grows, and growth takes time. It's infatuation that hits hard, fast and suddenly. It is impossible to know the real person after only a few dates. Early in a relationship people wear masks while putting on their best behaviour. Any unpleasant traits are closely guarded, hidden and controlled. For this reason it takes months and even years of seeing a person under varied circumstances before it can be said that you know someone really well. Many people successfully hide negative personality traits until after they are married. That is why some people say their partner changed after they got married, or complain they married a stranger.

Don't jump to conclusions. Allow your relationship to grow slowly. Begin as friends and don't try to rush through the getting-to-know-you stage. Leisurely beginnings can make for pleasurable dating relationships and they are much safer. Eventually such friendships can lead to a genuine love that resembles infatuation in intensity but is rooted in reality.

2. Love relies heavily on compatibility; infatuation relies more on chemistry and physical appearance. Steve met a new girl who was good-looking and very interesting to him. He got a good feeling the minute they met. He felt a definite chemistry between them. 'Either it works or it doesn't,' he says with a shrug. 'You either feel it or you don't. I felt it.'

If only discovering true love were as easy as Steve thinks it is! Where did he come up with the idea that chemistry and love are the same thing? Probably from all the love scenes portrayed in the movies he's seen. The script reads something like this: 'Her heart races with excitement; she melts into his arms. He kisses her passionately and their bodies merge.'

More often than not, people pretend this happens. Most likely they are conditioned for it and it happens because they desire it so intensely. Many people who allow chemistry to dictate their behaviour and future wake up later to deal with disastrous results. Relying on 'chemistry' to guide you towards true love is foolish and dangerous.

This is true because chemistry is based mostly on physical or sexual attraction. I believe there needs to be that spark and pull between the two of you that make your eyes light up and make you feel more alive than you have ever felt before, but to base a relationship on this alone is ludicrous.

I cannot accept the 'love-at-first-sight' theory. I can accept 'like-at-first-sight' or even 'like-very-much-at-first-sight', but *love*? No. You may feel strongly attracted to a person you just met. You feel the chemistry working. You like what you see – body build, actions and responses. You may like everything about that person. But there is still a long way to go before you can *love* that person.

Although true love includes chemistry and physical attraction, it springs from many other factors as well, including character, personality, emotions, ideas and attitudes. When you're *in love* you are interested in the way the object of your love thinks and responds to situations. You focus on the values you hold in common. How does the other person respond when he wins or loses? To the pitfalls or challenges of life? Is he or she kind, appreciative and courteous? Do your attitudes on religion, family, sex, money and friends match? What interests do you share in common? Can you enjoy an evening with family or friends or must you always go somewhere? Are your backgrounds similar? The more you have in common in these areas, the better your chances are for developing true love.

The Young Adult's Number One Dilemma
– How to tell if you are really in love

Compatible personalities, along with common interests and values, go a long way towards developing a lasting relationship.

3. Love centres on one person only; infatuation may involve several persons. An infatuated person may be 'in love' with two or more persons at the same time. And these two individuals may differ markedly in personality. For instance, Jan says she is in love with two guys and finds it impossible to choose between them. One is mature, stable and responsible, whereas the other is an irresponsible, fun-loving spendthrift. Most likely Jan is in love with neither one. Chances are it is her adolescent responses that draw her to the fun-loving spendthrift while her maturing emotions tell her that the qualities of the other man hold more importance. In her mind she combines their qualities and thinks she has fallen in love with both. True love focuses on one person in whose character and personality are found the qualities you believe are most essential. You no longer have to combine people to form an ideal.

4. Love produces security; infatuation produces insecurity. When in love, a person has a sense of security and trust after considering all the factors in the relationship. An infatuated person, on the other hand, will probably struggle with feelings of insecurity and may attempt to control the other through jealousy. This does not mean that when you really love someone you will never feel jealous. In a love relationship that has developed over time, however, jealousy is less frequent and less severe. Love trusts.

Some people feel flattered by jealousy at first. They think it indicates true love and assume that the more jealous a boy or girlfriend is, the more they are loved. Jealousy, however, does not signify healthy emotions, but rather insecurity and low self-image. Whatever the root cause, a jealous person wants to fence the other person in, keeping her or him to himself. Jealousy produces selfishness and possessiveness. Real love doesn't act in this way.

5. Love recognises realities; infatuation ignores them. True love looks at problems squarely without trying to minimise their seriousness. Two teenagers in love will strive to finish their education before they marry, because their know their marriage will be

107

stronger if they can build it on a solid educational foundation. They will not jump into a quick marriage for fear love will leave them.

Infatuation ignores the differences in social, racial, educational or religious backgrounds. Sometimes infatuation grips a person who is already married or is in a situation that precludes open dating. Infatuation argues that such things don't really matter. If you love one another, such problems can be worked out.

A couple in love faces problems frankly and attempts to solve them. If certain problems seem to threaten their relationship, they discuss them openly and attempt to solve them intelligently. Under infatuation a couple will disregard or gloss over the differences. A couple in love intelligently anticipates problems most likely to occur and negotiates solutions in advance.

6. Love motivates positive behaviour; infatuation has a destructive effect. Love will have a constructive effect on your personality and bring out the very best in you. It will give you new energy, ambition and interest in life. Love produces creativity and interest in personal growth, improvement and worthy causes. It engenders feelings of self-worth, trust and security. Love will spur you on towards success. You will study harder, plan more effectively and save more diligently. Life takes on additional purpose and meaning. You may day-dream, but you stay within the bounds of reality by centring your thoughts on plans within reach. Your love will encourage you to

function at your highest level.

By contrast, infatuation has a destructive and disorganising effect on the personality. You will find yourself less effective, less efficient, less able to reach your true potential. Family members or close friends may notice this effect immediately. They might say, 'My, what's come over you? You won't go anywhere or do anything. What's the matter with you? Are you sick or something?' Then someone else will comment, 'No, she's not sick. She's in love.' But that observation is incorrect. You are infatuated, not in love.

Infatuation thrives on unrealistic dreams in which the two of you lead a beautiful, blissful life in perfect agreement at all times. These daydreams cause you to forget the realities of life, school, work, study, responsibilities and money.

If you are in love, you will naturally idealise about your love, but this will tend to grow out of an understanding and appreciation for the other person that you have checked out against real circumstances. If you are infatuated, you will idealise with complete disregard for reality.

7. **Love recognises faults; infatuation ignores them.** Love will lead you to recognise the fine qualities in the other and help you build a relationship on those. But even though you recognise those good qualities and idealise them to some degree, you do not see the person as faultless. You freely admit areas of his or her personality or character that fall short of perfection, but you see so much to respect and admire that you accept the person on the basis of the good qualities.

Infatuation, on the other hand, will keep you from seeing anything wrong with your friend. You idealise to such a degree that you will not admit that the other person has any faults. You defend him or her against all critics. You admire one or two qualities so much that you fool yourself into believing that these can outweigh all the faults and problems.

Love also recognises all the good qualities, but it does not blind you to problem areas in the other person's personality. It will, however, enable you to love despite these faults.

8. **Love controls physical contact; infatuation exploits it.** A couple who has found true love tends to hold in check their expression of physical affection. Each respects the other so much that they voluntarily put on hold their desire for sexual intimacy. Infatuation demands physical expression much earlier. Furthermore,

physical contact makes up a smaller part of the total relationship for a couple in love, in contrast to an infatuated couple. The reason for this is that infatuation depends largely on physical attraction and the excitement felt when exploring the other person's physical equipment. The person experiencing this for the first time naturally concludes that this must be something very special, because he has never before felt such a response.

When a couple experiences such strong sexual attraction, they assume they are in love, and often marry on the basis of sexual excitement alone. They ignore the fact that their values, goals and belief systems are at odds. They may have few common interests and incompatible personalities and character traits. As their relationship continues they discover they differ on everything else, from where to go on a date, to what kind of food they like, to how to spend money. They begin to doubt they ever even liked each other. In the midst of such chaos they find their sexual interest declining. They finally wake up to what everyone else could see all along, and they part. They weren't in love; they were 'in lust'.

Although true love includes physical attraction, it springs from many other factors as well. For the couple in love, physical contact usually has a deeper meaning than sheer pleasure. It expresses how they feel towards each other. Unfortunately, physical contact expressed in infatuation often becomes an end in itself. Pleasure dominates the experience.

When you really love someone with a genuine love, you will do two things; always protect that person and provide the best for him or her.

9. Love is selfless; infatuation is selfish. Being in love involves more than just the emotions. True love is acted out in everyday life. You expect to be treated with love and consideration and you also express love and consideration to your partner, even when you don't feel like it. Any of us can be loving when our needs are met and our partner behaves in a caring manner. But the test of love is whether you can be loving even when your partner has treated you unfairly, neglected your needs, forgotten your birthday, or been inconsiderate.

One of my favourite *Peanuts* cartoons shows Charlie Brown dressed in pyjamas, carrying a glass of water to Snoopy, who is lazily perched on top of his kennel. The caption reads: 'Love is getting someone a glass of water in the middle of the night.' Chuck has the right idea.

It isn't easy to get up in the middle of the night and put someone else's needs before your own.

Infatuation is self-centred. You think more in terms of what the relationship can do for you than what you can do for the other person. You enjoy the feeling of pride you have when your partner is with you and others realise she belongs to you.

10. Love brings the approval of family and friends; infatuation brings disapproval. The divorce rate in Japan is one quarter of the divorce rate in the United States. The fact that most Japanese choose partners who are approved by their families, while American couples choose regardless of family approval, might explain the discrepancy. Apparently Japanese families have a clearer vision of who is suitable for their son or daughter than does the son or daughter! When your family and close friends see that you are well suited to a boy or girlfriend, they usually approve. They see how well your personalities blend, the many interests you share and how you complement and motivate one another.

If your parents or friends do not approve, beware! If they are convinced that the friend you

have chosen is wrong for you, they are probably right. Family and friends are extremely interested in your future welfare and don't want you to get hurt. Since they are not as emotionally involved as you, they may be able to see certain aspects you can't see.

Marriages that lack the blessing of parents have a high failure rate. One researcher compared complaints registered by happily married persons with those of divorced persons. The divorced were almost four times as likely to complain that their spouse had little in common with mutual friends. It was also found that happily married couples were far less likely to have problems with one another's parents. It's short-sighted and immature to say or even think, 'I'm not marrying his or her parents. They play no part in what goes on between us.' Oh, yes, they do. Just wait. If parents and friends object, take care. If they approve, take heart. With approval, there's a good chance you have found true love.

11. Love ends slowly; infatuation ends rapidly. You cannot test this factor, of course, until the relationship ends. But in retrospect a person can ask two questions: How long did the romance last? and How long did it take to get over it? Just as true love takes time to develop, so it also takes time for such feelings to vanish. It can

happen in no other manner. If the two of you have grown and shared many experiences together, you may not get over a break-up for a long period of time.

Infatuations end much the same way as they begin – fast – with one exception. Infatuation will not end rapidly if you have become involved sexually. Sex complicates the emotional responses. A couple may stay together, not because of true love, but because of mutually satisfying sexual relations. Therefore the length of time it takes to recover from a break-up does not indicate anything significant if the couple has been sexually involved.

12. Love survives separation; infatuation cannot. Love may even grow during a separation. Absence *does* make the heart grow fonder. If your love has been genuine, you will have been uniting your life more and more with your loved one. When he or she is separated from you, you will feel as though part of your own self is missing. Absence helps you recognise how much the relationship means to you.

Infatuation dies quickly once the other person fades from sight. 'Out of sight, out of mind' holds, because infatuation bases itself largely on physical attraction and one or two other qualities. Interest will die rather rapidly when the relationship is not sustained by contact. Infatuation cannot survive the test of time.

Part 13: To Make Sure . . . Give It Time

Infatuation wants to rush the relationship. Pulsating emotions overrule good sense and rush the couple into commitments that may be regretted in all the years to come. Don't make quick commitments that you will regret later. True love can survive the test of time, which is two years of dating to make sure you are well suited for marriage.

Even though your sexual urges are exploding and throbbing at an all-time high, hold off sexual involvement. Sex now will confuse the emotions and complicate the process of separating infatuation from the real thing. This calls for self-denial, patience and discipline – traits that go a long way in building a relationship that lasts.

Given time, infatuation may grow into true love. So there is no reason to end the relationship the minute you diagnose infatuation. Breaking up immediately, without allowing the initial intense feelings to run their course, may preclude knowing if infatuation would lead to true love.

Instead, adopt a 'wait-and-see' attitude. If the relationship lasts a year – great. During the second year, carefully evaluate your partner's behaviour and character as well as how the two of you work together.

A six-to-nine month engagement period is needed to give a couple time to prepare for a church wedding; but more important than the wedding is time to prepare for the marriage. Remember, after every wedding comes a marriage. I strongly recommend in-depth premarital guidance with a qualified counsellor. These sessions, which extend over several weeks, should include a series of discussions, outside reading and written homework.

The Young Adult's Number One Dilemma
– How to tell if you are really in love

Such an approach to marriage might sound unromantic and clinical, but where such programmes have been implemented, a divorce rate of only 3-5% is reported. Compare this to the US national average of 50%!

To win the love and respect of their partner, most people show only their better sides and attempt to hide their faults and shortcomings. They believe that if the other person knew about their faults or idiosyncrasies they would not be good enough or lovable enough. So they act a part – act as if these faults are not a part of themselves – for a time, allowing their loved one to see them only at their best.

Since it is difficult to play a role or wear a mask for long periods of time, it can eventually become tiresome and the masks will slip. This is when you can begin to see some of the hidden traits in your partner. So it is important to stay in a relationship long enough for the masks to slip. It may be possible for a person to mask a fault for a year, but longer than that would be difficult. It is for this reason that I strongly urge couples to go together for two years. During the first year you measure compatibility and wait to see the masks slip. After the masks slip, you begin to see the real person. Then decide if the good qualities outweigh the negative qualities now appearing. To marry someone before the masks have slipped is like marrying a stranger.

You simply do not know what you are getting

or what unpleasant surprises lie ahead.

If you analyse your situation carefully but still can't decide whether or not you have found true love; if the more you try, the more confused you get, allow yourself more time. Time will give you experience and perspective as it offers more contact with your friend. It will provide more opportunities for you to find out what you need to know to make the final decision. When all is said and done, you have found true love when your mutual relationship fosters individual growth for both of you and increases the depth of your love for one another.

More than a million divorces occur annually in the United States. The average duration of these marriages is seven years. Half of them disintegrate within three years after the wedding. Each of these couples stood at the altar, eyes bright with joy, promising love and faithfulness forever, never anticipating that they were making the greatest mistake of their lives. What happened to their starry-eyed talks, the tender promises, lingering looks, close embraces, passionate kisses and whispers of love?

Most failed to understand that you don't 'fall' in love. You decide to love – to think about, spend time with, and have strong feelings for someone. 'Falling' is the easy and fun part of love. The hard part, the commitment to love unconditionally an imperfect person, follows. True love says, 'I will love you unconditionally, even when you fail to meet my needs, reject or ignore me, behave stupidly, make stupid choices I wouldn't have made, hurt me, disagree with me, and treat me unfairly. And I will love you like this forever.' This is what true love is and it involves much more than sexual excitement or infatuation. Infatuation is little more than a cheap substitute for the real thing. Attempting to build a relationship on infatuation is risky, to say the least.

This doesn't mean that you should view all romantic involvements with fear or suspicion. An exciting infatuation can be fun and a glorious booster to self-worth, while making you feel great. When you find one, enjoy it rather than fighting it. Just don't allow your pulsating emotions to overrule good sense! Call it by its right name – infatuation – not love.

Love Is . . .

So far we've looked at love the way society views it. But what does Scripture say about love? In the New Testament five Greek words are used to define love.

Epithymia is never translated 'love' yet it is an important part of love. It means a strong desire of any kind, to long for or even covet. When used negatively it is the equivalent of lust. Within marriage, *epithymia* means the strong physical desire a couple has that results in sexual intimacy.

Eros is sensual love. It means devoted to or arousing sexual desire. To feel *eros* is to be strongly affected by sexual desire. It can be controlled and positive, or uncontrolled and sinful. The English word *erotic* is derived from the word *eros*. Whereas erotic love is important within marriage, outside of marriage erotic love lacks the commitment and staying power needed to hold a relationship together, because it is based solely on intense physical desire. Feelings of *eros* alone can be very selfish and self-serving.

A third type of love, **storge**, describes natural affection and a feeling of belonging to each other. Loyalty and commitment are fulfilled through *storge* love.

Phileo is friendship love, a type of love that should have high priority in marriage and long before. It means companionship, communication, co-operation and pure enjoyment in being with someone who is a 'friend'. Thoughts, attitudes, experiences, feelings and dreams are shared through *phileo* love. It cherishes and enjoys the presence of the other.

Agape love, the highest type of love expressed in the Bible, values and serves the loved one. It loves the unlovable. It keeps erotic love alive and possesses the power to rekindle what has died. It is an act of the will, not based on feelings. *Agape* love is a deep reservoir that provides stability even during times of stress and conflict. It is perhaps best described by God's love for us as exemplified in John 3:16. *Agape* love originates from God, not from within us. *Agape* love costs. God models this love for us throughout Scripture. It is an art that may take a lifetime to learn.

The Young Adult's Number One Dilemma
– How to tell if you are really in love

True love has bits of all five types of love but must be dominated by *agape* love. To experience this kind of love, you have to be willing to risk being rejected or feeling unloved. It means wanting the best for your loved one, even if the best opposes your personal wishes. Love means encouraging and supporting each other's dreams, even if it costs you something. It means wanting your partner to achieve and become all he can be, even if it becomes threatening to you. Love also means giving security when it is needed as well as space when privacy is desired.

This kind of love is God's creative gift to us and can be enjoyed to its fullest only within the safety and security of marriage. We are only able to love because he first loved us. It is

through his love that we are freed from the hurt of past relationships and are willing to risk loving again. Through him we no longer need to be dominated by rejection and failure.

Even true love changes over the years. The intense love you feel for someone now can grow stale or intensify. That's the way love is. It is fragile and needs constant nourishment to flourish.

Love Without Limits

Society programmes us through the mass media and other forums to believe that love will solve all personal problems. Such a concept leads people down a dangerous path because they expect romance to offer what only Jesus can supply.

Rather than securing all your hopes and dreams to a human being, why not secure yourself first and foremost to someone who will never change? Jesus is always the same, yesterday, today and forever. Any promises he makes, he will keep. You can count on it. His love is completely unconditional. He will always love you, regardless of your appearance, failures or mistakes. When others fail you, he will be there to love and care about you. He is the only one who loves perfectly.

Jesus is the only one who can supply all your needs, fulfil all your desires, and meet all your expectations. Anchor yourself to him first and then you will be less likely to be disappointed in love and more likely to find a satisfying love on this Earth.

Too Young

There's an old ballad that says, 'They tried to tell us we're too young, too young to really be in love . . .' I am not trying to tell you or any other young person that you are too young to be in love. (However, the younger you are, the more likely it is to be infatuation than true love. But that's not the problem.) Anyone, young or old, can fall in love. The problem comes with staying in love.

Smart Love

chapter five

Many young people play with sex – as if it were a game. Their concept of love is perverted and confused. To see how far they can get in a relationship, to see how much personal and sexual fun they can enjoy without getting hurt or trapped, becomes a challenge. Others play with sex because they don't know any better. They are insecure and use sex to boost their sagging self-esteem, forget some problem they are dealing with, or to get over some hurt from the past. Both sexes play with sex, but they tend to do so differently.

Part 14: What's My Line?

A professor who taught sex education classes at a large university asked his students to discuss the various lines they had used to entice someone into petting or sexual encounters. At first all the guys did was snort, giggle and laugh at the request, but eventually they got serious and gradually exposed the lines they had heard or used. Halfway through the course, however, the boys complained that the discussions were ruining their sex lives! In other words, once the girls understood what the boys meant by what they were saying, they weren't so quick to dish it out. Follow-up reports confirmed that there were no pregnancies among the group of girls who attended that course during the

ensuing term.

The role of 'lines' and other devious tactics used to entice the opposite sex into sex play is stronger than most young adults realise. What's a line? Lines are anything said or done to pressure or manipulate someone into sex play. And never underestimate the power of a good line delivered in the heat of passion. Many highly principled young people have found themselves victims of a well-timed, well-chosen, even if well-used line. Every young person should know how much stock to put into what is said or done at the time and where to draw the line when sex play begins.

Lines Guys Use

The True Love Line. One study revealed the most prevalent line is: *'If you love me, you'll let me.'* Boys have been using this line since the beginning of time. But the real question is: If he does get what he wants, what proof will you have when it is all over that he really loves you? It is more likely that he used you to satisfy his own urgent needs. The boy who uses this line is usually a slow but steady operator who tends to hang in there and wear you down over time until he gets what he wants. Girls, a good response to this line is: *'If you really love me, you won't put that kind of pressure on me.'*

The Flattery Line. *'You have such a gorgeous body I can hardly control myself!'* Or *'You are so beautiful I can hardly take my eyes*

off you.' Or *'You have the most beautiful eyes in the world.'* Under questioning, boys who use this line reveal they do so because they can think of little else to say. In other words, there is so little attraction between the two that he flatters (and sometimes outright lies) to get what he wants. This reinforces what an attractive girl wants to hear, and flatters an unattractive girl. Now get this: One researcher showed pictures of women to males who were sexually aroused as well as to males who were not sexually aroused. The ones who were sexually aroused rated the women in the pictures as much more attractive than did the males who were not sexually aroused when viewing the same pictures. In other words, the greater the sexual need, the better any female looks!

Girls, a good response to this line is: *'Thank you. I'm glad you appreciate my appearance, but this package can't be opened until my wedding night.'*

The Situational Ethics Approach. *'Everybody's doing it'* is a line used by the situational-ethics crowd. These men imply there's something wrong with the female who won't jump into bed with them. They accuse her of being a prude. *'Times have changed,'* such guys chant. *'Keep up with the times.'* These guys put such pressure on a girl she begins to wonder whether she is the only one who is still holding out.

In the age of AIDS, however, a good response might be: *'Everybody is not doing it because I'm one who is not and proud of it. I plan to live guilt free.'*

The Sympathy Approach. *'Nobody understands me but you. Everybody else is against me – my parents, the school, the law. All I need is you to help me and everything will be OK.'* This guy isn't doing very well in life and cries on your shoulder. It's effective because it appeals to the mothering instincts of a female. You know his reputation isn't the best, but that could change if only others would give him a chance. You want to help this boy, who could amount to something if only he had the opportunity! Whatever the version, beware of this line. This guy has mastered the technique of playing on a girl's sympathies. Just as soon as you smother him with sympathy, he'll prepare you for the pushover.

A good response is: *'I understand more than you think I do. Go home to Mummy.'*

The opposite version of the sympathy approach offers comfort to the hurting girl: *'You poor little girl. Nobody has cared much for you, have they? You've had it tough, haven't you, sweetheart? But I can show you real love, right now, right here . . .'* Any time sympathy is the primary motive, beware. This line is especially dangerous to a young woman who comes from an unhappy home and has never enjoyed a warm, loving relationship with her mother or father. She is vulnerable because she feels sorry for herself and is open to anyone who offers her sympathy. She wants and needs a man who understands her, of course, but she needs a man who understands more about life than how to engage her in instant lust.

The Big-shot Approach. *'Girls are standing in line to date me. You don't know how lucky you are to get this great opportunity.'* He probably doesn't verbalise all this in just this way, but you get the idea by how he acts. This youth is probably good-looking, tall, athletic, intelligent, personable and popular. He has the ability to make you feel  super-special. You'll be especially vulnerable to his attention if you are very young or inexperienced or have a potent case of inferiority.

A good response to this one might be: *'Thanks anyway, but I'll pass. Move on to the next in line.'*

The Logical Approach. *'I thought*

we were going to get married.' 'Who needs a slip of paper to legalise a love like ours?' 'It only makes sense to see if we are sexually compatible before we marry.' This line comes on so gradually that it is often difficult to recognise. It occurs often in long-term, steady relationships with a basically nice boy who you 'know' is right for you.

A good response to this line is: 'Guess we'll never be compatible, as I'm holding out until it's legal. In case we ever changed our minds about each other, I wouldn't want you to feel obligated to me.'

Then be prepared for protests! One report revealed that more than 33% of the sexually experienced girls believed when they first had sex that they would marry the man – but few of them did. However, only 7% of the sexually active men polled thought they would marry the young woman. Now one of two things was taking place – either she was fooling herself or he wasn't telling the truth. Take your pick.

The Abnormal Approach. 'What's the matter with you? Are you frigid or something? You don't want word to get around that you can't make it, do you?' Every normal girl looks forward to a sexually fulfilling relationship with her husband some day, but this boy plants seeds of doubt about her ability to function. She wonders whether she might be undersexed, if she is normal, or maybe she's simply undesirable. Warning: Boys who use this approach think of women as 'things' to be used by males. Chances are the 'pro' with this line would and could produce real sex problems for a girl.

A good response might be: 'Rest assured the plumbing works. There's no need to try it out in advance.'

The Intellectual Approach. Here the fellow promotes heavy 'think' sessions regarding sex. 'This article I read said that religious women make better lovers than non-Christian women. What do you think?' 'How often do you think a couple should have sex?' 'How important do you think sexual compatibility is for a couple?' He doesn't 'do' anything at first – just gets you in the habit of talking with him about sex. He's an excellent conversationalist, easy to talk to and wows you with his thinking and ideas. His objective is to lead you through the natural sequence of events. Such discussions can be sexually enlightening and very stimulating. When things get too natural, better call a halt.

A good response might be: 'This conversation is getting too hot to handle. Either cool it or take a hike – a permanent hike.'

The Threat. 'If you don't, I'll date someone else.' 'If you aren't interested, there are plenty of others who are.' This line attempts to intimidate you by implying that unless you give in to his desires, you will have to sit at home alone for the rest of your life. He probably won't have any trouble finding a willing partner. But you know exactly what he wants, and any female will do.

Tell this one to: 'Move on while I look for someone who respects my decisions and appreciates something besides my body.'

Promises, promises. 'I won't get you pregnant. You won't catch a disease from me. I promise we'll get married some day.' Under the pressure of sexual tension, some boys make promises they can't keep. They mean every word at the moment but quickly forget a promise once urgent sexual pressure has been relieved. Girls fall for promises because they desperately want to believe them.

Whenever a girl thinks she owes a boy sex, it is because he wants her to think that. In this case he manipulates her into thinking this through his words and actions. He cares little for her; his behaviour is manipulative and disrespectful.

A logical response works best with promises: 'Are you prepared to be a father should I get pregnant?' or 'Let's make absolutely sure you don't have AIDS or an STD by getting tested at the nearest STD clinic and then waiting six months to be sure.'

The Guilt Line. 'I'm so tensed up I can't stand it! You've let me go this far. You can't stop now! You're driving me wild. I've just got to have it!' No, he doesn't have to have it. If he doesn't get a sexual release right now, nothing bad will happen. He won't suddenly develop a hernia or suffer brain damage or

go bald. The worst thing that might happen is that he might have to run around the block a time or two before he can go home and say goodnight to his mum and dad, but that won't hurt him either.

A good response to this one is: 'I'm not driving you wild, but I will drive you home.'

There are many other lines. Guys who use them run the gamut from the suave, sophisticated, smooth-talking 'player' who knows exactly what he is doing, to the totally inexperienced 'innocent abroad' who accidentally stumbles onto a young lady's weakness. Not everything a guy says is a 'line'. But many boys do have an ulterior motive and when sexually aroused tend to say anything to get what they want. Commitments and promises are meant at the time but later are either forgotten or denied. They do not consider this to be dishonesty or lying.

The intent here is not to put males down or produce a negative picture of them, but to equip unsuspecting, naïve girls with awareness that sexual game playing is part of the romance cycle for many males. A guy who was into

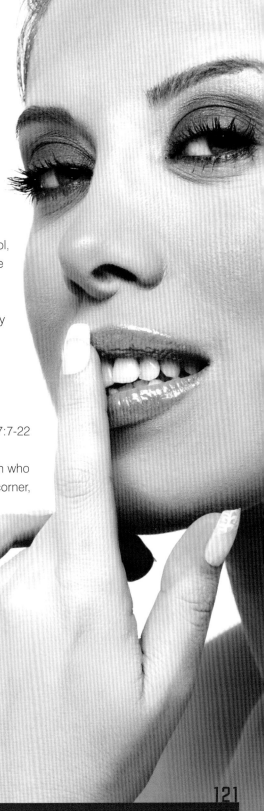

pornography said that when he began to date he threw away his pictures for the real thing. The excitement of casual sex was like winning a game to him. He learned to manoeuvre his opponent into a position where she couldn't say no. If he sensed hesitation or a moral dilemma in her mind, he would play *any role* to get what he wanted.

Guys tend to approach girls sexually, not because they have dirty minds, but because it is part of our Creator's plan. God designed the male to be the aggressor when it comes to sex. But he does not want or expect a male to misuse this God-implanted desire. When a man's sexual drive is placed under God's control, it produces positive results. This way God can always be honoured.

A person with self-worth does not manipulate others. And one who possesses self-worth cannot be swayed by manipulative actions.

Lines Girls Use

Guys certainly have no monopoly on using lines or pressuring someone for sex these days. Women have approached men sexually since Bible times. Proverbs 7:7-22 tells us about one such seductress:

'I saw among the simple . . . young men . . . a youth who lacked judgement . . . going down the street near her corner, walking along in the direction of her house . . . as the dark night set in. Then out came a woman to meet him, dressed like a prostitute and with crafty intent. (She is loud and defiant, her feet never stay at home . . . at every corner she lurks.) She took hold of him and kissed him and with a brazen face she said . . . "I looked for you and have found you! I have covered my bed with coloured linens . . . with myrrh, aloes and cinnamon. Come let's drink deep of love till morning; let's enjoy ourselves with love!" With persuasive words she led him astray; she seduced him with her smooth talk . . . he followed her like an ox going to the slaughter.'

The man mentioned in the passage is simple because he has no purpose, no goals, and doesn't know where he is going. But the seductress knows exactly where she wants him. And she has her strategies down pat. She dresses to allure her man (verse 10); her approach is bold (verse 13); she invites him to her place (verses 16-18); she cunningly answers every objection (verses 19-20); she persuades him with smooth talk and delivers her 'line' (verse 21); she traps him (verse 23). These verses outline her scheme. Her strategies are clear and recognisable. During the present era of sexual liberation, sexual pressure is very much a two-way street, and males are being openly pressured and seduced by women. Today females are less dependent on men and feel more in charge of their lives both in and out of the bedroom. Contraception is widely available, and it is more socially acceptable for a girl to come on to a man.

The question is: What kind of a girl approaches a guy in this manner? What drives her to do so? What type of home is she from? What psychological forces drive her to go against God's plan for male and female and push her to approach a guy sexually?

US agony aunt Ann Landers once published letters from mothers whose sons had been propositioned by girls. Some 20,000 outraged parents responded with similar stories about girls pursuing their sons. A high school guidance counsellor in a small conservative mid-western US town said: 'Girls seem

desperate to connect and they use sex as the connection.' A therapist added, 'Young women who are emotionally needy but don't know how to engage the man verbally or emotionally approach him sexually.'[1]

The danger of such behaviour is more profound than merely shocking the neighbours. Since these young women aren't emotionally ready to handle the psychological ramifications of sex, they learn only how to relate to men sexually. And girls who learn how to relate to men sexually make pitifully poor marriage partners and pathetic mothers who are likely to lead their own daughters into the same type of behaviour.

From the many dating seminars I've taught over the years, I've collected lines from the guys that the girls have used on them. They go something like this: *'I thought you were a man.' 'You're not scared, are you?' 'Maybe you're not as experienced as I thought.' 'Having sex is a part of nature.' 'If you don't, somebody else will.' 'I'm a virgin. You can be the first to break me in.' 'I want to make love to you – that's different from having sex.' 'You're different. I never felt towards my other boyfriends the way I feel towards you.' 'You look as if you'd be good in bed.'*

Some guys are disgusted by such sexual boldness. Others find it flattering and appealing to their egos. For others it provides the release they need when their sexual desire rages.

Most girls, however, send their messages non-verbally, through the way they dress or through their behaviour. Some girls send condoms in a greetings card, show up at inappropriate but convenient times, or even send bikini underwear to a guy to get their message across.

It takes two to play this game – simple men and bold, seductive women. Who wants to be married to a simple man? A bold, seductive woman may sound good (to a simple man) but she will be just as bold and seductive with other men.

If you are a Christian, you should have no part in leading or enticing another person (Christian or not) into sin. A basic principle of the Bible is that a Christian would not act in any way that would encourage another person to violate their morals or lead them into sin. To tempt another person towards sexual activity would cause a Christian to stumble and fall. It could distract an unbeliever from ever desiring to become a believer. As Paul says in Romans 14:13: 'Therefore let us stop passing judgement on one another. Instead, make up your mind not to put any stumbling-block or obstacle in your brother's way.'

There is no example in Scripture that demonstrates someone showing love by manipulating the 'loved' one. 'Lines' and sexual game playing offer only a cheap, temporary, conditional kind of affection. When you really care about someone you won't pressure or tempt this person into doing anything he or she does not really want to do or should not do. Love doesn't manipulate, coerce or force. It shows respect and reaffirms the other person's worth, while putting what is best for the other before your own selfish desires.

I'm Vulnerable! Handle With Care!

Girls are more vulnerable to sexual game playing because, from childhood on, most girls dream about a special guy who will hold and love them in a caring way. When she finally finds a guy who takes her in his arms, one who whispers words she has longed to hear, the moment she has waited for has arrived. *She has now reached her most vulnerable point.* To keep her dream going she has to believe everything he says and do what he wants or he might abandon her. This longing to establish a long-term, intimate relationship that will eventually end in marriage, along with the desire for children, makes her more vulnerable.

Whereas both males and females can get hurt in sexual game playing, it is the female who can be hurt the worst. It is she who faces the aftermath of consequences – pregnancy, abortion, adoption, and the emotional trauma that follows. For a man, sex is an exhilarating physical release for urgent feelings, but for the female, sex is a deeply emotional experience.

Girls with low self-esteem. Inferiority and premarital sex go hand in hand. If a young woman feels inadequate – that she isn't as attractive as other girls, that she isn't accepted by others, that she isn't part of the 'in' crowd – she's on dangerous ground. Erica had a reputation on campus with the guys. One fellow described her as a 'public neck'. Erica longed to be popular, to be accepted and loved, but she had such a low opinion of herself that she thought she had nothing but her body that would ever attract a guy.

Unconsciously,

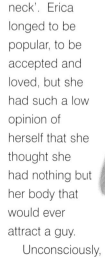

Erica is saying to guys: 'I don't have much personality or other admirable qualities to offer you, but I can offer you my body.' She knows from prior experience that she'll hate herself in the morning, but she needs someone so badly now to take away the pain of inferiority that she'll do anything he wants.

A girl who has learned to appreciate her worth can more easily make better choices. The more a girl respects herself, the less she needs to use sex as a means to get affection.

Broken homes. Girls whose parents are separated or divorced are *three times* as likely to be sexually permissive as girls from intact homes. Girls from such homes reflect the example and teaching of their parents. One said: 'At the time of my first encounter with sex, my parents were going through a hard time and almost divorced. This made me insecure and made me do anything to please my boyfriend, because I wanted security, since there was none at the time in my home.'

Girls reared in foster homes or by

guardians other than their parents are often very sexually aggressive with boys. Strong moral convictions and a desire to live right are developed in a home with affectionate parents who consistently teach positive values and encourage their teenagers to practise abstinence in their dating relationships. Young people from happy homes are much less likely to be sexually permissive.

Girls without fathers. Adolescent girls without fathers in the home behave differently around boys when they have not learned how to act and dress from their fathers. In other words, girls learn how to interact with boys by interacting with their fathers. When a girl overdoes it with provocative behaviour – in the way she walks or talks – she is showing she is starved of the male attention she never got at home due to divorce or separation.

Girls from homes where parents are divorced are often aggressive with the opposite sex. Their behaviour is seductive and often promiscuous. This results from the tension such young women feel with the opposite sex – tension they act out. They find it difficult to relate easily and openly with boys and respond more flirtatiously. Johns Hopkins University researchers found that 'young white teenage girls living in fatherless families . . . were 60% more likely to have had intercourse than those living in two-parent homes.'

A 14-year-old girl began dating an 18-year-old boy. After a month or so he told her he loved her and that if she loved him she would have sex with him. He also told her that if she didn't he would break up with her. She knew sex was wrong but wanted so much to have this boy love her. This girl felt her father didn't really care about her. So when her boyfriend told her he loved her, she gave in. In a few months she broke up with him and soon had another boyfriend. Did either of these relationships make her feel more secure? No – only a puppet in the hands of any boy who told her he loved her.

The search for her father's unconditional love and acceptance led her to make all the wrong choices. But what she needs will never be found in the arms of some guy who professes undying love while fulfilling his own lustful desires. The love and security she needs to make up for the daddy she never had can only be found in a heavenly Saviour.

A girl who exhibits such behaviour should certainly not be blamed when circumstances beyond her control have triggered her actions. But she can learn where she is vulnerable and why she behaves the way she does. Unless this girl takes the time to know herself and seeks help from a mature adult to solve the leftover business from her past, she will never achieve an emotionally healthy relationship with a male.

Part 15: Straight Talk About Petting

Lisa and Paul met at church where leadership meetings threw them together, and they began dating. Both had high standards and felt secure in their Christianity. To become sexually involved was unthinkable. But one night after watching a DVD at Lisa's home, they went further than either believed possible. They were so carried away, they were on the threshold of intercourse.

Lisa and Paul were brought up to believe that sex belongs exclusively to marriage. This is what they believed and their church confirmed it. Yet the best intentions of two good Christian young adults were forgotten in the heat of a steamy petting episode. Both were shocked it happened and remorseful afterwards. They promised each other that it would never happen again. 'It was an accident,' they rationalised.

Many couples get caught like Lisa and Paul did. Lisa needed Paul's hugs and caresses to satisfy her need for intimacy and closeness. But her belief system said that sex belongs in marriage. However, if she could be swept off her emotional feet or overwhelmed by the emotion of the moment, when there was no planning in advance, it provided the excuse she needed.

Petting is a powerful force. Those caught in its grip tend to make up their own rules as they move along because they don't know the rules to start with. Petting is a step beyond hugging and kissing and yet not as far as sexual intercourse. This leaves a wide range of body-exploring activities open to question, guess and negotiation.

When a guy begins fondling a girl's body, he is testing the waters. How far will she let me go? he wonders. He enjoys this testing immensely since it is pleasurable and brings on strong sexual excitement. His mind races with anticipation as he thinks about what lies ahead. It's at this point that he may deliver his best line: 'I've never loved anyone the way I love you.' His hormones are pumping, and he is likely to say or do anything to get what he wants now that he is this close to satisfying his urgent sexual desires.

Her agenda is most likely very different.

She enjoys the hugging and kissing more than the sexual aspects. She craves his kisses and touch because her need for love and emotional security is being met.

Wait A Minute!

To use such intimate caressing outside of marriage, just for the sexual thrills to make you feel good, is very selfish and self-centred. And to use someone else's body in such a manner hardly shows respect or caring for the other person. This violates the principles of love that should govern a relationship between male and female.

Particularly is this true in a casual relationship, when a couple is not in love and has no plans to marry. Petting cheapens a relationship. The risks are high and the rewards are low.

It's risky because petting takes advantage of the other person. At no time is a person more vulnerable to exploitation than when in a petting situation. The unloved feel loved, the unattractive feel attractive, the lonely feel as though someone cares – all because one is caressing the other's body, pretending they care when those feelings may not even exist. An intense desire for love can easily translate petting into a message of caring, when nothing but lust exists.

Likewise, to allow someone to fondle your body outside of marriage, just to make you feel loved, special and cared for, is equally selfish. To allow someone access to sexually excitable areas to fill your needs for love, security or worth, is also selfish and immature. Let's

clear something up. Petting is not dirty. It will not curl your toes or stunt your growth. Within the bonds of marriage, petting is a beautiful experience. It is the natural expression of love between a husband and wife called *foreplay*. Foreplay is designed to lead directly to sexual intercourse. What, then, is the difference between petting and foreplay? The activities are the same but the purpose is different. Petting is the exploration of another's body by two unmarried persons who should not or do not intend for intercourse to occur. And that's the trouble with petting. It doesn't stand alone. It moves naturally to intercourse. By itself, outside of marriage, it is more frustrating than satisfying. Our bodies were designed and created by God to respond to petting by becoming sexually aroused and desiring intercourse. Ideally that arousal culminates in intercourse.

When an unmarried couple engages in petting with the intention of not having intercourse, they must constantly be on guard to stop, lest things go too far. Petting, or foreplay, was not designed to stop on command. Therefore one who habitually proceeds to French kissing and petting, and then stops, risks the possibility of sexual problems in marriage. Even though this person marries, their sexual response may stop, due to prior programming and the habit of going so far and then stopping. Their bodies never get the message that now it's OK to go further. God's plan for us is that sexual relations after marriage should be fulfilling. Starting and stopping, however, leaves one very unsatisfied and frustrated.

Petting might be likened to crossing a bridge that spans a wide gorge. On one side is sexual intercourse and on the other side there is no expression of caring – no touching or kissing. When petting you begin on one side of the bridge and move towards the sexual intercourse side. It's so exciting and stimulating that it's easy to find yourselves across the bridge before you realise it.

Crossing the bridge doesn't always happen all at once. Sometimes it takes weeks or even months. But petting is dangerously progressive. Each time you begin petting, the desire accelerates, but the thrill of the previous level declines. In other words, if you really enjoyed French kissing last time, next time you'll want more. Each level of excitement demands the next level. It is a powerful force for those who feel the sexual chemistry between them heating up.

About Guys and Petting

Petting affects guys differently from the way it does girls. But since members of both sexes wear masks, they often do not understand what the other is feeling.

The male is stimulated sexually in ways that few females realise. He is more sex-driven than the female, and this holds true for him throughout life. Since God implanted this desire for sexual pleasure, when a male acts in this manner he is responding in the way God planned. He is not being dirty or evil when he responds to sexual stimuli. He is being male, and that is good – to a point, at least!

Studies have consistently shown that the sexes have little or no conception of the vast gulf between their own feelings and those of the opposite sex. Some men guilty of rape are caught because they return to the scene of their crime, assuming the woman enjoyed the experience and would like to repeat it. Peeping Toms are often caught because they make a noise to alert the woman, thinking she will enjoy the attention!

Males are more visually oriented than females. Most girls do not understand how their appearance affects men. Because women are not aroused by merely looking at the male body or the way he dresses, they have little realisation of their effect on men.

Psychology Today found that girls who wear skin-tight jeans and no bra think of themselves as being stylish. However, young men read sexual come-ons into such dress. None of the young people felt that a guy's open shirt, tight trousers, tight swimming trunks or jewellery indicated that he was on the prowl for sex. Both sexes agreed that a see-through top on a girl was probably a come-on, but the males tended to see other clothing as deliberately encouraging as well – a low-cut top, shorts, tight jeans or no bra.

To a large extent girls do not understand that female clothing is designed by the fashion industry to be seductive and attention-grabbing. Most young women don't realise that guys don't look at the way a girl dresses as she does and that certain types of dress do cause problems for guys. To put it succinctly, any article of clothing that accents the sexual aspects of a woman is immodest. With a little common sense, girls can look attractive and stylish without dressing provocatively. (See 1 Timothy 2:9.)

A young woman does not have to wear revealing clothing to play the teasing game. A boy will read a lot into the movements of a girl's body. If she acts 'loose' or 'easy', she'll get that kind of treatment. The choices a girl makes in

regard to her clothing and behaviour become signs for men to read. She is either saying, 'I am a person of worth and high ideals. I respect myself, and I expect others to respect me also.' Or 'Hey, look at me! I'm available. I'm ready and willing. Come and get me.'

Since external stimuli easily arouse a male, sex lurks close to the surface of his thinking at all times. A billboard, a dirty joke, a suggestive picture, a movie, a television programme, all help him along. Add music with suggestive lyrics and a girl, and you've got the whole plot.

Because a guy is created by God to respond visually, his mind can remember scenes so vividly that when he is with a girl what he recalls pushes him to act out what he 'sees' in his mind. One boy said: 'My brain recalls what I've seen so visually that I must carefully guard what I watch or I can recall those scenes instantly – which could stimulate me to act on them.'

A girl who doesn't understand how males respond may think it is she who brings on such a strong sexual desire in him, as well as his deep love for her. Not necessarily so. He could be recalling vivid pornographic images. The girl in his arms may be little more than a toy through whom he will now act out what has passed through his mind. He may care nothing for her. But the scenes he recollects may drive him to seek release when his mind isn't even in the same room.

For many males it begins like this: He holds hands with her. She permits it. He thinks that if he can hold her hand, she will permit him to put his arm around her; and if he can get his arm around her, he knows he can kiss her. After he gets that far, he'll try French kissing. If she allows that, he begins to fantasise about touching her breasts. If she permits that, he pushes her to the next level, until intercourse occurs.

After a few minutes of close body contact or prolonged kissing, he will usually have an erection. This is not nasty or dirty. God designed the penis to become erect when mental or physical stimulation occurs. At this point he is ready for intercourse, although he does not *have* to have it. Nothing bad will happen to him if he doesn't, but he *is* ready, nonetheless.

The erection occurred because he is thinking about sex. You see, it doesn't take long for a stimulus to propel him towards wanting to go further. Scripture, however, forbids intercourse outside of marriage and labels it either fornication or adultery. So unless he is married to this girl, he is not at liberty to have sex with her if he has claimed Christ as his Saviour.

If the couple have engaged in an extended period of petting, he is very likely to experience an uncomfortable ache in his testicles. He may be aching enough to use every means at his disposal to accomplish his purpose. *Any words spoken now, any promises made, should be discounted*. He is simply under too much pressure to think straight and will probably say *anything* to get what he wants.

This pressure build-up that he feels will not cause him any permanent damage or injure him in any way, despite his claims! He will not become sterile, go bald, nor will his teeth fall out. The ache usually passes in half an hour or so.

Males feel a strong need to prove their masculinity. A boy needs to prove to himself and others that he can function just as a man should. Some boys think the only proof of manhood is having sex and lots of it. To them the measure of masculinity relates to the number of females conquered. A college textbook told of a 21-year-old student who belonged to a fraternity and maintained a B average while participating in sports and campus activities. He had dated ninety-seven girls and had intercourse with sixty-four of these. He went on to map out the number of times he had sex with each of these girls, and averaged three to four times a week for a total of 950 to 1,100 times.

Behind a girl's back guys engage in a lot of laughing, joking and crude talk about sex. Their primary concern is to build their own shaky egos, and they will use any female to do it. There is no caring or concern for what these encounters may do to the girls or the effect on their future. The sexual pleasure they receive is not as important to them as the fact that they succeeded in exerting their masculine charm over the girls involved.

Studies show that men far outdistance women in the number of sex partners they have and in the number of casual sex encounters. Often such boys have a long history of unsuccessful relationships and are incapable of commitment. A high percentage also become impotent because their misuse of sex numbs their sensitivity and they cannot integrate tender feelings with sexual feelings.

Peer pressure exerts strong pressure on males. These men use sex as a means of improving their position with their crowd. Older males may exert pressure on younger boys, urging them on. One of the strongest urges young people have is to conform to what the group is doing. So if all the others are engaging in sex – or they say they are – these men will want to do it, too.

Other men try to exploit women. Some males deliberately try to see how far they can go. One study investigated sexually experienced 20-year-old men. On average, they had already had more than three partners each. Thirty-four percent had picked up women exclusively for sexual purposes and reported having no feelings for the girls.

Some young men use sex as a form of rebellion. Some young adults use sex as a method of rebelling against parents, teachers, church or other symbols of authority. Many authority figures warn teenagers against premarital sex. Therefore, a man who resents authority and feels that those in power cannot force him to act against his own wishes may rebel just to show he can do it. Young people from overly strict homes frequently express their rebellion through sexual promiscuity. Sex is often sought as a short-term escape from a troubled life. Sex acts like a drug, an anaesthesia to dull the pain.

But the effects are only temporary and short-lived.

The adventure-loving male seeks thrills.
The excitement of seeing if they can get away with it leads some men to sexual aggression. This 'devil-may-care' attitude prompts them to drive too fast, court danger, and take risks with their lives. Premarital sex offers several risks – detection, infection and conception! To play the game and not get caught or hurt serves as a motivating force for some.

About Girls and Petting

Men who do not really understand females often assume that girls are as eager to make out as they are. In reality, females respond much more slowly. It isn't that a woman cannot respond; it is just that she takes longer. Due to the erection of his penis, the male is immediately more aware of his sexual responses than she is. His responses are more localised; her responses are more complicated. He responds more to physical factors; she responds to emotional ones. Males can have sex with women they care little for; females desire affection prior to sexual intimacy.

For the female, petting sets off a slow chain reaction of physical sensations. The first thing she may feel is a general uneasiness, a restlessness, an excitement and possibly a tightness in her throat. These feelings may be followed by a tingling in the spine or in other parts of the body, or perhaps a choking sensation caused by the heart's pumping faster and necessitating faster breathing. She may not recognise these sensations at first as a stirring of sexual response. But these first vague feelings of discomfort are the beginnings of physical desire.

So here we have a boy and girl involved in petting. He's secretly hoping she'll get carried away and give him what he really wants. What she is enjoying, however, is not so much the physical thrill as the feeling of being 'loved'. Suddenly she decides that things have gone far enough. Disengaging herself, she walks into another room. She feels little or nothing, because she was never particularly excited to begin with. But her boyfriend feels very different! She has left him feeling tense, uncomfortable, and somehow defeated. If he is clever, he'll swallow his pride and work on her another time when he can push her further. Each encounter weakens her defences.

Therefore a girl who allows prolonged kissing and caressing but who has no intention of following through is actually *leading him on*. But most girls don't understand what a man goes through when she permits intimacies that stop short of intercourse. One girl responded in the survey: 'Petting is really boring. I rarely get stimulated. I usually just sit there waiting for it to end. I really wonder what he gets out of it.'

You can rest assured that he didn't feel the same way; yet she was totally unaware of it!

I do not wish to leave the impression that a girl never enjoys petting. The more experience she has, the better acquainted she will become with her body responses. She can begin to train and 'will' her body to respond to sexual stimuli. Petting can be an extremely pleasurable and exciting adventure for the more experienced female, though not nearly as urgent as with the male.

Now let's consider some of the reasons why young ladies engage in petting.

To get love. Every woman has a consuming desire to be loved the way she has always dreamed of being loved. These dreams, which centre on being cherished, protected and cared for, begin in early adolescence and last till old age. This desire for love forms the core of a woman's emotional security. However, such a goal also puts her in competition with every other female for the attention of a male. This pressure is tough; and she's ready to believe a boy when he says, 'I love you,' because she wants to believe it.

When he goes on to argue that intercourse will make their love more secure, she finds his words persuasive because this is exactly what she wants – not intercourse, necessarily, but love and security. Therefore, girls commonly colour the facts to fool themselves into believing what they want to believe. Most males quickly learn this and use it to their advantage.

One other fact works against women and romance. Many girls do not realise that just when they feel the most romantic coincides with their monthly cycle when they are the most fertile. Just when intercourse appears most desirable, they have the least control and pregnancy is most likely to occur.

To gain popularity. Some young women think that being sexually co-operative will ensure popularity. Some of these girls are popular. But you should hear what the guys say about them! Furthermore, their dates always end up doing the same thing in the same place. Hundreds of girls have complained, as this one did: 'When he wants to make out, he calls me; but when a nice event is scheduled, he takes somebody else.'

To work out feelings of rebellion. Feelings of rebellion against parents or others can provide a springboard for sexual activity. The rebellious girl has something to prove, an axe to grind, and lessons to teach adults. This young woman often has grown up under demanding or distrustful parents. She aches to get even with them for their lack of faith in her. Subconsciously she may even attempt to get pregnant – just to hurt them the way she feels they have hurt her. One girl wrote on the survey: 'When I had sex the first time, it wasn't because I loved him. It was because I was bored and it was something new. Also I was feeling very radical and rebellious towards my parents and life in general, so nothing really mattered anyway.'

Caution: A man can want sex without being in love, and his wanting sex affords no proof that he loves. He may interpret his strong sexual desire as love and try to convince her that his love is the same as hers. She assumes that he would not ask unless he deeply loved her. She therefore gives in to his wishes, feeling they have sealed a compact through intercourse. But it only reinforces the observation that he gives love to get sex and she gives sex to get love.

When all is said and done, couples usually pet for *security* – not *love*. They feel they need to do it in order to tell the other person they love them, to have a basis for their relationship, or to hang on to someone. But unless a couple develop something besides physical intimacy, the relationship will crumble. Sex alone won't suffice when you have to live together daily. If you feel insecure now and need petting in order to build up your feelings of worth, then later you will have to find something else to help you cope with your insecurities. Better to back off for a while from dating until you mature.

Part 16: Pressure . . . Pressure . . . Pressure . . . How Far Do We Go?

Trish and Tim are an inseparable couple who have been going out together for six months. After school Tim walks Trish home. Trish opens the door with her key. Tim gives her a playful pat on the behind as she goes in the door. 'What time will your mum be home?' he asks. 'Five thirty,' Trish replies. Tim glances at his watch. 'We've got plenty of time,' he replies.

Trish giggles and grabbing Tim by the hand she leads him to her bedroom. At 5.30 when good old Mum comes home from work, Trish and Tim are at the kitchen table working on an English assignment. Mum smiles. She's so proud of Trish and pleased with her boyfriend.

It may appear that it just 'happened' one day for them. It did happen, but it didn't happen without warning. Trish and Tim actually progressed through a series of steps that neither was aware of. Each step led them to the next level. Let's follow Trish and Tim from the day they met and find out how they ended up sexually active even though they had no intention of that happening.

Whenever I talk with young adults about 'touchy situations', they tend to ask similar questions: How far should we be going? What's right and what's wrong? Is it all right to kiss and hug? What about French kissing? Can I touch my girl as long as I stay outside her clothing? Above the waist? Can I go as far as . . .? Is it OK to . . . ? How far can we go anyway?

Since the Bible provides no clear-cut guidelines for the grey areas of petting, I have searched for answers to these probing questions in order to help young adults make choices about what's right and what's wrong prior to marriage. I believe knowledge about 'pair bonding' is the best way of helping you make choices for setting boundaries.

Pair bonding describes the attraction between a guy and a girl that blossoms into love. The word *bonding* means 'that which binds or holds together; a uniting force; a substance that cements or unites'. The term describes the emotional attachment that develops as a couple's affections grow and ripen. An almost predictable pattern of intimacy unfolds without the couple's awareness.

Pair bonding was first reported by zoologist Desmond Morris in *Intimate Behaviour*

and then popularised within Christian circles by Dr Donald Joy in *Bonding: Relationships in the Image of God*. Morris notes that the twelve-step bonding process tends to be present in all human cultures but does not appear as a step unless at least 50% of the cultures engaged in it. Not all cultures followed all twelve steps and some cultures took extra steps. The twelve-step process certainly provides a predictable pattern for western culture.

Although each pair of lovers sees their relationship as unique, love affairs do tend to follow a pattern.

The Twelve Steps to Pair Bonding

Stage 1: No Touch

Step 1: Eye to Body. First glance is not so much a sexual look but more the look of discovery. *Wow! Where have you been all my life?* First glance takes in size, shape, colouring and age. Immediately an almost unconscious grading process begins, ranking the person on a scale of 1-10 as to interest or desirability. Unless the person is ranked around an 8, 9 or 10, a second look will probably not take place. Ordinarily great importance would not be attached to Step 1 and yet this first step determines whether or not the relationship progresses.

Step 2: Eye to Eye. This might occur in the study hall or library. You are studying, minding your own business. When you look up, your eyes meet with someone interesting across the table for the first time. You blush with embarrassment, your heartbeat quickens, and you glance away. You are dying to look again to see if the person is looking at you but you're not ready for prolonged eye contact. Usually direct eye contact is reserved only for those we know and trust. So two people who see each other for the first time usually look each other over when the other isn't looking. If you like what you see, you might add a smile to the next look. Unless the eyes convey a message during future glances, the relationship will probably not proceed. Eye contact now is brief, but later will dominate.

Step 3: Voice to Voice. The couple begins to talk. At first their conversations revolve around small talk such as each other's name, where they live, their favourite subject, the weather, and so on. This exchange of small talk, however, permits further opportunity to look the other person over as well as time to evaluate their tone of voice, rate of speech, accent, how they use words, and how they think. This provides more information for evaluation.

During Step 3 a couple can learn much about each other, including opinions, pastimes, hobbies, ideas, likes and dislikes, hopes and dreams for the future. A couple should spend many hours at Step 3 voice bonding before moving to Step 4. During this step, they will probably love to talk on the phone. They can learn about each other but without the eye contact which would rush them up the pair-bonding scale. Over the phone they can discover each other's inner worlds, learn about themselves and how to share that knowledge with a member of the opposite sex. They can explore their inner selves and become vulnerable, a major task when intimacy is developing. I believe so much in what is taking place here, and the safety in which it takes place, that I recommend a couple spend *one thousand hours* on the phone before moving up to Step 4. (If your parents

object, have them call me and I will remind them of what takes place during Step 4 and beyond!)

This step cannot and should not be ignored. This is where a couple can learn a lot about one another and where the relationship needs to be slowed, before romantic gestures begin. After romantic affection begins, the couple will convert everything said and done to idealised romantic notions and will look at one another differently, talk about different things and interact differently. It is during Step 3 that a couple can learn if they have enough in common and if the relationship should continue – all before getting romantic.

Stage 2: First Touch

During the second stage of bonding, the couple spend much time talking, but eye contact is still limited as they remain more in a side-to-side position rather than face to face. They tend to steal glances at one another. Touch begins, but none of it is directly sexual.

Some light hugging and light conventional closed-mouth kissing may take place during the next three steps. Prolonged periods of face-to-face embracing or open-mouthed kissing would become troublesome as it would awaken sexual responses ahead of schedule and rush the bonding process.

Step 4: Hand to Hand. First touch is almost always innocent and non-sexual – a handshake, accidentally touching hands while reaching for something, or the touch of a hand on her back as when a guy assists a girl through a doorway or into a car. First touch may not seem significant but he can learn much about how far he can go with her if she pulls away from his first touch. However, if she freely accepts his touch or moves closer, he'll know she's ready for more. Much can be read into all these non-verbal signals.

First touch also includes hand holding. It is only four square inches of skin on four square inches of skin, but 10,000 volts of electricity shoot through the bodies when a couple holds hands for the first time. The heart races and the cheeks flush. At first hand holding may be only occasional and then become constant. The couple continues to talk, but from a side-to-side position, avoiding direct eye contact but stealing glances at one another.

Hand holding shows a growing attachment. It is also a social statement which says: 'I am no longer alone in this world. I am attached to someone who enjoys being with me.'

Step 5: Arm to Shoulder. Eventually the thrill of holding hands subsides and another plateau is needed to show continued interest and bring back the thrill. In Step 5 a fellow slips his arm around the shoulder of his girl. The arm-to-shoulder embrace pulls their bodies closer, and the thrill returns. Whether the couple is seated or standing, they maintain closer body contact in the side-to-side position.

This is an easy step up from Step 4, is usually less censured by adults, and says more than holding hands does. In effect it states, 'This relationship is going somewhere.' The couple continues to talk, with limited eye contact but closer body contact.

Step 6: Arm to Waist. Arm to waist displays more ownership of the body. Usually the girl will slip under the armpit of the guy and their arms crisscross at the back, making it appear almost as if their hips are 'glued' together. Arm to waist clearly signals romantic interest.

Notice, the hands are moving down the body closer to the genitals. You might observe a couple each wearing jeans, walking across the campus in the Step 6 position. Sometimes each will slip a thumb inside the back pocket of the jeans for the sake of easy walking. Picture where his hand rests . . . directly on her buttocks. She may not be aware where her hand rests, but he knows exactly where his hand is. He is probably entertaining some interesting thoughts: If I can touch her here outside her clothing, I wonder if I might touch her inside the clothing?

Couples can frequently be observed at this stage of bonding on a school campus. Their bodies are close, but they appear to be looking down, talking to their feet, kicking dirt, playing with something in their hands, picking grass, keeping their bodies close, but avoiding prolonged eye contact.

Deep levels of communication develop now. Personal disclosures are made and elaborated on. The topics for discussion are endless, but basic issues of life are discussed and evaluated. Many personal secrets are shared and a couple really get to know one another at a deeply emotional and personal level.

This is where a couple explores their values, goals and beliefs. Some serious questions need to be explored: Do our life goals and personal beliefs

blend well? Do we bring out the best in each other, motivating one another to higher challenges and accomplishments? Do we know each other's expectations for the future? Can these expectations be fulfilled? Can each allow the other to develop talents and be himself or herself? Will this person allow and encourage me to make my own decisions? Boost my self-worth? Contribute to my happiness and well-being? Do our values regarding family life, fun, leisure time, travel and religion mesh? Is this person emotionally healthy? Does he have a mature understanding of life? Is he capable of earning a living? Is he free from anxiety, fears and other emotional handicaps? Free from addiction to alcohol and drugs? Capable of developing a friendship without emotional baggage from the past?

It is now that a decision regarding the future of the relationship must be made – whether it should progress or end. Enough personal disclosures have been shared so that compatibility can adequately be evaluated. If serious doubts or questions regarding any facet of the relationship exist, now is the time to say goodbye. Proceeding to Step 7 or beyond and then breaking up can leave deep scars, because by then the bond is so well formed. The pain can equal that of a divorce.

For these reasons and more, don't rush through Steps 3 to 6. Remember that anyone can talk (granted, some better than others), but not everyone can carry on a meaningful conversation. Take time now to explore values, goals and beliefs. Once Step 7 begins, romance will dominate and control the relationship, allowing less time for getting to know one another in non-sexual ways.

Stage 3: Intimate Contact

The most significant change during Stage 3 is that the couple turns to face one another. Although no direct sexual contact occurs, the change in body position puts sex on a hidden agenda that both become acutely aware of. Any genital touching would trigger intercourse and could scar the formation of a healthy bond. Intercourse would also introduce an undercurrent of mistrust and high levels of anxiety that would haunt the pair later, should they marry. Communication is vastly different. Until now the couple has been developing their communication skills. Now the verbals shut down and eye contact and non-verbals take over.

Step 7: Face to Face. The body position shifts from side-by-side to facing one another. Three types of contact take place: face-to-face hugging, open-mouth or French kissing, and prolonged eye contact.

Close body contact in this frontal position combined with open-mouth French kissing brings on strong sexual arousal, particularly when repeated or prolonged. Those who engage in French kissing must realise they are simulating intercourse. Much restraint must now be exercised, since the body position and activity quickly excite sexual arousal. Even though they are several steps away from genital contact, sexual desire has been activated and becomes a factor to deal with.

Since kissing dominates, the verbals shut down. It becomes obvious why compatibility and the quality of the relationship must be decided before Step 7. If the couple has taken the time to talk through all the important issues of life and the foundation has been well laid, deep communication can still take place with fewer words. Eye contact becomes long and pronounced. The couple focus on reading one another's face and kissing. An unmarried couple must guard their display of physical affection carefully from this point on, as *all sexual motors are racing.*

Step 8: Hand to Head. Here one's hand is used to caress or stroke the head of the other while kissing or talking. This intimate gesture is generally reserved for those who have earned the right. In other words, a high level of trust has developed between the two.

Very few people allow anyone to touch their head unless they are in love, are family members, or are trusted, as with a doctor, dentist, barber or hairdresser. This act, then, shows emotional closeness. The sight of someone gently running his fingers through a loved one's hair or stroking the face is tender indeed. It signals a deep bond of friendship, love, caring and trust. The bond is well formed.

Step 9: Hand to Body. The hands now explore the partner's body. Breast fondling becomes important to some males. But Step 9 includes any type of hand-to-body touching – back rubs, leg rubs, and so on. In the early stages of Step 9 the hands remain outside the clothing. In the latter stages of Step 9, the hands move underneath the clothing but stay above the waist. Hand-to-body touching, or what is commonly referred to as petting, is dangerously progressive. Sexual excitement escalates; and the couple experience increased difficulty stopping at Step 9, because Step 4 demands 5, 5 demands 6, and 6 demands 7 – right up the pair-bonding scale. At this point the female usually recognises she must call a halt or it will be too late.

This is the point of no return before the protection of marriage is needed.

Stage 4: One Flesh

During these final three steps the couple will achieve ultimate sexual intimacy.

Step 10: Mouth to Breast. Step 10 requires the partial or full baring of the female breast. This act, then, is usually conducted in the utmost privacy. Mouth-to-breast contact once again changes the focus of the relationship. A couple at Step 10 is not just concerned with pleasure and arousal but intends to complete the sex act. Anyone progressing to Step 10 would find it extremely difficult to stop here without proceeding to Steps 11 and 12.

Step 11: Hand to Genital. The hands now slip below the waist to the genitals. Sexual arousal and foreplay are well under way in this last, most intense and intimate stage of petting prior to intercourse. By definition, this includes stimulating a partner to climax through what is commonly called 'petting to climax' or 'mutual masturbation'. By the age of 15, between 25 and 27% of teens had been masturbated by a partner and 33% by the age of 16. Thirty-six percent had masturbated a partner.[2] Most of these young adults do so to retain virginity or to avoid pregnancy and sexually-transmitted diseases.

Stopping at Step 11 to retain virginity until marriage is faulty thinking. *The Oxford English Dictionary* defines the word *virgin* as 'a person of either sex remaining in a state of chastity'. This definition shows that the line of purity has

already been crossed – for both, not just the female partner. Hand-to-genital touching would hardly be considered chaste, pure or virtuous behaviour in any culture.

The Old Testament in several passages associates nakedness with illicit sexual conduct, and I suggest that when an unmarried couple caress breasts or genitals, whether outside or underneath the clothing, or remove their clothing, they have gone too far. This is true for any sexual activity from Step 9 on. Such intimate steps should be reserved for marriage only. Technically it is only a breath away from intercourse.

Sex play is so stimulating and addictive you may lose your ability to judge it clearly. Proverbs 13:19 says, 'A longing fulfilled is sweet to the soul, but fools detest turning from evil.' A 'longing fulfilled' certainly includes such stimulating sex play. Intense desire blinds judgement and can cause you to proceed further than you ever intended.

Petting to climax provides a great deal of sexual gratification, but it has several hazards as well. Psychologists and physicians have found that women who have trouble achieving climax in marriage can trace the problem to sex before marriage when their bodies became programmed to stop short of intercourse. In the male it can result in premature ejaculation where he has become programmed to quick sex. It can also result in impotence, of which 90% is a psychological reaction to a real or imaginary experience.

Another hazard is the spread of STDs. Genital stimulation produces a lot of body secretions. Therefore, if STD germs are present on either him or her, they can be passed on through the secretions.[3]

Some question where oral sex fits into the pair-bonding scale. It did not show up as one of the twelve steps, since many cultures have taboos against it. In oral sex the mouth is used to provide sexual pleasure by kissing or sucking the sexual organs. This activity may or may not be continued to the point of orgasm. For some teens, oral sex comes before intercourse; 41% of 17-year-old girls say they have performed *fellatio* (oral sex) on their boyfriends.[4]

Oral sex is way beyond petting to climax in the hierarchy of sexual experimentation. I was chatting with a large group of young men on a college campus after presenting pair bonding and was questioned about a pair-bonding number for oral

sex. 'I'd place it at eleven and a half,' I responded. One young man from the group called out, 'I'd place it at twelve and a half!' Whatever the number, a person must overcome more inhibition to expose themselves to such nudity and sexual openness. It should have no place in dating.

Both petting to climax and oral sex require a nakedness of body and soul that should be saved

for marriage only. Since both activities border on intercourse, the term 'technical virginity' applies. Only a legalistic attitude would permit the idea that because you avoid penetration you also avoid intercourse.

Those who engage in oral sex also need to reckon with health factors. The herpes simplex virus type II causes genital herpes. The virus is passed from person to person through genital-to-genital intercourse and mouth-to-genital sex. Within a week following sexual contact with someone with the herpes virus, fluid-filled blisters may develop around the sex organs or in the mouth. The sores will heal on their own within two to four weeks, but the herpes virus remains in the nerve tissue. The infected person will probably experience successive attacks of blisters and ulcers accompanied by extreme pain.

Herpes is one of several sexually-transmitted diseases for which, at the time of writing, there is no cure. Anyone with an active infection will, of course, pass it on to his or her sex partner. For anyone considering sex and/or marriage to a partner with herpes simplex II, remember that any time the infection is active you too will get the virus and have it for life. Medication can help suppress the symptoms and pain, but it is extremely expensive and needs to be planned into your budget.

Essentially, all STDs can be transmitted by oral sex.[5] And most STDs can be transmitted from genitals to mouth, or from mouth to genitals. Oral sex isn't 'safe sex'. Pregnancy can be avoided, but STDs can occur. STDs are not always obvious on a person's body since diseases like Chlamydia, gonorrhoea and HPV can be hidden inside the mouth.

Step 12. Genital to Genital. The highest level of sexual desire is complete with penetration and intercourse and, in most cases, orgasm. Intercourse can result in pregnancy and the formation of a new family. The bonding cycle will continue, with a new bond forming between parent and child. Whether the child is able to form strong bonds with others is, to a large degree, determined by the strength of the bond formed between mother, father and child.

Once you know and understand the twelve steps of pair bonding you can almost determine where a couple is in the pair-bonding steps by observing their hands, body positions and eyes. After I taught this at one seminar, young people lined up to talk with me privately. From my peripheral vision I could see a couple waiting to talk to me. He was seated on a table. His girlfriend was standing facing him. They were holding hands, and she was rocking back and forth between his legs. By observing this action and their body position, I guessed them to be sexually active. When I finally heard their story, I learned they had been living together. Recently they'd been converted and felt living together was sinful. 'Having sex is like being addicted to a hard drug,' this young man agonised. 'We really love each other, but we aren't ready to get married. How can we make this right?' I provided guidance for their question, which is given in the next chapter. But the point I want to make here is that their non-verbal interaction told me, as well as the rest of the world, what they'd been up to. So does your interaction with a boy or girlfriend.

Sexual purity or true abstinence, then, not only means avoiding penetrating sex, but also includes avoiding oral sex, mutual masturbation and any other sex play until your wedding day. Such activities simply do not fall within guidelines for 'purity of lifestyle' or for true abstinence since they can and do result in pregnancy and STDs. True abstinence, then, is a commitment to a monogamous lifestyle after marriage. Monogamy means one partner for a lifetime and not as defined by college women who consider any relationship lasting longer than six months to be 'lengthy monogamy'. Abstinence has a 0% failure rate for STDs or pregnancy.

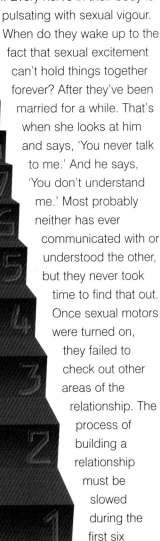

Part 17: Why Wait?

What happens when you rush or skip steps? When the twelve-step bonding process is altered, several harmful things can happen to the development of the bond. **When steps are skipped, missed or rushed, the bond is weakened and tends to break or be deformed.** Does the couple realise they are forming an imperfect bond while dating? Of course not! They are having so much fun indulging in petting and sexual experimentation. Every nerve in their body is pulsating with sexual vigour. When do they wake up to the fact that sexual excitement can't hold things together forever? After they've been married for a while. That's when she looks at him and says, 'You never talk to me.' And he says, 'You don't understand me.' Most probably neither has ever communicated with or understood the other, but they never took time to find that out. Once sexual motors were turned on, they failed to check out other areas of the relationship. The process of building a relationship must be slowed during the first six steps, during the communication process, or there is a high probability of a weak marriage later on.

Once sexual motors get turned on, people tend to forget to talk through the important issues – values, goals and beliefs – which must be done prior to getting physically involved or it very likely won't get done at all. The couple spends their time getting to know each other physically rather than emotionally because it is easier, faster and more exciting. **After a couple breaks up, the tendency is to rush the steps with the next partner.** Take Justin and Katie who have been going out together for six months and have been doing some light petting (Step 9). Almost without warning Justin loses interest in Katie and begins dating Christina. Immediately he moves Christina to Step

9 since he is used to this level of excitement and doesn't want to mess about with less exciting activities.

Katie looks around for a boyfriend and finds Ralph. Ralph has never had a girlfriend before and is very shy. Once in a wild moment of passion he held a girl's hand, but that is as far as he has ever gone with a girl. When Ralph takes his time getting to know Katie, she feels he must not care much for her when he only holds her hand (Step 4) and attempts no sexual liberties. So now Katie, who is more sexually experienced, encourages and actually pushes Ralph towards Step 7 and beyond. Neither Justin nor Katie takes time in this relationship to get to know their partner as they should. Steps are rushed and sometimes skipped entirely; and they never stop the sexual motors long enough to check on their compatibility in other areas. Should Justin or Katie marry these new partners, they will most likely

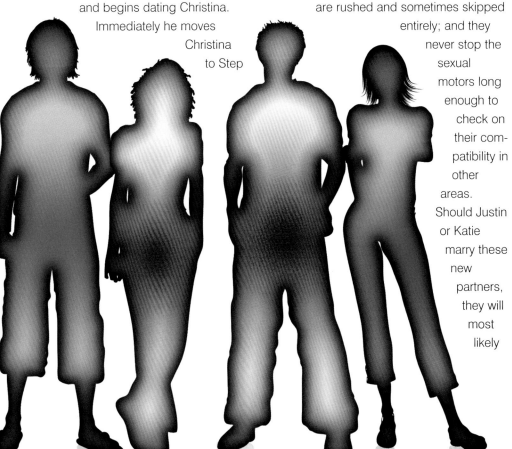

find themselves in very troubled relationships, and never fully understand why until it is too late.

Each level of physical affection establishes a new plateau, making it extremely difficulty to break up once it has been reached. Each level is so immediately rewarding it becomes almost impossible to be satisfied with lower levels of excitement. Each step in the pair-bonding process, then, must be carefully thought through and chosen. Such thinking runs against the popular 'if-it-feels-good-do-it' philosophy. The long-term consequence of unrestricted sexual freedom is difficulty in settling down to one partner after promiscuous behaviour.

A sexually experienced person will tend to rush a new partner to intercourse. This tracks the previous point. A person used to Step 12 finds it difficult to slow the process or stop at Steps 7, 8 or 9. This presents a real problem for any sexually experienced person as well as the formerly married. Since they are not accustomed to stopping, intercourse is achieved without thinking through levels or steps. When a relationship ends and this person begins dating again, the pair-bonding steps become a blur. Many become sexually involved immediately, thinking it 'normal'. If a young person begins dating an older, sexually experienced person, or one who has been married before, parents are often against the relationship for this very reason. Rushing to

sexual intimacy before marriage is one reason for the higher divorce rate in second and third marriages.

After a break-up, deep hurt results because intercourse intensifies the bond. Sex binds a couple together psychologically. The sex act increases feelings of intimacy and closeness. In temporary relationships (all those outside of legal marriage), there is a high risk of hurt. Usually one partner cares more than the other. Since the marriage vows have not been exchanged, all this couple shares is *promises* of love as long as . . .

Although both may have said, 'We'll have sex with no strings attached,' the break-up will be especially difficult. The tearing apart of a couple who have become sexually intimate is particularly wrenching. It inflicts pain and suffering which may take years or even a lifetime to heal. We are all vulnerable to rejection. This is especially true for the female.

A similarity has been noted in the muscle contractions of a woman during childbirth and contractions during orgasm. The muscle contractions during labour trigger a nurturing instinct for the new mother to love, protect and nurture her baby. Similarly, when a girl has sex with a boy, the sex act and orgasm cause those same muscles to contract, triggering like instincts. Only now the object of her affection is a boy, not a baby. This is why a girl's feelings often run deeper, because a deeper set of emotions has been tapped – feelings that go beyond the emotional or intellectual. Once these feelings have been activated, a break-up becomes all the more devastating.

Think about it. If a girl's instincts to love, protect and nurture are triggered every time she engages in sex, when the relationship ends she must ignore the deeper feelings of longing for him when she moves on to someone else. With each new partner she must repress past memories and emotions that surface. This repression of emotion weakens the strength of the bond with the new partner. Her body is so confused by multiple rejections of the bonding instincts that she will have difficulty forming a permanent bond with anyone. She has systematically destroyed, through multiple bonding, her ability to 'glue' herself to one person for a lifetime. This also destroys her ability to nurture her children.[6]

We have underrated the complexities of our physical make-up and the wisdom of obeying God's laws. We think of the Bible as a mere rulebook rather than an owner's manual. Since God created us, he knows best how we are put together, why we break down, and what we need to run efficiently. He doesn't always explain the scientific reasoning behind his laws; he merely asks that we trust and obey.

Now that the twelve pair-bonding steps have been outlined, you can better determine what demonstrations of physical affection are appropriate for each stage of dating. What dictates your choice is your self-worth and what you value for your future, as well as your commitment to obey God's Word. As you map out your intentions for your current relationship, as well as your standards for all future relationships, remember that everyone crossing the boundary from Step 6 to Step 7 risks exposing him or herself to the same trauma that follows a divorce, due to the intensity of the bond that is formed.

In my

estimation, Steps 9-12 belong in marriage only and have no place in a relationship prior to the wedding ceremony.

Remember also that bonding goes beyond physical intimacies to include emotional, intellectual, and spiritual bonding as well. True bonding is more than sexual intercourse, more than falling in love. It is the fusing of two separate and different lives, two separate and distinct minds. The couple blend their values, goals, beliefs, all their ideas, hopes and dreams for the future.

Note that this can happen without a formal agreement. Being bonded and married are not the same thing. Some coupes are *bonded* but not married. Other couples are *married* but not bonded, since they have a weak or damaged bond. The bond is like an expensive car. If you owned a Ferrari I doubt if you would park it on the street to get damaged or stolen. The car represents the bond. A garage represents the ceremony of marriage to protect the bond.

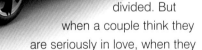

A well-bonded couple can survive almost any problem or stress to their relationship. They survive because they have taken time at each advancing level of their relationship to communicate and solve problems. Day by day they keep their bond strong through affection, touch, eye contact, and other intimacies. A strong bond is developed by advancing slowly up the steps of pair bonding.

Who Should Call a Halt, and Why?

Many researchers have asked young people who they think should draw the line when it comes to petting. The trend today places the responsibility on both. Fewer and fewer people think the female must bear the full brunt of drawing the line. And today males are willing to accept more responsibility for limiting sexual experimentation.

When a couple begins petting, however, verbal communication breaks down. And it isn't always clear to the two involved which of them is taking the initiative and which is responsible for limiting. Ideally, the responsibility for calling a halt should be equally divided. But when a couple think they are seriously in love, when they have unlimited opportunity to be alone and express affection, it becomes difficult to stop. Aroused sexual feelings respond reluctantly, if at all, to intelligence, reason, logic, ironclad decisions, previously determined guidelines, or anything short of sexual release.

When a couple reaches this point, it is left to the female to call a halt. The male, because he is more sexually aggressive, usually proceeds about as far as she will allow. Society, along with parents and others – all expect her to say No when conditions require it. This double standard may not be fair, but is a fact that girls must live with.

Society still tends to look the other way when guys are caught with their trousers down, but brands young women who do likewise as 'bad'. This same system proposes equality in so many other ways that it has become nauseating. Yet in one of the most basic and important aspects of our lives – our sexuality – the system remains silent.

The double standard can be erased in one of two ways: either both partners can willingly accept premarital sex in their partners or both can demand sexual purity prior to marriage. The latter choice has more advantages.

The female has more to lose than the male, and people tend to blame her more than him when they are found out. There are two main reasons for this attitude:

1. **A woman can control her sexual impulses more easily than a man.** Men become sexually stimulated more easily than do girls. He can become excited simply by watching a girl in revealing clothing or a bikini. Add a few intense kisses and you have turned him on. A girl may consider this next to meaningless and get no thrill at all. As his excitement mounts he feels less and less desire to stop. His natural urge is to proceed so that he can gain release from the mounting tension.

Because tension mounts in a girl more slowly, she becomes the logical one to apply the brakes. If she does not call a halt, she is usually the one who bears the blame. Society rarely considers a fellow a poor prospect for marriage because he has a sexual past, but few guys want to marry a woman who has had as much sexual experience as they themselves have had.

2. **The female runs the risk of pregnancy and suffers the greater social rejection when pregnancy results.** More than one million unmarried teenagers become pregnant each year – most of whom thought they wouldn't get pregnant. But pregnancy is *always* possible – even when the couple practises 'safe sex'. If a girl chooses to keep the child, she'll raise it alone, since 85% of the guys who impregnate girls abandon them.[7] And since 90% of marriages between teenagers end in divorce, there is a negligible chance for a marriage to survive.

My husband and I were guests in the home of a woman in charge of an adoption agency. In this home a 16-year-old unwed girl in her eighth month of pregnancy was boarding until she gave up her child for adoption. She lumbered out of the kitchen after meeting us. The next day, after feeling more comfortable in our presence, she showed us a picture of

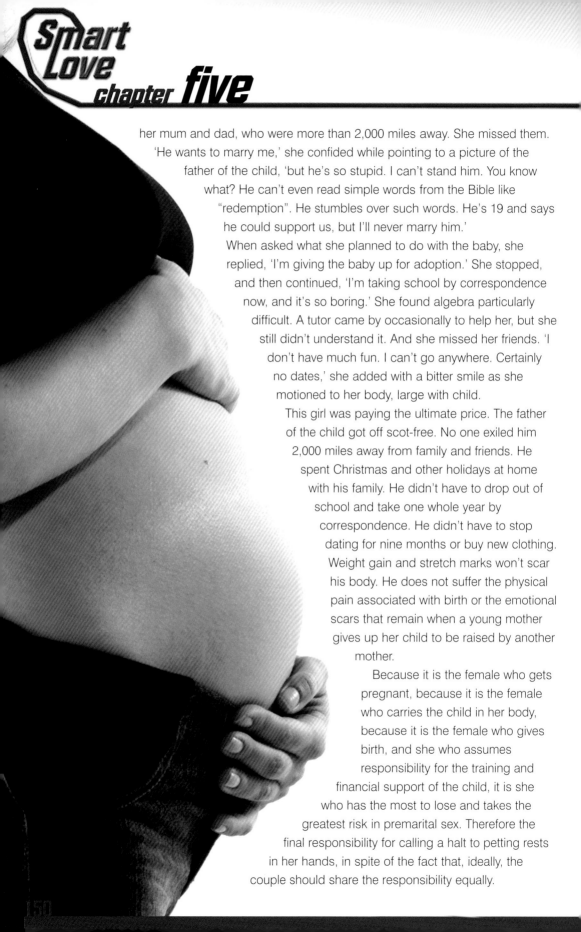

her mum and dad, who were more than 2,000 miles away. She missed them. 'He wants to marry me,' she confided while pointing to a picture of the father of the child, 'but he's so stupid. I can't stand him. You know what? He can't even read simple words from the Bible like "redemption". He stumbles over such words. He's 19 and says he could support us, but I'll never marry him.'

When asked what she planned to do with the baby, she replied, 'I'm giving the baby up for adoption.' She stopped, and then continued, 'I'm taking school by correspondence now, and it's so boring.' She found algebra particularly difficult. A tutor came by occasionally to help her, but she still didn't understand it. And she missed her friends. 'I don't have much fun. I can't go anywhere. Certainly no dates,' she added with a bitter smile as she motioned to her body, large with child.

This girl was paying the ultimate price. The father of the child got off scot-free. No one exiled him 2,000 miles away from family and friends. He spent Christmas and other holidays at home with his family. He didn't have to drop out of school and take one whole year by correspondence. He didn't have to stop dating for nine months or buy new clothing. Weight gain and stretch marks won't scar his body. He does not suffer the physical pain associated with birth or the emotional scars that remain when a young mother gives up her child to be raised by another mother.

Because it is the female who gets pregnant, because it is the female who carries the child in her body, because it is the female who gives birth, and she who assumes responsibility for the training and financial support of the child, it is she who has the most to lose and takes the greatest risk in premarital sex. Therefore the final responsibility for calling a halt to petting rests in her hands, in spite of the fact that, ideally, the couple should share the responsibility equally.

An Invitation to Sexual Purity

The Bible addresses the subject of sex openly. In Scripture, sex is neither dirty nor the ultimate experience. God's Word clearly states, however, that sexual intercourse is reserved only for those who have entered the state of marriage.

Some feel they aren't disobeying God's Word as long as they are having sex with only one person and they intend to marry – 'someday'. They feel as long as they are not promiscuous they will suffer no remorse or guilt, regardless of their past. When we disobey the laws of health, we will at some point suffer the consequences of our choices. Likewise, when we violate God's law regarding sexual purity, we will reap a harvest of devastating consequences, although we may not be aware of them immediately.

God's plan for our lives is perfect and has never changed. Sexual intimacy for marrieds is God's special design for our enjoyment and for bringing children into the world. This is the only lifestyle that offers complete happiness.

In the eyes of the secular world, the choice to remain sexually pure prior to marriage seems unrealistic and Victorian, but the facts supporting such a choice remain in your favour. Your sexuality might be considered a gift from God marked, *'For greatest enjoyment, do not open till married.'*

Whenever a relationship is based on physical pleasure rather than friendship it will eventually burn itself out. It's the qualities found in friendship that will get you through a lifetime bonded to one person.

At one time Christ walked this Earth. Scripture records that '[He was] tempted in every way, just as we are – yet was without sin.' (Hebrews 4:15.) This means that he faced sexual temptation. Yet he did not falter, toy with the idea, or give in. In the face of temptation he was able to turn away and remain pure. His life serves as an example for us today. If you will commit your life to Jesus, you can be assured that he can and will control your sex life when you ask for guidance. He will provide the strength to resist temptation. You do not have to fight this battle on your own. He will guide in this area of your life. It is possible to slow the pair-bonding instinct and make wise choices that will lead to a life of purity.

Regional HIV and AIDS statistics, 2001 and 2007

	Adults and children living with HIV	Adults and children newly infected with HIV	Adult prevalence (%)	Adult and child deaths due to AIDS
Sub-Saharan Africa				
2007	22.5 million [20.9 million–24.3 million]	1.7 million [1.4 million–2.4 million]	5.0% [4.6%–5.5%]	1.6 million [1.5 million–2.0 million]
2001	20.9 million [19.7 million–23.6 million]	2.2 million [1.7 million–2.7 million]	5.8% [5.5%–6.6%]	1.4 million [1.3 million–1.9 million]
Middle East and North Africa				
2007	380,000 [270,000–500,000]	35,000 [16,000–65,000]	0.3% [0.2%–0.4%]	25,000 [20,000–34,000]
2001	300,000 [220,000–400,000]	41,000 [17,000–58,000]	0.3% [0.2%–0.4%]	22,000 [11,000–39,000]
South and South-East Asia				
2007	4.0 million [3.3 million–5.1 million]	340,000 [180,000–740,000]	0.3% [0.2%–0.4%]	270,000 [230,000–380,000]
2001	3.5 million [2.9 million–4.5 million]	450,000 [150,000–800,000]	0.3% [0.2%–0.4%]	170,000 [120,000–220,000]
East Asia				
2007	800,000 [620,000–960,000]	92,000 [21,000–220,000]	0.1% [<0.2%]	32,000 [28,000–49,000]
2001	420,000 [350,000–510,000]	77,000 [4,900–130,000	<0.1% [<0.2%]	12,000 [8,200–17,000]
Oceania				
2007	75,000 [53,000–120,000]	14,000 [11,000–26,000]	0.4% [0.3%–0.7%]	1200 [<500–2700]
2001	26,000 [19,000–39,000]	3800 [3,000–5,600]	0.2% [0.1%–0.3%]	<500 [1,100]
Latin America				
2007	1.6 million [1.4 million–1.9 million]	100,000 [47,000–220,000]	0.5% [0.4%–0.6%]	58,000 [49,000–91,000]
2001	1.3 million [1.2 million–1.6 million]	130,000 [56,000–220,000]	0.4% [0.3%–0.5%]	51,000 [44,000–100,000]
Caribbean				
2007	230,000 [210,000–270,000]	17,000 [15,000–23,000]	1.0% [0.9%–1.2%]	11,000 [9,800–18,000]
2001	190,000 [180,000–250,000]	20,000 [17,000–25,000]	1.0% [0.9%–1.2%]	14,000 [13,000–21,000]

Eastern Europe and Central Asia

2007	1.6 million [1.2 million–2.1 million]	150,000 [70,000–290,000]	0.9% [0.7%–1.2%]	55,000 [42,000–88,000]
2001	630,000 [490,000–1.1 million]	230,000 [98,000–340,000]	0.4% [0.3%–0.6%]	8,000 [5,500–14,000]

Western and Central Europe

2007	760,000 [600,000–1.1 million]	31,000 [19,000–86,000]	0.3% [0.2%–0.4%]	12,000 [<15,000]
2001	620,000 [500,000–870,000]	32,000 [19,000–76,000]	0.2% [0.1%–0.3%]	10,000 [<15,000]

North America

2007	1.3 million [480,000–1.9 million]	46,000 [38,000–68,000]	0.6% [0.5%–0.9%]	21,000 [18,000–31,000]
2001	1.1 million [390,000–1.6 million]	44,000 [40,000–63,000]	0.6% [0.4%–0.8%]	21,000 [18,000–31,000]

Total

2007	**33.2 million** [30.6 million–36.1 million]	**2.5 million** [1.8 million–4.1 million]	**0.8%** [0.7%–0.9%]	**2.1 million** [1.9 million–2.4 million]
2001	**29.0 million** [26.9 million–32.4 million]	**3.2 million** [2.1 million–4.4 million]	**0.8%** [0.7%–0.9%]	**1.7 million** [1.6 million–2.3 million]

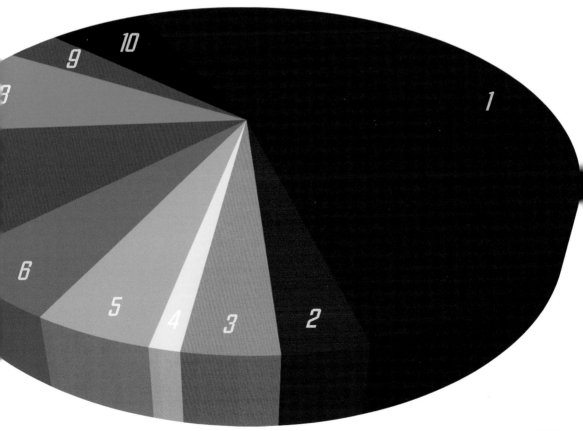

rce: http://data.unaids.org

Smart Love

chapter six

Boy meets girl.
Boy likes girl.
Boy kisses girl.
The entire sky explodes with
   rockets and fireworks.
Boy and girl head for bed.
And the camera fades out.

Research on television proves that portrayals of intercourse occur 49% of the time between unmarried lovers; 29% of the time between total strangers; and only 6% of the time between married couples. Both the media and secular society try to convey that sex is the ultimate experience. Sex makes life worth living. Life without sex is unfulfilling and laughable. If you take a stand for abstinence until marriage, we'll put you on a talk show and encourage the world to ridicule you and your standards. We'll make a sideshow freak of you.

I don't want to downplay the importance of satisfying sex in marriage. But a healthy sexual relationship is only one of several essential factors critical to marital happiness. And note that if the average married couple had sex three times a week and spent thirty minutes in each encounter for one year, they would spend only seventy-eight hours making love. That's three days out of 365 days in a year. What will they do the other 362 days of that year?

In other words, 97% of their time is spent out of bed, engaging in other activities. This is when the quality of the overall relationship outweighs the importance of the few hours spent enjoying sexual pleasure.

Evidence on Abstinence

For years I've been collecting data on why it is wiser to wait until marriage for sex. Sociological, psychological and medical evidence all support an abstinence stand. Sex outside of marriage has some extremely dangerous consequences. It destroys family life as well as the purpose and meaning of marriage. It erodes a person's ability to love and turns people into objects, which degrades their self-worth. It can lead to disease and results in unwanted children.

Furthermore, sex outside of marriage is a sin against God. The Bible is clear on the subject. In the *King James Version* of the New Testament, the word fornication refers to sexual immorality in general (John 8:41; Acts 15:20, 29; 21:25; Romans 1:29; 1 Corinthians 6:13, 18; 2 Corinthians 12:21; Ephesians 5:3). Two passages (Matthew 5:32; 19:9) use fornication as a synonym for adultery. In four passages both *adultery* and *fornication* are used together, indicating a definite distinction between the two words (Matthew 15:19; Mark 7:21; 1 Corinthians 6:9; Galatians 5:19). Both words refer to voluntary sexual intercourse between unmarried people or between an unmarried person and a married person (1 Corinthians 7:2; I Thessalonians 4:3-5). In 1 Corinthians 5:1 Paul applies the word *fornication* to an incestuous relationship.

In the final analysis, then, thirty-seven out of thirty-nine biblical passages exclude sexual intercourse from God's plan for unmarried young adults. The two exceptions are where fornication is used as a synonym for adultery. God asks his followers to confine sexual intercourse to marriage. This biblical advice is simple, clear and straightforward.

Most young adults are aware that Scripture says no to sex before marriage, but they either ignore or forget it when faced with a close encounter. Others say that times have changed. People are more sophisticated now and biblical restrictions are archaic. But what Scripture says against sex before marriage is as relevant today as in biblical times. I, along with Scripture, teach abstinence – total sexual purity – until marriage.

God didn't prohibit sex to see how good we are at jumping through hoops or scoring points. His purpose is to protect us, because he knows his laws are in our best interests. If we follow them, we will live longer, happier and more fulfilling lives. This is true even though his laws may not make sense to us now.

Some argue that it is all right to break God's law against sexual sin if nobody gets hurt. In truth, somebody always gets hurt. Even if you escape disease and pregnancy, the ability to commit or to bond with one person for a lifetime is scarred, as well as the ability to trust, to feel sexual desire, and to be fully open with another person. God's laws are not arbitrary. They do not forbid sexual pleasure; rather they preserve sexual pleasure if we abide by them and keep sexual intimacy for marriage.

It's foolish to tempt God, to wait and see what will happen. The best time to learn the dangers of going after forbidden sex is long before temptation occurs. Resistance is easier when you've already decided that you don't want to indulge in premarital sex.

Part 18: Fifteen Benefits of Sexual Abstinence Before Marriage

I've found that young people are tired of pious preaching. Therefore, I won't preach. There are a multitude of benefits to total and complete abstinence before marriage. I will present medical and psychological information, facts that show that abstinence until marriage is better. If one precedes another, that does not mean it carries more weight. They are not listed in order of importance.

1. Abstinence before marriage helps prevent unnecessary break-ups. In one of the most careful studies on the subject, it was found that couples who engage in sex before marriage are more likely to break up than those who do not. Even formally engaged couples who have intercourse are more likely to break their engagements.[1] Some studies show that twice as many engagements are broken among couples who have intercourse. Such couples are also more likely to divorce, separate or commit adultery after getting married.[2]

And studies show that 50% of those who get married have been engaged before. So being engaged means nothing as far as knowing for certain that you will marry that person. The more frequent the sex, the more engagements were broken. It's hard to end a steady relationship, harder to end an engagement, harder still to end a marriage, and even harder to end a marriage with children. The further you go, the more difficult it becomes and the more painful the results. One reason for the increased number of break-ups is that the male's need for marriage lessens when his sex needs are being satisfied outside marriage.

Premarital sex destroys trust and proves that a person is not in control of his desires but instead is controlled by them. When neither has control of their desires, sex controls them. Trust is undermined, and now they become victims of selfish desires; the relationship suffers and weakens, thus making it more likely to end. And when a break-up occurs, it is far more painful – because of the bonding that has taken place.

2. Abstinence before marriage helps prevent divorce. Divorce rates among those who were sexually active in their teens run extremely high (an estimated 75-80%). This finding dovetails with another study which reports that 'Those who cohabit before

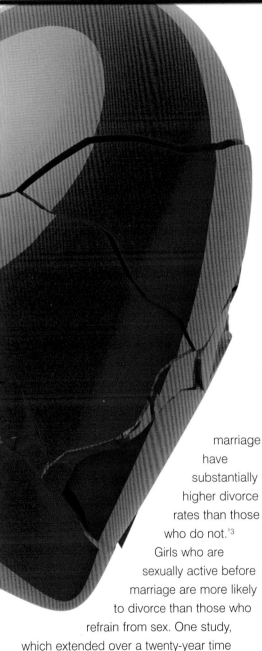

statistics by saying that virgin females are more likely to be religious and brought up in homes with strict moral values. Such evidence proves that those who practise biblical standards can increase their odds for a lasting marriage.

3. Abstinence prior to marriage helps prevent cervical cancer. Young women who engage in sex with multiple partners are at a high risk of contracting cervical cancer later in life. About the time menstruation begins, the entire endocrine system is putting the finishing touches on the uterus, fallopian tubes and ovaries. Delicate tissue surrounds the opening of the uterus or the cervix. In addition, the tissues of a young teen girl grow rapidly. This rapid growth increases susceptibility to cervical pre-cancer and cancer. Young women have a higher risk of cervical infections because their cervix has not completed age-related developmental changes. Thus they have fewer protective antibodies. In a few more years, the tissue surrounding the cervix will be replaced by a more mature, less moist, and tougher lining.

The cervix is extremely vulnerable during this time. If her cervix is exposed to semen, from one or multiple partners, a girl is placed at risk of cancer of the cervix later in life. Semen contains 'antigens' that sensitise or code the cervix and may cause abnormal development when a girl is exposed to it too early, too often, and by multiple sexual partners. *When a girl has three or more sexual partners, her odds of getting cervical cancer jump fifteen times over a girl who has only one partner.*[5]

4. Abstinence prior to marriage eliminates the risk of contracting a sexually-transmitted disease (STD). An interesting study among teenagers

marriage have substantially higher divorce rates than those who do not.'[3] Girls who are sexually active before marriage are more likely to divorce than those who refrain from sex. One study, which extended over a twenty-year time frame, showed that virgin brides were less likely to end their marriage through divorce or separation than those who had not been virgins at marriage. How much less likely? An astonishing 53-71% higher than non-virgins.[4]

The researchers elaborated on these

found that 42% of those surveyed couldn't name one STD outside of HIV or AIDS. Yet 30% could name someone who had one! This won't do. Now let's get educated about STDs.

Teens and young adults aged 10 to 24 are at a higher risk of getting STDs than older adults.[6] This is true because of physical immaturity, the tendency towards more sexual partners, and selecting partners at high risk. Because this age group is at greater risk than adults they have a disproportionate amount of STDs. About 20% (one in five) of sexually active young adults become infected with an STD every year.[7]

HPV (human papillomavirus) infection is the most common viral STD in America. It causes genital warts, warts of the vulva, perianal areas, and the throat. One study of female college students treated at a university health centre showed that genital HPV infections were five times more common than all other STDs combined! Forty-six percent of all sexually active students tested were infected with HPV. HPV is dangerous as it places a woman at risk of cervical cancer, the second most

common cancer among women, and is the cause of most pre-cancerous cervical lesions found in women. HPV causes at least 93% of pre-cancerous and cancerous growths of women's cervixes. And condoms do not protect against this most common and dangerous STD.[8] HPV infects men as well, but it is often undetectable since it is not painful. He may not know he has one or ignore small growths, yet he puts his partner at risk.

Chlamydia. STDs infect 33,000 people a day in the United States alone, or 12 million cases each year.[9] Chlamydia is the number one bacterial STD in America. Many men have no symptoms, and most women have no symptoms until complications set in. Chlamydia can cause infertility in both sexes. It also causes infections in the eyes, ears and lungs of babies, along with possible death. Teen females are more susceptible to Chlamydia, because cells lining the cervix of adolescents are less resistant to infection by certain sexually transmitted organisms.

Gonorrhoea. There is an epidemic of gonorrhoea among 15 to 19-year-olds. Women frequently have no symptoms, so the disease progresses painlessly until it results in pelvic inflammatory disease

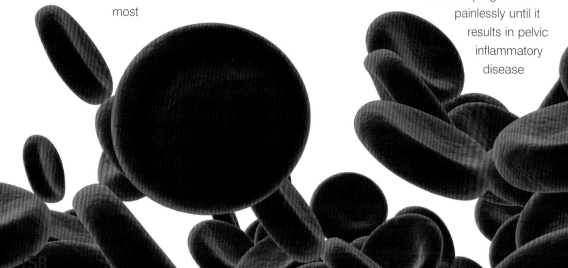

(PID), which results in infertility or ectopic pregnancy.[10] Babies of infected mothers may be born blind. Males show a pus-like discharge. The gonorrhoea rate among teen girls has increased 400% over the last thirty years and is the highest of any age group.

Trichomoniasis, genital warts, syphilis and herpes constitute an ever-growing list of STDs. Herpes type 2 now infects one in five persons 12 years of age and older in the US, and results in painful genital ulcers that keep recurring. These sores are extremely tender. Often a woman will be unable to urinate due to severe pain caused by urine flowing over the sores. The ulcers can be treated, but infection persists and recurs. Herpes can be transmitted to sex partners even when no genital ulcers are present. Don't be fooled. Herpes can also be transmitted by oral-genital contact. If a baby is born when a mother has a primary outbreak, the baby has a 40-50% chance of becoming infected and a 50% chance of dying. If the child survives, there is a 50% chance it will suffer severe brain damage. Since there is no cure for a viral infection, the infected person will carry this affliction for a lifetime. And yes, it is something you have to tell a partner before marriage.[11]

HIV and AIDS. One of the fastest-growing AIDS populations in the US is among teens. Persons who become HIV infected will usually develop AIDS. Only 5% live for ten years without developing AIDS. Persons who develop AIDS will usually die from the disease unless death results from some other cause first. All HIV-positive people will probably be infectious for the rest of their lives and should consider never having penetrative sex again. Homosexuals still make up 40% of infected individuals, but women acquiring HIV from heterosexual contact are the fastest growing risk category. Young women are at even higher risk. In New York City, heterosexual infection in teens rose 135% between 1992 and 1997.

In 2007 the global estimate for adults and children living with HIV/AIDS was 33.2 million, of which around 2.5 million were new infections. (Source: UN AIDS – Joint UN programme on HIV/AIDS.)

AIDS has now reached pandemic proportions, affecting almost every family. Unmarried partners simply do not know one another's sexual histories. Studies reveal that such persons are very uncomfortable discussing STDs, contraception or condom use and think they can sense or know when a partner isn't safe. *No one can intuitively know.*

Sub-Saharan Africa (the region south of the Sahara Desert) is more heavily infected by HIV and AIDS than any other region in the world. Although Africa has only 12% of the world's population, it is estimated to have 60% of the AIDS infected population. Millions are dying from AIDS while still young or in early middle age. The average life expectancy in the Sub-Sahara region is now 47 years, when it could be 62 without AIDS. AIDS kills some 6,000 people every day in Africa and is the Number One overall cause of death in Africa. It is estimated that AIDS will kill more than one third of young adults in parts of Africa.

How is this deadly disease transmitted? Let's get the facts. The HIV virus which develops into AIDS is transmitted in body fluids, including blood semen, vaginal fluid, and breast milk. It is most commonly passed on during sexual intercourse, shared hypodermic needles, or from mother to child through breast milk. It can also be transmitted by blood infusion, but not by ordinary social contact.

Young people are especially at risk. Youth in Africa begin their sexual activity in early to mid teens. High levels of pregnancy among teens and pregnancy outside of marriage tell us two things – young people are very sexually active and few are using condoms. *Remember: condoms will not totally prevent pregnancy, AIDS or other STDs, but are 'safer'.* When young people have unprotected sex, especially with multiple partners, they are exposed not just to pregnancy but to infection with STDs, including the one that can kill them – AIDS.

In Sub-Saharan Africa about 59% of those living with HIV are female. The reason behind this lies with social inequities between men and women. Men most often dominate sexual relations, forcing themselves on a woman, which means the couple will not practise 'safe sex' – he won't take the time and she won't have the chance. This can occur even when they both know and understand the risks involved. Some studies show that nine out of ten young adults never use condoms even in casual encounters.

Girls often become infected at younger ages than boys. The age gap indicates that young girls are getting infected by having sex with older men. Many girls choose such relationships because the men come with gifts, money or other favours attached. Often these girls are powerless to refuse and are forced or raped. When a girl is forced in this manner, the vagina is dry and cuts and abrasions are more likely. With ejaculation, the virus is injected into a woman's vagina (or mouth or anus) and produces infection in her body. If the male is already infected with HIV or AIDS the virus can easily find its way into the girl's bloodstream.

Because there is a stigma in admitting to an HIV infection and in the use of condoms, many continue to engage in unsafe sexual practice which spreads HIV to new sex partners. Others deny that HIV causes AIDS. And there are many myths attached to the use of condoms. In countries where strong educational programmes are in place, such as Uganda, youth are delaying the age at which intercourse first occurs and the HIV rate is decreasing.

Remember, there is no cure for AIDS presently, and no vaccine against HIV,[12] but there are drugs that can slow down the spread of the virus. Infection can occur from just one act of intercourse with an HIV-infected person who may look and feel totally normal and not know he/she is infected. Both HPV and HIV organisms can be found in the semen of infected males with no symptoms. With ejaculation, these germs are injected into a woman's vagina (or mouth or anus) and produce infection in her body.[13]

Just remember, it is possible to catch more than one STD at a time. One chance encounter can infect a person with as many as five different diseases.[14] And there are many recorded cases of syphilis being transmitted through kissing. About half of those who have it are unaware of it since primary lesions do not appear for ten to ninety days.[15]

If you have sex before marriage, you become a prime candidate for STDs. Unmarried partners simply do not know one another's sexual histories. Studies show that teenagers are very uncomfortable discussing STDs, contraception or condom use and think they can just 'know' when a partner is or isn't safe. No one can just 'know'. One survey showed that 20% of all the guys and 4% of the girls *would not* tell a potential partner they had tested positive for HIV. Forty-seven percent of the girls said they would understate the number of previous sex partners if they were asked.[16]

Even an honest answer to whether a person has an STD can't be counted on as truth. STDs can lie dormant and still be transmitted to another. Herpes is contagious even when it is dormant and no lesions are present.

Females are more vulnerable to AIDS than males because the vagina is highly susceptible to cuts or tearing during intercourse. Another reason females are at higher risk is because the virus is more concentrated in semen than in vaginal fluid, and susceptible cells of the vagina are exposed to the semen for a prolonged period of time.[17]

Safe sex isn't safe. The failure rate in preventing pregnancy for couples using condoms is at least 15.8% of the time annually. Among young unmarried minority women the failure rate for preventing pregnancy is 36.3% annually. Medical journals report the failure rate in preventing pregnancy due to slippage and tearing of the condom to be 26%. Obviously anyone who relies on condoms for birth control can be called a parent! This super high failure rate exists in preventing pregnancy – where a girl can conceive only one to five days a month. The egg only lives one day, but sperm can survive in the mucus of the cervix for several days. Therefore, we can only guess the failure rate for preventing STDs which can be transmitted 365 days a year![18]

Condoms cannot be accurately tested for AIDS protection. The AIDS virus is 450 times smaller than sperm and can easily pass through the smallest detectable hole in the condom. Furthermore, condoms must be used correctly, reliably and consistently to

have any chance of STD protection. And they offer little or no protection against bacterial vaginosis and HPV.

Now get this: If you have had two to three sex partners and your partner has had two to three sex partners, you have a 100% chance of getting an STD. To help you understand this, look at Peter and Paula, who are in love and are considering becoming sexually involved. Both know the other has had previous partners but neither has been specific or truthful. Let's look at the whole picture. (See the following diagram.[19])

Peter   Paula

Adapted from *Risky Times* by Jeanne Blake.
Used by permission of Workman Publishing Co., Inc.

Peter's former girlfriend is Diane. Peter and Diane had sex. Diane had sex with two other men, Charles and John, before she had sex with Peter. Charles's three partners before Diane were Pat, Deborah and Judy. Deborah had sex with one person, Jason, before Charles. Jason's former partner was Janet. Judy's first partner was Steve. John's former girlfriend was Betty. Betty had two previous sexual relationships, with Tom and Kevin. Kevin was bisexual and involved with Jack.

So if Paula thinks she is safe with Peter, she is forgetting about the other thirteen people in the picture. When you sleep with a person, you, in essence, sleep with all his or her previous sex partners.

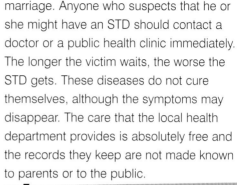

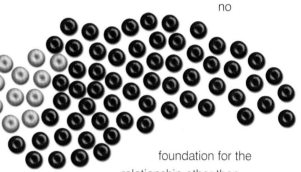

Here is a progression worked out, assuming all partners have the same history – one partner a year, beginning at the age of 15. At the end of the first year you would have had sex with one person. At the age of 16, three persons – last year's partner, your current partner, and the person your current partner had sex with last year. At age 17, seven persons. At age 18, fifteen persons. At age 19, thirty-one persons. At age 20, sixty-three persons. At age 21, one hundred and twenty-seven. The cumulative effect builds yearly. This type of promiscuity is the reason for the soaring rates of STDs in young adults.

The only way to be sure you will not get an STD is complete abstinence until marriage. Anyone who suspects that he or she might have an STD should contact a doctor or a public health clinic immediately. The longer the victim waits, the worse the STD gets. These diseases do not cure themselves, although the symptoms may disappear. The care that the local health department provides is absolutely free and the records they keep are not made known to parents or to the public.

5. Abstinence before marriage improves chances of distinguishing real love from infatuation. Most young people find it difficult to distinguish between what feels good and genuine love. When there is no foundation for the relationship other than sexual excitement, the ardour soon cools unless the couple stays together for sex. For instance, sometimes a girl will continue with a sexual relationship so she can keep her boyfriend. Sometimes a guy will use a girl he barely likes just for the physical thrills. In most instances, the longer a couple dates, the greater their chance of finding genuine love. But once they become sexually involved, they may stay together for sex and not because they share common interests, goals and values.

It works like this: A couple begins dating. As the relationship progresses, their compatibility is tested. When mostly compatible, they stay together. When incompatible, they break up. This is the way it works when a couple is not sexually involved. But as soon as a relationship becomes sexual, the dynamics change, whether either will admit it or not.

Sex before marriage inevitably masks areas of concern that should be discussed as a relationship moves along. Often, when a sexually active couple encounters a problem, rather than dealing openly with it, the problem is masked by having sex, which makes things better temporarily. Thus the couple never develops the ability to talk problems through. On the surface their relationship is fine, but they never really learn how to communicate their feelings. Sex masks their problems until after they are married.

When sex begins before a couple learns how to solve problems and communicate their thoughts in a meaningful way, sex invariably becomes manipulative. If all you have going for you in the relationship is sex, it won't hold you together permanently anyway.

Abstinence can help a couple learn to communicate and solve problems when they are committed to spending time learning about themselves and their relationship.

6. Abstinence before marriage eliminates guilt feelings. The Sorenson Report, the most complete sociological study of teenage sexuality to date, asked girls to describe their reaction to their first sexual experience. Words like *afraid*, *guilty*, *worried* and *embarrassed* headed the list. Words like *happy*, *joyful* and *satisfied* ranked much lower.

Another study targeted the reaction of college girls to their first sexual experience and found that one third of them had a negative experience, with little or no pleasure and high levels of guilt and anxiety. Another third of the girls had a mixed reaction but still experienced considerable guilt and anxiety. The final third felt exploited and used.[20]

Premarital sex has some serious adverse effects on the self-image of the person indulging in it. Emotionally crippling guilt, not happiness and freedom, accompanies it. A study of unmarried women showed that 86% of those under a psychiatrist's care were sexually active, while only 22% of those not under care were not. Premarital sex and emotional instability are directly related.[21] A study conducted at the University of

Wisconsin showed that 86% of the psychologist's patients interviewed had engaged in premarital sex. The main cause of their problem was guilt over premarital sex.[22]

Premarital sex, because it is so expressly forbidden by God, causes intense emotional damage. It flies in the face of God's plan for the family. Females generally feel more guilt when breaking their moral codes than do males. And the more devout the female, the greater the likelihood she will experience regret and guilt following the incident.[23] But males also experience regret as a result of promiscuous behaviour prior to marriage.

When you indulge in premarital sex over and over again, the guilt, fear and loss of self-respect compound. You feel more and more guilty. And it is possible that you might always associate guilty, negative feelings with sex even after you are married. Such feelings do not end once the wedding takes place, for most of us have trouble shaking off previous attitudes. To the degree you associate premarital sex with

fear, guilt and shame before marriage, to the same degree you will experience the same emotions after marriage. Such attitudes may take months or even years of professional counselling to cure. And they may never be cured.

By limiting sex to marriage, God is trying to protect us from the devastating emotional consequences that accompany sex before marriage. The consequences of such actions may be immediate or they may drag on for years. We must recognise the wisdom of his Word and the value of keeping his commands.

When two people have sex, it is more than a mere physical act. There are emotional consequences. Each time you have sex with someone, you mesh a part of your non-physical self with that person. Sex makes such a definite impression that you leave a part of yourself with that person forever. Therefore, there really is no such thing as 'casual sex'. We humans are put together in such a way that we know even then we've violated God's intentions. Whether the partners acknowledge God's laws or not, they *feel* guilty before a holy God because they *are* guilty. **Abstinence eliminates guilt. Period.**

7. **Abstinence before marriage totally eliminates the risk of pregnancy.** Girls who first have intercourse at the age of 15 or younger are almost twice as likely to become pregnant within the first six months of sexual activity as those who wait until they are older. This is due partly to ignorance about methods of birth control and to their maturity level. Girls at this age frequently don't understand or don't believe the relationship between sex and pregnancy. They discount it by saying, 'It will never happen to me.'

About 500,000 teen girls run away from home each year. Forty percent of them do so because they are pregnant. 'My dad told me he'd kill me if I got myself pregnant,' or 'My mum told me not to come home if I got pregnant,' is the way they put it. And the most prevalent reason for suicide among teen girls is pregnancy.[24]

Unmarried girls in their teens have a higher risk of becoming a parent than older females, even though they are on birth control pills. And when a woman takes 'the pill' for contraception along with other medication, she may be more likely to become pregnant. Some drugs change the way the body handles birth control pills, thereby decreasing the contraceptive effect. And remember that oral contraceptives provide no protection against STDs.[25]

Health risks. The health risks to teen mothers and their babies are enormous.[26] The teen mother is more likely to begin premature labour and have a more difficult labour. Non-fatal anaemia and toxaemia are more likely. Babies born to girls under the age of 15 are almost two-and-a-half times more likely to die during their first year. Babies also have a lower birth weight and have more brain and nervous system disorders, which usher in complications such as blindness, learning disorders, cerebral palsy and behavioural problems. These babies also have lower IQs. These children also have more difficulties in life. They have more trouble in school, perform significantly lower in tests and their performance in school does not improve as they get older. They are more likely to drop out of school and boys are 2.7 times more likely to go to prison.

One quarter of the girls who become pregnant between the ages of 15 and 19 will have a second baby within two years of their first delivery. These girls end up in poverty, relying on the state for support. Only three out of ten girls who become pregnant at the age of 17 or younger will ever complete their education. (Seventy-six percent of girls who abstain until the age of 20 do complete their education!)

Regardless of why a teenager becomes sexually active, most of them do not want a baby. But some girls have such low self-esteem and feel so unloved that they deliberately try to have a child – 'someone I can love who will love me back.' A teenage girl with major self-image problems who can't discipline her own behaviour is hardly in a position to train and discipline a newborn! She also puts a tremendous onus on her child by expecting a baby to solve her self-image problems. Babies compound problems, not solve them. Others want to get pregnant as a means of keeping a boyfriend or to get him to marry her.

A girl who becomes pregnant has four choices: give the baby up for adoption, marry the father of the child, raise the child alone, or abort the child. Regardless of her choice she will have to raise the child alone, since 85% of boys who impregnate teen girls eventually abandon them.[27]

Since 90% of marriages between teens end in divorce, there is negligible chance for a marriage between the two to survive.

Some years ago my grandson,

Jamison, as part of a senior family living class, received his newborn infant 'Shelby' to care for over a forty-eight-hour period. This programmable Real Care Baby has a computer inside that records the baby's problem along with the care given by his 'parent'. The caregiver wears a sensor on his arm that works only on his baby, thereby preventing the parent from leaving his child with a babysitter. If you remove the sensor you fail the course. The baby can cry for many reasons: wet nappies, hunger, needs burping, rocking, neck support, bad position or fussy. The 'parent' has to work out what the problem is and the computer records the care given. Your grade for the course depends on your care. The computer also notes if the baby is neglected, spanked, shaken, and records its abuse. Each Real Care Baby has a personality and Jamison's Shelby was programmed to be a 'difficult' child.

Shelby woke Jamison at 3am and kept him awake for two hours the first night needing to be rocked, and three hours the second night needing little more than a burp. This project occurred on Jamison's birthday. 'The best birthday present I got,' he said, 'was giving up Shelby!' All class members agreed they never wanted to have a child!

8. Abstinence prior to marriage excludes the need for abortion. One girl became pregnant after drinking too much and having casual sex with a boy she barely knew. After weeks of painful deliberation, she decided to have an abortion. In the waiting room of the abortion clinic, she was embarrassed to see a girl from school she knew. Eventually both began to talk about their situation and learned, to their horror, that the same man had fathered both of their children! This man had a lot of 'love' to give! Abortion terminates about 40% of teen pregnancies in the US,[28] and millions of girls suffer intensely following an abortion. Physically, they suffer from nervous disorders and stomach problems; and some, because of complications, have to have hysterectomies – which means they can never have a child of their own. They also suffer from depression, feelings of rejection, guilt, suicidal thoughts, and seem unable to forgive themselves.

Yes, abortion has an aftermath of consequences that has largely been ignored until recently. One study found the following: 81% reported preoccupation with the aborted baby

73% reported flashbacks of the abortion itself

69% reported feelings of mental instability after the abortion

54% reported recurring nightmares related to the abortion

35% felt they were having visits from the aborted child

23% suffered hallucinations related to the abortion.[29]

These symptoms occurred in spite of

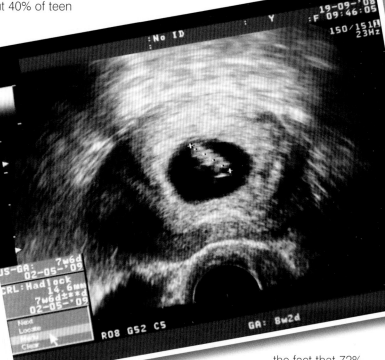

the fact that 72% of the women said they held no religious beliefs at the time of their abortion! We can only guess about the repercussions on the mothers (as well as the fathers) of the children who were raised in Christian homes and broke their values in seeking abortion as the answer to pregnancy before marriage. In addition to the emotional consequences, there are health risks. Abortion can damage a woman's female organs which can result in infertility, or if pregnancy occurs, in premature delivery with all its risks.

Any girl who has had an abortion needs to seek repentance, healing and the assurance of Christ's forgiveness. Once she understands Christ's mercy and forgiveness, she can let go of the guilt and hurt. It takes time to heal and the process of forgiving oneself cannot be hurried. And you cannot always predict when these symptoms will occur. Sometimes they do not occur until five or ten years after the abortion, which means that many girls marry unsuspecting guys. Problems surface years later and cause stress to the couple and their marriage.

9. Abstinence protects the value and meaning of the honeymoon. The lingering memories of a happy and special honeymoon are treasures the couple should cherish all their years together. A couple should be able to look back on their honeymoon as a tender time when they got to know one another in new ways. One study showed that 87% of the couples who had been sexually abstinent until their wedding took a honeymoon. But only 47% of the couples who had had sex took a honeymoon.[30]

One recently-married man said: 'Having sex before we were married greatly took away my expectations for our honeymoon. After we were married, I was truly sorry I'd let it happen, but it was too late.'

When you wait for something, it brings anticipation and excitement. When you wait for it, you develop character through patience; and, in turn, this increases self-esteem. And the longer you wait and dream about it, the greater your response will be when the time finally comes.

10. Abstinence before marriage prevents much sexual dysfunction for the female. Some studies indicate that half of all married American women have such poor attitudes about sex they cannot achieve orgasm. Women are more apt to carry guilt and fear about past sexual encounters with previous partners. When this happens, negative attitudes connected with these guilt-producing experiences rob them of their ability to achieve orgasm after marriage.

In studies conducted on girls who have had sexual intercourse before marriage, it was found that the more premarital sex girls have prior to marriage, the more likely they are to experience orgasm in the first year of marriage. This held true for those who had sex only with their future husband as well as for those having multiple partners.

If we stopped here, it would appear that abstinence doesn't pay. But despite their ability to reach orgasm, *far more of these women had sex difficulties during the early years of marriage.* Significant numbers reported long-term difficulties and dysfunction that began during the first two weeks of marriage. Others reported feeling like 'sex servants'.

Girls who freely allowed boyfriends to have their way before marriage were confronted with emotions and difficulties after marriage that they had been unaware of just weeks before. And the more religious the girl, the greater the likelihood of her experiencing regret and guilt.

The study also showed that girls with no previous sexual experience quickly learned to achieve orgasm after marriage and were at no disadvantage. Whether a woman is able to achieve orgasm seems to be connected to guilt. When sin is indulged in repeatedly – in this case, sex outside of marriage – guilt is the natural outcome. Fear and loss of self-respect for not following moral codes and religious values follow. As remorse is felt and compounded with each sexual indulgence, negative feelings become associated with sex. Such feelings do not go away even after the marriage ceremony takes place.

11. **Abstinence before marriage prevents much sexual dysfunction for the male.** Impotence affects one out of ten males and is caused by a variety of physical and emotional factors. Anger, fear, resentment and guilt can cause impotence. Ego or self-worth problems in which a guy feels his masculinity is threatened, including fear of rejection, can also be contributing factors.

One man who experienced impotence after he was married said, 'My sex drive was greater while we were living together than now.' Another guy admitted to his first bout of impotence after he and his girlfriend were 'caught in the act' by her parents. A third man who began having sex with his fiancée just weeks before the wedding told his pastor, 'I go limp every time we go to bed and my wife can't take much more.' The common denominator in each of these situations? Sex before marriage.

Another problem for males, premature ejaculation, can result from poor sex habits prior to marriage. A male suffering from this problem cannot withhold ejaculation. This problem plagues younger men and usually can be traced to a variety of sex experiences: frequent sex play where he became used to ejaculating without a girl (as with masturbation), steamy petting episodes where he feared 'getting caught' and had to hurry, or involvement with pornography and prostitutes.

Sex experiences seem to be written in indelible ink in our memories, *never to be erased*. It happens due to the manner in which long-term memories are stored: (1) through the intensity of the experience; and (2) through how often we rehearse or review the experience in our mind. Sex involves both of these. Since the experience is usually intense and often reviewed, and because of the emotions involved, it can never be erased.[31]

Sex cannot be locked in a compartment isolated from the rest of our lives. How someone conducts his sex life before marriage will affect his mental, physical and psychological processes after marriage as well. Abstinence before marriage protects one from negative effects on the psyche.

12. Abstinence before marriage predicts greater sexual satisfaction after marriage.

A study by the Family Research Council found that 72% of those who strongly believe sex before marriage is wrong report high sexual satisfaction. This is thirty-one percentage points higher than those who thought sex before marriage was OK.[32] In other words, it was those with the least sexual experience who were more likely to report their marriage as always warm and supportive. Another survey indicates that when a couple abstains from sex prior to marriage, they are 29-47% more likely to enjoy sex after marriage.[33]

Another survey on sexuality by the *US News and World Report*, dubbed the 'most authoritative ever', sheds further light on the subject. This survey found that of all of the sexually active people, those who reported being most physically pleased and emotionally satisfied were the married couples.

A chance of this kind of sexual enjoyment alone would make it worth waiting for!

13. Abstinence prior to marriage decreases the likelihood of extramarital affairs.

A strong link exists between sex before marriage, and extramarital sex. This is true even when there was only one sexual partner prior to marriage. Studies on the subject show that those who have had premarital sex are twice as likely to have extramarital affairs as those who are virgins at marriage. And those who have had affairs once admit that they are likely to do so again. This finding can certainly be used to predict unhappiness in marriage as well as a major cause of divorce.[34]

Those who have been promiscuous prior to marriage find it difficult to do an about-face at their wedding and commit to only one partner within the sacred bonds of matrimony. Sexual attitudes practised before marriage strongly affect and direct sexual appetites after marriage.

Those who have been sexually active find themselves comparing the performance of their current partner with the performance of a previous partner. This places sex on a performance level, rather than being an act of love. Many women become so anxious over how they perform that arousal is blocked. When people are put on a performance basis, they feel as if they are accepted and liked only when they do something their partner wants or expects. They do not feel loved for who they are – only for what they give. This gives rise to insecurity. 'You'll only keep me around as long as I please you. When I no longer please you, you'll toss me aside.' This leads to perpetual insecurity.

Once a young person becomes involved in premarital sex, his body begins to associate sex and arousal with guilt and the fear of getting caught. Such feelings may be so strong he will forever associate sex with fear and guilt and never experience the fulfilment it should bring to a committed relationship. Such a reaction may follow a person into marriage, and he/she may endlessly pursue extramarital affairs in order to stimulate sexual arousal – which in this person can only be accomplished through fear and guilt.

14. **Abstinence prior to marriage ensures a more perfect bond.** It is impossible to predict before having sex with someone what your attitudes or the attitudes of your partner will be following the experience. Sex changes the dynamics of the relationship. You may look at yourself, the other person and life through different eyes.

For instance, after having sex a girl often feels a strong attachment to a boy – an emotional bond that cannot be forgotten

years later, even though she may have married someone else. After hearing about the twelve steps of pair bonding, an 18-year-old girl told me about a break-up she had with a boyfriend. She just couldn't seem to get over it. She thought about him every day and was extremely troubled about why she couldn't get over him. She had become sexually involved with this boy when she was only 14. Four years later she still couldn't get over the after-effects of this relationship. Sex had solidified their bond.

Sometimes a girl who gives in reluctantly will begin to think of sex as something a woman has to do to please and hold a boyfriend. Other young people feel used, dirty and ashamed because they have lost their innocence and virginity and it can never be reclaimed. Still others suffer from intense confusion and bewilderment.

All the consequences apply when you have sex outside of marriage, but the toll is infinitely greater when multiple partners are involved. Bond. Break. Bond. Break. Bond. Break.

A painful and unhealthy lifelong pattern of relating to the

opposite sex in a series of easy-come, easy-go relationships. This pattern becomes difficult to break – even after you find someone you want to settle down with and marry. There is even less opportunity for establishing one perfect bond.

15. Abstinence promotes self-worth.
Repeated indulgence in known wrong destroys self-worth. Girls frequently engage in sex for non-sexual reasons. A girl goes out with a boy and then has sex with him, not because she wants to or cares deeply for him but because she thinks it is expected of her. She thinks that unless she plays the game his way, she'll not hear from him again. Having sex because she thinks it's part of some unspoken deal eventually makes a woman feel guilty and used. Guilt and feeling used lead to increased feelings of rejection and self-loathing.

Boys also admit that a one-time sexual experience with a girl outside of a committed relationship isn't as great as it's made out to be. Someone has said that instant sex is about as satisfying as a sneeze.

Sex isn't the answer to feeling lonely and unloved. Sex outside of marriage only complicates the problems we already have. The answer to such problems can be found when we have a committed relationship with Jesus Christ.

Not having sex outside of marriage is called abstinence. Abstinence here refers to abstinence from all forms of sex play. And it's 100% guaranteed to work. You won't get hurt, get an STD, get pregnant, or suffer a host of other problems. You can choose abstinence at any time, even when you've previously been sexually active.

Abstinence. It works! And it has some great rewards.

Part 19: Ten Key Habits of Sexually Abstinent Youth

If you've already chosen abstinence and want to stay that way until you are married, here's how to maintain your choice. And for those of you who are already sexually experienced, here are ten sure-fire strategies to help you reform.

1. Develop positive feelings of worth. Having positive feelings about yourself is the most important factor in avoiding sex prior to marriage. If you live up to your values, others will think highly of you, and inner conflicts will not tear you apart inside. You will respond to others' opinions of you with personal integrity and self-confidence. Your appearance, abilities and popularity will not unduly worry you and this leaves you free to love, study and play.

A. C. Green, one of the great all-star basketball players, said that as a professional athlete he was constantly confronted by women who wanted to meet and spend time with him. From the time he arrived in a city until he left, women pursued

him. Professional basketball players often have a larger-than-life image, and such women were everywhere, he said – in the airports, hotel foyers, restaurants and sports arenas – trying to catch his eye.

A. C. wasn't blind. He recognised the kind when he saw one. Furthermore, he heard the locker-room talk about the sexual conquests of other players. But this celebrity chose to remain sexually pure until marriage, to follow God's rather than secular standards. This was verbalised to his team-mates. He told them what his stand on sex before marriage was and that he believed God has reserved sex for marriage. His team-mates did not all agree with his stand, but they respected him for standing up for it. A. C. was proud to be a virgin till he married. 'I have to respect myself before I can respect others,' he said.

If you are going to practise abstinence from this day forward, you must first improve your feelings of worth. (See Chapter 1 on how to do this.) When you truly see yourself as a valued child of God for whom Christ died, you will feel more capable of making tough choices that will benefit your future rather than weakening it.

2. **Set rules for conduct in advance.** Most young adults have never set limits on their conduct, especially not their sexual conduct. Phrases like: 'I never really thought about it,' or 'I just do what comes naturally,' or 'I just go with the flow,' are commonly used. Such attitudes create opportunities for pressure situations to develop.

Think through your standards and develop criteria for showing physical affection based on your personal values as well as God's Word. Take time for a thoughtful self-inventory and decide what limits you will put on your dating behaviour. Decide at what point in the steps of pair bonding you will never go beyond until you are married.

After carefully thinking through and setting your standards, plan how to maintain them. Develop a specific plan to follow so that you can continue a dating relationship with someone without compromising yourself. The following eight habits will help you develop this plan.

Babe Ruth, the legendary baseball hero, once played before a hostile stadium. Amid the boos and hissing of the crowd, he pointed his bat to the exact spot in the grandstand where he intended to hit the next pitch. Then he hit the ball to precisely where he had pointed – for a home run. When you set standards for your own conduct, think of Babe Ruth. Everyone else might say you'll never make it, but your standards can never be too high. The more clearly your standards are defined and the better you know yourself and your standards, the more likely you are to achieve them. Just keep thinking about where the bat is pointed.

And remember, if you aim for the barn door and miss, you end up in cattle-produced barnyard soup. But if you aim for the stars and miss, you end up in stardust. So aim high!

3. Talk it over with your dating partner.

This doesn't mean that you introduce yourself to a new date by saying, 'Hello, I'm Jennifer and I don't sleep with anyone.' You can be both straightforward and tactful about letting the other person know your limits. Those who let their dating partner know what their standards are usually receive a positive response.

An easy way of bringing up the subject might be to talk about something you heard in a class you are taking or a book you are reading. 'Our teacher said studies say more teenagers today are choosing abstinence prior to marriage than ever before.' Or you can tell about your choice for your future: 'It is only fair to tell you about what I've chosen for my life. I am only interested in dating relationships that do not include sex until marriage. I hope you will respect my choice.'

At first you may find it a bit stressful to be so up-front about your no-sex-before-marriage policy, especially if you have a new dating partner and you don't know that person well yet. This may be someone who has not approached you sexually in any way, someone you have done little with besides hold hands. But once you bring your values out in the open, you will notice that it actually eliminates stress and uncertainty about where the relationship is going. Even then you will have to be very careful about advancing in the pair-bonding steps.

This discussion about your limits and values needs to take place before you are about to get 'carried away'. Any predetermined limits may be quickly forgotten in the heat of passion and can be rationalised away. Select the right time and place where both of you can be objective about your limits. Then once your limits are set, follow them to the letter.

One caution: it's better not to share your weaknesses with your partner, as it could be used against you. If a girl tells a guy that she gets 'turned on' when he French kisses her, she has just given him ammunition to use on her in a moment of weakness.

Once a couple puts their standards on the table and discusses them openly, it clears the air. It minimises the frustration about false expectations. It frees both to enjoy a developing friendship. And once the other person knows what your standards are, it's easier for you to remember them also.

Then, stick to them!

4. Develop and abide by a dating agreement. I recommend that teenagers develop a dating agreement to share with their parents. Many teenagers encounter problems with their parents when they begin to date. Their parents are constantly worried about their choice of companions, their activities, and curfews. You could eliminate much trouble by drawing up a 'Dating Agreement' and presenting it to your parents.

5. Develop an action plan should you ever be faced with a 'close encounter'. One thousand sexually experienced teen girls were asked what they would most like to know about sex. Eighty-five percent said, 'How to say No without hurting the other person's feelings.' Let's look at it in three stages:

A light threat: If a guy or girl even jokingly makes reference to a suggestive activity, you can say No and mean it. Or you could begin talking about how to share your faith. Get up, change the activity and say: 'I'm starved. Let's go and get something to eat.' Or tell a joke.

A girl was in a rowing boat floating on a quiet lake when a fierce storm hit and drove her towards a dangerous waterfall. A man on the shore saw her and offered to throw her a rope. She refused, saying, 'God will save me.' Then a helicopter lowered a ladder so she could climb to safety. Again she refused, shouting, 'God will save me.' Finally, the coastguard sent a boat. Once again she insisted, 'God will save me.' Then the rowing boat crashed

over the waterfall as she cried out, 'God, why didn't you save me?' From the heavens an answer came: 'I sent a man with a rope, a helicopter, and finally the coastguard. What else did you expect me to do?'

When there is no serious threat to your standards and it remains in the suggestion stage only, any one of these ideas may take care of the situation.

A medium threat: This situation is even more serious. A simple 'No' didn't cut it. This time his hands slide over her breasts or she turns her body so his hands rest on her breast. An invitation for a sexual encounter has now been offered, whether verbal or non-verbal. Another tactic is required. A firmer 'No!' through an I-statement is needed: 'I feel uncomfortable or threatened when you pressure me like this.' Or 'I need you to

respect the values I have chosen or we have no basis for a relationship.' You may need to repeat a statement like this firmly more than once before they understand that you mean business. This is where 'What part of No do you not understand?' comes into play. Immediately get to where others are present. Girls should carry a mobile phone, enough change to make a phone call and/or cash for a taxi in an emergency.

A serious threat: Your requests to stop have been ignored, your values and standards are being trampled on. This is not the time to be afraid of hurting the other person's feelings. Trust your instincts – if you feel threatened or scared, act on those feelings. Get out of there fast. Escape any way you can. Use whatever resources necessary to get away. Slap or run. Girls may want to carry pepper spray, just in case.

Don't wait for a real threat to occur; develop a plan of action *before it happens.* Think of it as practice fire drill. The time to find the exit is before the flames are singeing your feet.

If I encountered a light to medium threat to my moral convictions, I would:

6. Become accountable to someone. One of the best ways to abide by the standards you have set for your conduct, as well as to remain sexually abstinent until you are married, is to become accountable to someone for your conduct. A parent would be a good choice – a youth pastor, a counsellor, a trusted teacher or friend. It could be a group of friends who are holding each other accountable. You need to feel comfortable with your accountability partner and respect the person chosen.

One 16-year-old boy was disgusted after totally messing up. One night when a group of friends were together he began drinking (the first violation of his standards). While under the influence of alcohol he had sex with one of the girls present. Although he had little recollection of what happened that night, he vowed to clean up his act. He tried repeatedly to change on his own. Nothing happened until

he became accountable for a change in his lifestyle to a counsellor. No drinking, no sex. Immediately there was a dramatic change in his lifestyle.

A couple desiring to maintain their standards must report in person weekly to their accountability partner(s). On a regular basis you share honestly with this person areas of your life with which you are struggling. While looking him or her in the eyes, each must give a full account of their time, activities, conduct and their thoughts. Knowing you have to answer to someone for your conduct is powerful. I recommend it.

7. Plan your dates carefully in advance. Before going on a date, know where you are going, who is going to be present, what activities there are to participate in, how you are getting there, and what time you will return home. If a date can't provide this information or hesitates when asked – beware!

Dating should include a variety of interesting activities. Time spent participating in activity dates should far outweigh time spent in spectator dates (see Chapter 2, 'The Dating Game'). Plan a variety of fun activities where you can get to know your date's likes and dislikes, total personality, values, goals and beliefs. In the early stages of a relationship, group dates are best. You can be together, but when with friends or another couple there is less stress. This allows you to observe how your date interacts with others and her sense of humour. In a group you can size up your date faster than you ever could on ten formal dates alone. Among friends, he will relax and be himself. It cuts out 'masking'. Group dating leaves room for friendship to grow.

Group dates also make it easier to maintain moral standards and prevent many dangerous 'close encounters'. 'Touchy situations' do not lend themselves to public viewing.

8. Choose your dates with care. Your dating partners should be people who have similar interests, ideals and values – and those who are about your age. Teenagers should restrict their dating partners to those who are no more than two years older or younger than they are. Even two years during the teens produces a wide gap in experience and maturity. Your best dates should come from your circle of friends at church or school – those with whom you have already established a friendship, young people you already know something about. Avoid blind dates with anyone you do not know or have never met unless it is arranged by a trusted friend.

Under no circumstances date a married person. This includes anyone whose divorce is pending or one who is separated from his/her spouse. Until the divorce is final, this person is still married. Dates with those who drink, are known to be drug-users, or anyone not in a position to date you openly are off limits. Don't be so hard up that you would date someone twice who doesn't measure up to your standards, persons you've met over the Internet, or in a chat room.

9. Avoid situations designed to stimulate sexual pleasure. Scripture advises that we 'flee from sexual immorality' (1 Corinthians 6:18), not toy with it!

Teenagers are known for taking daring, calculated risks. Couples who spend hours at the beach nestled on a blanket, necking and petting; couples who sleep together but try to refrain from having sex; couples who lie down together intending only to hold each other; those who engage in mutual masturbation without going to Step 12; or those who are having sex but use no birth control – all are gambling with danger! No one can continue to take such risks and beat all the odds forever.

Since 54% of teens say they first had intercourse at their own or their partner's house, the first rule of conduct involves boy or girlfriends entering your home without adult supervision. No young person should invite a member of the opposite sex into their home when a responsible adult is not present – not to study, watch TV, listen to music, watch a DVD, or any other excuse. This also means you will not entertain a member of the opposite sex in your bedroom, even when your parents are at home. Bedrooms are private areas designed for rest and sleeping. Should you need to study with a member of the opposite sex, it can be done in the living or family room or in the kitchen, but *never* in the bedroom. Any time spent together in a bedroom breaks down resistance and barriers to propriety.

One girl went home with a boyfriend in his car rather than waiting for the school bus.

This put her at home earlier than usual. Although she didn't recall her parents ever forbidding her to enter their home with a boyfriend when they weren't there, she just knew it wouldn't be wise. She desperately wanted to appear 'mature' so rather than telling him her Mum and Dad wouldn't like it if they were alone in the house together, she suggested they wash his car. When Mum and Dad came home, this couple was outside merrily immersed in suds and water – a healthy and fun activity. This girl proved to her parents that she could be trusted to make wise choices, even when they weren't present.

Periods of cuddling and cooing in front of a cosy fireplace, especially with the lights low and music with lyrics that suggest 'Let's Spend the Night together', 'Go all the Way', 'Get Physical', or the more sexually-explicit ode to intercourse, 'Bump and Grind', will eventually lead to sexual intimacy. Not only should you avoid settings that are sexually tempting, but also avoid movies, TV and DVDs that would encourage sinful desires and fantasies, ones that cause you to long for illicit sex or to laugh or snigger at what God says is sinful.

Others think they can travel together, share a hotel room, go camping and share the same tent – all foolish choices. No one can play with sexual fire for long without getting burned. God would have us flee the 'appearance of evil' – not flirt with temptation. (1 Thessalonians 5:22, KJV.)

Once your limits are defined, stick to them. Regardless of how magic the moment, remind yourself that re-negotiation of your standards is permitted only in broad daylight, when the passion has cooled and your accountability partner is present. Only then do you possess the rationale to rethink your position. Not only will this help you translate close encounters into rational behaviour, but it also allows you to keep intact a very precious commodity – your self-esteem.

10. Know the facts about sex. Some parents, teachers and church leaders think the best way to keep young people pure is to keep them ignorant. They pretend that sex doesn't exist in the hope that young people won't experiment. But knowledge is your best safeguard. Sexual experimentation is highest among those who have not had proper sexual instruction. Curiosity can create problems. Frequently boys say that the easiest way to score is with the girl who doesn't know what the score is. As one boy put it: 'A girl who is really ignorant often lets a fellow go too far before she knows what's happening. Then she can't stop him.' Another sexually experienced boy dated a girl for some time but never made any sexual advances. When asked why, he said, 'I'd never try anything with her. She knows too much. Her dad is a doctor!'

Many young people who pride themselves on being sexually savvy do not have reliable data regarding basic facts. What about you? Do you really know the score on sex? In addition to the basics, you need to understand the emotional whys and wherefores of what males and females want from sex and the implications of premarital sex on both sexes.

Hopefully you have parents who have instructed you faithfully regarding God's plan for sex after marriage. Your local school or library may also have some authoritative books on the subject. Some churches offer seminars and group discussions for young people. Whatever avenue you choose, get informed! And reading *Smart Love* is a step in the right direction.

Sex desires are very real, but they are more real when you are doing nothing. So take your mind off the subject and plunge into an absorbing activity. You will find it nearly impossible to concentrate on sex if you must practise two hours a day in preparation for a swimming competition, are working on perfecting your part in an upcoming school play, or are involved in active leadership in your youth group.

Ask God for Help

An important part of your commitment to abstinence is relying on God. Ask your heavenly Father for his help to remain pure. If you and your date discuss and pray about your commitment to abstinence, it will produce a bond of conscience between you that can serve as a roadblock to temptation. Discuss your relationship in terms of 'we three – God, you and I'.

Sexual immorality is a seductive sin. Two of the most difficult sins to resist are pride and sexual immorality, since both are seductive. Pride says, '*I deserve it.*' Sexual desire says, '*I need it.*' In combination, their appeal is deadly. Solomon says that only by relying on God's strength can we overcome them. Pride appeals to the empty head; sexual excitement to the empty heart. But by looking to God we can fill our heads with wisdom and our hearts with his

love. You may not be able to resist sexual temptation, but God can. Turn that part of your life over to him too.

Part 20: For Those Who Have Already Gone Too Far: A Fresh Beginning

What should you do if you have already gone too far? First of all, you need not feel unclean or subhuman. And you are not obligated to marry because of pregnancy. For a couple to marry just to give a baby a name is stupid reasoning. (Babies always get names, whether their father and mother marry or not.)

If you are currently having sex with someone, the remedy may not be easy, but here are some suggestions:

Admit your mistake. One girl sobbingly told her youth pastor how she 'accidentally' went 'all the way'. Let's look at this situation realistically. She should have said that she and her boyfriend did not mean to go all the way. But they did not keep a close watch over their emotions and actions and lost control. This was no accident! Both of them freely and wilfully made several choices that made intercourse more or less inevitable. They went to a place where they could spend time alone without anyone else present. They progressed from light petting to intercourse. These are decisions, whether they realise it or not. Both agreed to proceed. She agreed when she allowed fondling below the waist. He decided when he attempted intercourse.

To call this progression of choices 'an accident' is self-deceiving. In reality both partners refused to draw the line at several stopping points along the way. They threw their moral and spiritual values to the wind when they became emotionally and sexually aroused. This is not an accident, but a choice, and the sooner a couple admits it, the sooner they will be able to handle the problem and cope with the guilt connected with it.

Ask God for forgiveness.
Once you admit personal guilt, you can move to the second step and confess your wrong to your heavenly Father. Confession cleans and purifies the soul, and we serve a God who will totally and completely forgive our sins when we truly repent. If we face our wrongs and are sincerely sorry, God has a wonderful way of using these experiences for our good. He can actually help us, through our mistakes, to become a stronger, finer and more complete person. Your present attitudes towards the experience can help you grow to be more loving, understanding and mature.

Forget the tears and sleepless nights. Refuse to whip yourself endlessly with guilt. Stop punishing yourself. Stop cutting yourself off from spiritual activities due to your guilt. Ask for divine forgiveness, and then accept it.

Even though God can forgive your sins, you still have to live with the consequences of your actions. If you lost your virginity so long ago you can't remember where, when or with whom, that fact will always be a part of you. If you have had a sexually-transmitted disease (or still do), been pregnant or have been responsible for a pregnancy, had an abortion, or put a child up for adoption, the recollection will recur from time to time. There's no way of escaping the dreaded reality of the past. But God has an amazing way of healing memories so they won't haunt or destroy you. When God says that he forgives your sins, he means that he not only forgives them but he forgets them as well.

Scripture tells us that he casts our sins into the depths of the ocean. (See Micah 7:19.) Did you know that the ocean is so deep in places and the pressure so great that anything dropped to the bottom cannot be brought back to the surface? And that's exactly where God casts our sins, in a place where they can never be found again. In this way he frees us to begin afresh. Once again your slate is clean in his sight. Your sins are forgiven. It is as though it never happened.

You no longer need to carry self-hatred or guilt concerning the past, only gratefulness to a heavenly Father who is big enough to forgive even sexual sins. Go forward with a smile on your face and a pure and honest heart.

Stop seeing one another. This is the hard part. If you are currently involved in a sexual relationship and want to test whether it is real love or infatuation, there is only one way to find out. You must isolate the sexual factor. In any scientific experiment, the variable must be isolated. In this case the variable is sex.

Studies indicate that satisfying sex can hold a couple together for three to five years but no longer, if that is all they have going for them. For this reason alone a couple should resist sexual temptaion early in their relationship. Sex deceives the emotions. A couple needs to be very sure of other factors before clouding and complicating the picture with powerful responses that surface when sex takes over.

Refuse to see one another for six months. You may write and phone one another, but you can never be alone together. Vowing never to have sex again won't work. Once a couple has had sex, it is next to impossible for them to be together without indulging in it again. Sex is like being addicted to a hard drug: during serious moments you vow you will never again touch the stuff, but when the craving and opportunity arise, you can't control yourself.

You and your dating partner must initiate and carry out the decision not to see one another. It won't work if parents, a pastor or even a friend tries to talk you into it. When forced against your will you will just rush back into one another's arms the minute you get the chance. Or, worse still, you might begin to sneak around and lie in order to get what you want. Only you can make the decision to stay apart. Undeniably this will be a difficult period for a couple who are really in love, but it offers the only way to analyse the quality of your relationship. An accountability partner

can help by providing motivation and encouragement to abide by your decision.

Should your partner be unwilling to forgo sex for this period of time, several things become crystal clear. If your partner is more interested in filling urgent sexual needs now than in establishing a long-term, emotionally healthy relationship, maybe sex is the only thing you have going for you. Before proceeding, find out for sure. Test your relationship for six months now so you don't have to spend a lifetime with a person who is totally unsuited to you. And if your partner can't hold out, then you know what he or she was really

interested in!

Many young people, even those from Christian homes, have 'gone further' than they may want to admit. Sexual sin has a way of making such young people feel hopeless, as if they can never live a life of abstinence. Often, due to one mistake, they feel resigned to a life of promiscuity because of that one bad experience. They think their future is lost due to their past. But it is never too late to begin saying 'No.' You don't have to keep going down the wrong path. You can always make a fresh beginning today. God's love and forgiveness are unconditional. He is always there with open arms to receive you when you approach him. He'll take those sins of the past and throw them into the depths of the sea.

Today can be the first day of the rest of your life. There's always an opportunity for a new beginning. All God asks of us when we begin afresh is that we recognise and respect his limits. When religious leaders dragged a half-dressed woman who had just been caught sleeping with someone else's husband to Christ, he had an answer adequate for the occasion. 'Jesus declared, "Go now and leave your life of sin." ' (John 8:11.) You can have a new beginning, just as the woman caught in adultery did. Claim it today.

Double Protection

OK. By now you should know that my position is that total abstinence from sex, before and outside of marriage, is the only good and safe way to proceed. But perhaps you are already sexually involved. This also goes for you who plan to be abstinent until you marry, but you get sidetracked and innocently or intentionally become sexually active. I don't want you to be at greater risk of pregnancy or STDs just because you didn't have information on how to protect yourselves.

So if you ever make that choice, I ask only one thing – proceed in the best way possible to protect both of you as well as everyone else concerned. *This means **never** having unprotected sex – sex without protection against pregnancy and STDs!*

Therefore both partners must protect themselves. Unmarried sex calls for *double protection*. For males, this means never having sex without the protection of a prophylactic in order to reduce the risk of picking up an STD. Although they are not 100% safe, the risk is reduced and it is better than using nothing at all. And remember, they give absolutely no protection from some STDs like syphilis and herpes, where the lesions are outside the area of the contraceptive device. Remember also this means *perfect use* – no mistakes can be made with the use of the device or it will increase your risk of infection. It is important that the male puts the device on *before* any intercourse takes place and removes it directly afterwards.

Even when their partners are considerate and careful enough to use such protection, females must also use contraception to protect against unwanted pregnancy. Male contraceptive devices fail almost 16% of the time in the first year of use. Among young unmarried minority women (USA), the rate is 36.3% and among unmarried Hispanic women it is as high as 44.5%. Contraception for females includes the female condom, vaginal jellies or foams, diaphragms, contraceptive injections, hormonal implants, or 'the pill'. (Do not try to obtain or use these last three items without medical supervision.) Contraceptive injections, hormonal implants and the pill are the most effective methods of birth control (outside of abstinence), and the female condom is also quite successful when properly used.

Many think that oral contraception or the pill provides perfect protection from pregnancy. Not true. Multiple studies show that unmarried teen girls have a 5.9-12.9% rate of pregnancy, even when taking the pill. Unmarried women 20 to 29 years of age get pregnant while on the pill 5.9-15% of the time.35 And if a girl on the pill takes other medications, she may even be more likely to become pregnant. This can be explained by the fact that some drugs change the way the body handles the pill. Ampicillin, tetracycline, tegretol and dilantin, plus other lesser-known drugs, decrease the effectiveness of the pill.

Girls, even though you protect against pregnancy, you have no protection against STDs unless your partner uses a male contraceptive device correctly. They must be used consistently and correctly to have any chance of STD protection, and they work best protecting against HIV and gonorrhoea, but are much less effective for protecting against genital herpes, trichomonias and chlamydia. They offer little or no protection from bacterial vaginosis and HPV. *Make sure you never proceed even once without using a contraceptive device or double protection.*

If you have been 'monogamous' for one year, you are still at risk. What does *monogamous* mean? Monogamous means one partner for a lifetime. So if you were with one guy for three months, and another for two months, and now you are with another and think you are monogamous because you were true to that partner when with that person, you were not monogamous. Every time you begin with a new sex partner you must wait, get tested, and then wait another six months and get tested again. There is a window of time from two weeks to six months for your body to produce antibodies for the HIV virus. *You must get tested for STDs every time you start with a new partner.* Ask yourself: Am I bringing any health risk to this new partner, or is he or she bringing any health risk to me?

When you have to slow down to double protect yourselves, you may find your passion cooling slightly and becoming easier to control. Taking time for protection provides time to think about the risks you are about to take. It isn't very romantic. It's serious and businesslike, but then so is parenthood . . . sexually-transmitted disease . . . abortion . . . pregnancy . . . as well as all the emotional risk to your future happiness.

God's Plan for Sex

Sex by itself is little more than animal passion. True love combines sexual desire with all the other components that build the highest kind of relationship between man and woman. Love is friendship, tenderness, self-control, selflessness, kindness and loyalty blended with sexual desire.

The sexual urge, when separated from other aspects of a relationship, selfishly desires to dominate, conquer, force or surrender. True love idealises, controls and conforms sexual desire to become more than pure passion. Love is other-person centred. Sex without love is self-centred, a craving for physical satisfaction, physical release. Love, on the other hand, craves an intimate sharing with another person.

Joe, a university undergraduate, was very popular with his classmates and had been voted president of the student body. In addition, he was voted best-dressed, best-looking and most likely to succeed. Joe really was intelligent, dependable, honest, a hard worker, and he had a dynamite personality to boot. Girls found it difficult to think straight when he was around and it was common knowledge that even married women had propositioned him. When Joe walked through an office, computers crashed. When Joe walked into the cafeteria, the girls stopped eating. When Joe bounded onto the football field, not only the girls from his school cheered, but the girls from the opposing team as well.

Furthermore, Joe loved God and possessed other rare character qualities that were a source of pride and joy to his family. He listened to his father's advice and because of his outstanding character development became his father's favourite. Such favouritism aroused resentment and hatred among his brothers. Eventually they refused to say a kind word to him.

One night Joe had an unusual dream. In this dream he and his brothers were in a field harvesting sheaves of grain. Suddenly his sheaf stood tall, and his brothers' sheaves bowed down to it. Then he had another dream in which the sun, moon and eleven stars bowed to him. If his brothers hated him before, they now became

more furious than ever. Their evil hearts carefully and deliberately plotted his murder.

You can find the rest of the story in Genesis 37 and onwards, a gripping and tragic tale, perhaps the greatest rags-to-riches story ever told. Joseph's brothers were so angry with him that they sold him to a raucous bunch of merchants, who sold him again when they got to Egypt. Potiphar, who was chief of Pharaoh's Bureau of Investigation, bought him and placed him in charge of his entire household.

One day, Potiphar's wife attempted to seduce Joseph, asking him to come and lie with her. Even though she was married to a man with power and wealth, she was not blind to Joseph's masculine charms. For weeks she plotted and planned a cunning seduction. Dressing as alluringly as possible, she made herself as available as she dared. One day she spent longer than usual dressing. She applied her make-up just so, arranged her hair youthfully, bathed herself in perfume, slipped into her

most revealing negligée and invited Joseph to sleep with her.

Joseph, very much male, had 20/20 vision, and a good-looking woman had just offered herself to him. He had reached the age when a man's sexual desire peaks.

Joseph did not have time to debate with himself about the proper course of action. He didn't play games, reasoning that Potiphar had given into his hand the entire house – and certainly Potiphar's wife was a part of his house. He didn't attempt to rationalise that the affair was of concern only to the two persons involved and that as long as no one else found out it wouldn't hurt anyone. He didn't argue with himself that she could get an abortion if the worst came to the worst.

He responded, 'No! A thousand times No!' But Joseph didn't make this decision when Potiphar's wife approached him. He had decided that long beforehand. He already knew what he would do. He made that choice based on other choices he had made dozens of times before.

Close Encounters of a Dangerous Kind

In the face of temptation Joseph could say 'No.' It wasn't because Potiphar's wife was unattractive that he fled, leaving his coat in her clutches. No, Joseph had learned to deny himself certain pleasures today in order to attain long-range goals. He knew the beauty of sacrificing something today in order to get a better reward in the future.

Most young people think they can choose correctly at the moment a decision must be made. But choices aren't really made at that moment. Choices are made according to the way the person has chosen a hundred times before. Our destiny is not that which we decide to do, but what we have already done. Your future actually lies behind you!

Some young adults try to rationalise that sex before marriage doesn't hurt anyone. Such claims turn a blind eye to the pain already evident in countless lives all around them. They cave in to situational-ethics thinking rather than setting a standard of absolute right and wrong.

It doesn't take a genius to figure out how premarital sex hurts people. Our entire society is hurting from unwanted pregnancies, STDs, abortion and sky-rocketing welfare costs.

And we haven't mentioned the emotional wreckage to individuals from broken relationships.

Those who think they can be spared such pain are lying to themselves. They think the rules don't apply to them. But they are just being wilfully ignorant.

God's standards are unchanging. They are as applicable today as they were in Joseph's time. There is no guesswork.

Those who are not willing to accept this black-and-white definition set forth in the Bible will have to find their values somewhere else. They will have to accept the situational ethics which say, 'The right thing to do in any situation is what makes me feel good or what I think is right for this situation,' and then accept the consequences.

This make-it-up-as-you-go-along morality has no foundation. Christian young people who have fallen into this kind of thinking must either turn back to God and his truth or continue as they are and move further away from any semblance of the Christian life. Their hearts will become more and more hardened to spiritual matters.

If you want to be a winner, as Joseph was, you, too, will have to give up some immediate pleasures for the sake of ultimate benefits. You will look away from wickedness rather than accepting it as normal. Just as Joseph found and followed the law of chastity and purity, so you can find and live by a code of decency and morality in a world that places little or no value on these attributes.

chapter **seven**

Date Rape

'My boyfriend and I went to a party at a friend's house one night. No adults were there and alcohol and drugs were brought out. My boyfriend asked me to go upstairs to a bedroom with him. I'd had a lot to drink, but even then I knew I shouldn't go. But I did. He tried to have sex with me. I tried to fight him off but was too drunk and confused. Then he raped me. Later he apologised but said he thought I wanted it since I went upstairs with him. Now I feel as if I asked for it since I did go upstairs with him. I broke up with him but never told anyone about this because I was drunk. I cry a lot and feel terribly guilty. I don't want to go to youth meetings and I wonder if God can ever forgive me for what I did.'

Date rape is one of the fastest growing violent crimes in the US. The National Victim Center reports that over 700,000 women are raped every year and 61% of all rapes are girls under the age of 18. Although males can also be victims of sexual assault, rape affects less than 5% of males.

More than 80% of rapes are committed by someone the victim knows, a fellow student, neighbour or relative. It frequently occurs on a date, in people's homes, at parties, during daylight as well as the night hours, where friendship and romance end in sexual assault.

Being raped by someone you know can often be more

traumatising than by a stranger since it represents a violation of trust. Secondly, family and friends may refuse to believe an assault by someone they all know, and take sides or blame the victim. This violation of trust often leads to alienation from family and friends, substance abuse, suicide attempts, depression, excessive anger or eating disorders.

Regardless of who the perpetrator is, rape is an act of violence – an obscene attack on another person. And the problem is getting worse due to Hollywood and the music industry who push the idea that No really means Yes. Pornography that is now available in home DVDs and on TV also promotes the idea that forcible sex is enjoyed by women and that no harm is suffered.

Alcohol and drugs play a significant role in date rape. It is estimated that 55% of females and 75% of males had been drinking or using drugs at the time of the rape. Drinking is touted as a popular way of setting the mood for romance. But after a few drinks, a woman can become too intoxicated to realise what's going on. Alcohol clouds the judgement and decreases motor skills which prevents her escaping from a dangerous situation.

Date rape is quite prevalent on university and college campuses. This can probably be explained by the fact that young people who have been constrained by their parents' rules are unprepared for so much freedom away from home. Such freedom often leads to unrestrained drug and alcohol use,

which in turn leads to irresponsible sex and frequently on to date rape.

What are referred to as 'date-rape drugs' are also being widely used on unsuspecting victims. Both Rohypnol and GNB are tasteless and odourless and can be slipped into a drink and within ten to fifteen minutes cause dizziness, drowsiness and confusion. Date rape drugs are yet another reason for avoiding alcohol and those who drink.

Preventative measures. Setting limits and respecting yourself are two of the most important defences. Remember that something as innocent as holding hands or a goodnight kiss might be interpreted by the other person to mean, 'It would be OK to go further.' When you go further it is almost impossible to back up. Therefore it is much better to stay on the conservative side. Rather than being old-fashioned, this is nothing less than 'smart'.

Some guys will test a girl by

touching her inappropriately, telling a sexual joke, or making a lewd comment. Depending on a girl's response he may push for more. But regardless of how far things have gone, if a guy tries to force you to have sex, it is a crime.

Another preventative measure is to avoid unhealthy situations where there is a major difference in age or authority as with a teacher, a boss, a doctor, counsellor, church leader or family friend to whom you might owe a favour. Also avoid control freaks who might try to get you all to themselves by controlling your friends, your time, and where you go. Guys who make crude comments, tell lewd jokes or enjoy pornography are very bad risks. If he wants you to watch sexually explicit DVDs or films with him, dump him straight away.

Rape is more likely to happen to those who do not have clear boundaries, those who have been sexually abused in the past, and those who are afraid of rejection. Such people become the perfect setup. Remember that rape exposes you to risk of pregnancy, STDs, injury and humiliation. Regardless of how handsome, popular, rich, desirable or respectable a boy might appear, rape remains a crime.

Beware of anyone who ignores your wishes; attempts to make you feel guilty or accuses you of being 'uptight'; is excessively jealous or possessive; ignores your personal boundaries; disregards what you say; is under the influence of alcohol or drugs; and/or gets hostile when you say 'No!' Pay attention to behaviour that doesn't seem right. If something feels wrong, it probably is.

Take action.

Defusing the situation. If someone tries to force you to have sex, stay calm and think: What options are open to me? Women who fight, scream and claw have a better chance of escaping than those who beg, plead and cry. Begging plays into the rapist's desire for power. And this is definitely not the time to turn the other cheek or worry about being polite. This is the time to protect your body and possibly your life!

Responses should be sharp and direct, such as, 'Stop this NOW!' or 'Get away!' If anyone is within shouting distance, shout loudly, 'I'm being attacked!' Avoid the word 'help' as nowadays people are afraid to help or get involved in others' problems.

Shouting 'Fire!' may also bring you help. Sometimes using the word 'rape' shocks a potential rapist into realising what he's about to do. Look for a way of escape or someone to help you. Distract him if you can. Act quickly. The longer you delay, the fewer your options.

Should the rapist be armed, passive resistance is best. Try to talk him out of it. Intimidation might work. Try to distract him or mention AIDS. Do whatever it takes to win this battle.

Should the rape occur. Let's say in spite of all your efforts a rape occurs. Get to the safety of a friend or relative's home and call the police immediately. Since it is of vital importance to preserve all evidence of the attack, do not shower, bathe or even change clothes. Most rape victims want to rid themselves of all traces of the attack. Sometimes they don't want to deal with what happened and wait days or weeks to report it. This reduces credibility and makes prosecution more difficult. Reporting the assault immediately helps the victim gain a sense of control and ensures proper medical treatment.

The vast majority of rapes, however, fail to get reported due to embarrassment or shame. But by taking action you can help prevent the rapist from assaulting other victims. Most rapists are repeat offenders. Remember: he has committed a serious crime and deserves punishment for it.

You will also need counselling from someone qualified to deal with the impact of the assault. Do not neglect this step, thinking you can just forget it and get on with your life. It takes time to recover from the emotional, psychological and spiritual after-effects of rape. You will need to rebuild your feelings of worth so you won't be vulnerable again.

Most important of all, remember the rape was not your fault. Nor did your behaviour cause it. The rapist caused the rape. Don't give him the satisfaction of ruining your life. Pick up the pieces, get well, and carry on. You owe it to yourself.

Sexual assault is an ugly reminder that we must always be on guard against Satan and his army. Strengthening your self-worth, staying alert and making commonsense choices will go a long way towards helping you avoid this tragedy.

Live-in Lovers

You've been dating someone terrific. You think you have found the real thing. Obviously he feels the same about you, because, after a delightful afternoon at the lake, he pops the question, 'We have something special here. How about moving in with me?' Before you pack, look at the cold, hard facts.

Living together before marriage is an almost sure predictor of failure. Seven recent studies concur that couples who live together before marriage have a higher divorce rate than those who don't![1] The number of co-habiting couples in the UK has increased by 65% in the last decade. Today more than four million unmarried couples in the US live together. More than half of all first marriages are now preceded by the couple living together first. And a US national survey of older teenagers found that nearly 60% felt that it was a good idea to live together before marriage to find out whether they really get along. Many are aware of such statistics but discount the data as they feel their situation is different.

About 40% of couples who live together break up before getting married. And marriages where couples live together have a 50% higher rate of divorce or separation which makes for a 75% divorce rate. Or another way to say it might be: Of every one hundred couples who begin living together, forty will break up before marriage. Of the sixty who marry, forty-five will divorce. That leaves only fifteen of the original one hundred couples still married!

Moving in with someone prior to marriage is an act of immaturity. There is no commitment. It blasts out a message: 'You don't have to do much to get me.' Then your live-in partner fools around. You stay, and another deafening message comes through: 'You don't have to do much to keep me, either!'

Living together is a difficult trap to get out of. When dating, if someone is immature or disrespectful or abuses you verbally or physically, you can back off and not date that person again. But once you're living together, it becomes more difficult to end what needs to be ended. You keep hoping and praying your partner will change. And after a year of living together, separating can be as painful as divorce – especially for women.

When asked why they live with a partner, the number one reason cited by women is that they want to get married. Yet few live-in relationships result in marriage. One study concluded that only one in three couples ties the knot. Males give a totally different reason for living with a woman. The number one reason cited by males is sex. As one male put it, 'Living together provides safe sex, when you want it, how you want it.'

Marriage has some definite advantages. It acts as a safeguard for moral standards, property rights and joint purchases. It also provides a legitimate family name for children. Marriage comes with many built-in legal protections. Live-in lovers might find it possible to avoid divorce lawyers and maintenance payments, but often there are no fewer problems, heartaches or tears.

The Riskiest Sex Practice of All

Often young adults do not understand the true risks of some of the sexual practices they participate in. And it is my duty to mention the practice of anal sex, even though it may be offensive to some. Anal sex is an activity that young people think they can engage in without causing pregnancy. Many girls are using anal sex as a method of contraception! This means that girls think anal sex is safer – that they are more afraid of getting pregnant than HIV.[2] Somehow, the idea that anal sex can lead to HIV infection has disappeared from their mindset. Furthermore, some young adults do not even consider this practice as 'sex'. Some young people

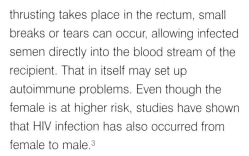

think, 'I can satisfy my boyfriend with this activity and still be a virgin.' In a *Seventeen* magazine survey, 40% of those surveyed did not count oral or anal sex as 'sex'.

Let's take a look at the facts. Half of all new HIV infections are among young adults under the age of 25, and the majority are infected sexually – including anal sex. Anal sex is the most efficient sexual means of HIV transmission and an easy way to spread hepatitis, HIV and all other STDs. Anal sex can pass STDs from one infected person to an uninfected one more readily than vaginal or oral sex can. Why? The rectal mucous membranes seem to have more receptors to bind HIV and the tissue is more easily torn or broken, leading to easier access for HIV or STD transmission.

In heterosexual anal sex, the female is at higher risk because the entire lining of the rectum is exposed, rather than just the head of the penis. If the female is exposed to infected semen from an HIV male she retains these infected secretions within her body while the male is only exposed during the actual sex act. Furthermore, the rectum lining is thin and fragile and is not made for thrusting. It is made for the absorption of the water in faeces. When

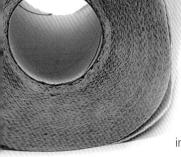

thrusting takes place in the rectum, small breaks or tears can occur, allowing infected semen directly into the blood stream of the recipient. That in itself may set up autoimmune problems. Even though the female is at higher risk, studies have shown that HIV infection has also occurred from female to male.[3]

A risk that is often not thought about is that the girl who has sexually transmitted germs in and around her anus can pass those organisms to the male who inserts his penis into her anus. And the reverse is also true. The guy who has STD organisms on his penis can pass these germs to a girl's anus and can cause an STD infection.

A common infection from anal sex is HPV condyloma or genital warts. These condyloma or genital warts can be very uncomfortable. One study at a university health centre shows that 46% of sexually active students were infected with HPV.[4] HPV is associated with the development of anal cancers. A man may not even be aware that he has a wart until his partner develops an abnormality. A man may ignore a small growth or may not want to admit that he has one. And it is difficult for his partner to know that he has an infection. But regardless of whether the warts are visible, the HPV infection can be passed from one person to the other. Some warts on men can be treated easily, but others need repeated treatment. Sometimes the use of a laser or surgery may be necessary.

STDs exist because of promiscuity, or multiple partners. There is no way for STDs to enter the closed, sacred circle surrounding husband and wife. One partner for a lifetime solves the problem of STDs.

Smart Love

chapter *eight*

I have presented a lot of information in *Smart Love*. We can't live in the twenty-first century without information. Yet information does more for us than merely inform – *it empowers us.* But just *to know* isn't enough either. All the information and knowledge in the world won't do you any good unless it helps you make better choices and decisions, which in turn influence your actions. You have to *do* something with what you know.

A few years ago the Southern Baptists in the US started a 'True Love Waits' campaign. This campaign encourages a commitment to God, family, future mate, and future children to be sexually pure until marriage. To prove the point that young people were willing to make such a commitment, 100,000 young people marched on Washington, D.C., with signed commitment cards. These commitment cards were planted in wire holders on the lawns surrounding the White House. What a statement by young people!

I believe the time has come to offer more young people an alternative to the sexually promiscuous lifestyle offered by secular society.

Society acts as if it expects young adults to be sexually active. I don't, and neither does God. Remember, thirty-nine times in Scripture God encourages moral and sexual integrity. He wouldn't ask us to do something that was unattainable.

I believe *today* is the day to take your stand for virginity and purity until marriage. Once you make that commitment and no longer straddle the

fence, constantly vacillating between Should I? or Shouldn't I? there will be a sense of peace, freedom and integrity in your life such as you've never before experienced.

Remember, virginity is not a prerequisite for making this commitment. Maybe you or someone you know has already had sex, but wish they'd waited. Such people join ranks with the Roper Starch Study of more than 500 teenage students, where 62% of the girls and 54% of all teens who'd had sex wished they'd waited.[1] It's clear from studies on the subject and young adults I've talked to that many wish to stop. If this includes you, here's something you need to know. *You can choose virginity all over again.* If you do, you can be a part of helping reduce STDs and premarital pregnancy. One of the greatest risks of becoming infected with STDs is an ever-increasing number of sex partners over your lifetime. And by choosing abstinence until marriage, there is zero chance of either! Previously sexually active young adults are going beyond *wishing* they could commit to sexual purity. They are going for the next best thing – 'secondary virginity'. And it can be done. One study showed that 30.5% of 14 to 15-year-old girls and 40.4% of boys of the same age who had been sexually active in the past were able to abstain from sex after taking an abstinence pledge. Others who had reached the ages of 17 and 18 showed much the same ability – remaining abstinent after pledging to do so.[2]

Regardless of which category you are in, by signing the following pledge to sexual purity, you are only committing yourself to purity *from this day forward*. The past is now behind you and you are allowing God to take care of that. But you can do something about your future.

Printed at the end of this chapter, you'll find a commitment card ready for you to sign. The sexual purity to which you are pledging yourself means avoiding penetrative sex, as well as any genital contact, mutual masturbation or contact with any sexually excitable body parts and/or oral sex. Such activities do not fall within guidelines for 'sexual purity' or true abstinence since they can and do result in pregnancy and STDs. And engaging in such activities also leads directly to sexual intercourse. True abstinence, then, is a commitment to save all sexual activities for the exclusive, lifelong, one-flesh relationship called marriage.

When you have carefully and prayerfully read My Commitment to Sexual Purity and the five items listed, and pledge to live by the conditions listed, sign the card and date it. Like any other major life choice, really think about this before you sign it. Choosing not to have sex until you are married is a Big Choice. So take time to work out how you are going to manage this choice so that it empowers you rather than being a burden.

You will need to remind yourself that you made this choice to honour God on a daily basis. So think through why you are making this choice. What do you hope to accomplish by it? And rather than thinking about it in negative terms, *I'm never going to have sex until I'm married*, think of it in positive terms: *I have chosen sexual purity until I'm married because I value my future and want to honour God.*

This choice of sexual purity doesn't mean your sexuality has vanished. Having sexual thoughts and feelings is part of being human. So just because you are choosing not to have a sexual partner right now doesn't mean you never will have sex or that you'll become a eunuch or a non-sexual person. It only means that you and God are choosing the time when you exercise your sexuality. So, whereas you have no choice in whether you are sexual, you can always choose how best to manage your sexuality and make it work with all the other life choices you have to make.

Choosing sexual purity because your religion or your parents or your belief system do not encourage or permit sex prior to marriage are also good and valid reasons. Any time you violate your belief system you'll feel guilty. That guilt is a signal that you

shouldn't be doing it. Or if you only have sex to defy your parents, family members or religion, it would be better to abstain. This is true because when sex makes you feel bad about yourself, it just isn't worth having.

In the future, whenever you are feeling sexually aroused, you can help yourself by engaging in some activity to help you get your mind off such feelings. And when you are feeling this way, it's a good idea to avoid going out on dates.

Many young people now say, 'I'm proud to be a virgin.' Others say it is 'awesome' to make a pledge of sexual purity. Still others say they want to be able to present this special gift to their future husband or wife.

If you are in a relationship with someone, you may want to have a copy of this card made and have your special friend sign one as well. I suggest you keep your card in your bag or wallet or maybe in your Bible. Some have it framed and keep it on their dressers at home or taped to the mirror they use every morning – although one young man said he was going to tape it to the dashboard of his car!

After making your commitment, it will work better if you surround yourself with family, friends and

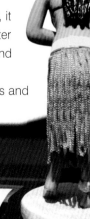

My commitment to sexual purity

for the benefit of my future mate and children I do solemnly commit myself

dating partners who support your stand. When you make a decision to abstain from all sex play until marriage, you are making a powerful choice that shows you care about yourself and wish to honour God. Anyone who uses that choice to mock you or tease you is ultimately someone who is intimidated because you have the strength to make that choice regardless of what others think. A lot of people are intimidated by strong people. They don't like to admit it and so try to make you feel small. So instead of feeling attacked when others ridicule you, be proud of the choice you are making. Let it go, and remind yourself why you have made that choice. The only person you have to live with is yourself. Doing things to please others may gain short-term results, but in the long run you and God are the ones to whom you have to be accountable. You are making this choice because you want what is best for you now.

Too many people have sex because someone else wants them to,

before they're ready, or for the wrong reasons – wanting someone to like them, or to keep a partner. When you choose to abstain from all sex play till marriage, for your own reasons, you are fully aware and alert to what you are doing. You want to choose a sexual partner when you are ready, when you are prepared for the intimacy and the responsibility involved. Then after marriage you can discover what is so wonderful about sex and how the experience can be used in ways that make us and others around us feel good.

Making the commitment to sexual purity will give you time to learn to trust, understand, and learn to communicate with your dating partner. It can help you learn about your own body, rather than be told by someone else how it should function. It can allow you to achieve other things which may have a higher priority for you right now than sex. And, above all, it can serve to let you know that when you are married, you can enjoy sex with a clear conscience, of your own choice, because you want to, and come to it prepared and ready for all the responsibilities as well as all of its joys. And, best of all, you can approach your honeymoon without guilt or any unpleasant baggage from the past. You come clean, honest and pure. Oh, what a night that will be!

Recording artist John Tesh, who was also former co-host of US television's 'Entertainment Tonight', and actress Connie Sellecca have learned that good things come to those who wait. This couple, who chose to wait until marriage for sex, have stated that they wanted to do everything right this time. Both were wary of entering a new commitment because each had had a disastrous earlier marriage. After John's first marriage was dragged through the divorce court with the kind of testimony the supermarket tabloids pounce on, John said that every couple should be forced to spend one day in a divorce court before they're given a marriage licence. He spent a lot of time in therapy making sure his relationship with Connie was not on the rebound.

After a year's courtship, the couple flew to Carmel, on the coast of California, where they helped serve Thanksgiving dinner at a mission for the homeless. They went on to nearby Monterey for a festive dinner at a restaurant on the water. When they arrived at the restaurant, Connie noticed the empty car park and a sign on the door that read 'Closed'. She hesitated, but John pushed ahead and led her to a table in the centre of the deserted restaurant. As she looked around in bewilderment a string quartet began to play 'Concetta', a love song John had written for her early in their romance. (Concetta Sellecca is her real name.)

Gradually it dawned on Connie that John had rented the entire restaurant for just the two of them! In the middle of their five-course dinner, John dropped to his knees, asking for Connie's hand in marriage. How did she respond? Completely overwhelmed, she cried buckets. Her acceptance of his proposal created fireworks. An offshore barge launched a magnificent ten-minute firework display.

But their engagement was not all fireworks, music and romance. Both Connie and John are deeply committed Christians. They had many serious talks about the responsibilities and demands of sharing their Hollywood lives together and spent thirty hours in premarital counselling with their pastor. In those sessions they learned to handle disagreements. When upset, 'I close down,' Connie said. 'He likes to talk it through.' They read books that probed into marital crises and how to solve them. They role-played. Together they studied the Scriptures. In addition they talked about religion, finances, the importance of communicating on every level, and sex.

They jokingly called it a bare-knuckle fight among four people – Connie, John, the pastor and God.

But now the best part. This high-profile couple chose premarital abstinence during their courtship – for religious reasons and 'to be a good role model to my son,' Connie added proudly. That's right. They chose to wait until their wedding night to consummate their vows. Snuggling close to John, Connie said during an interview before their marriage, 'Our honeymoon will be traditional in every sense of the word.' John added, 'This is going to be some honeymoon!'

John Tesh and Connie Sellecca have been good role models not only for her son but for the world. Abstinence is a choice to be proud of. Your future will be determined by the choice you make. The price is high but the rewards are limitless!

A Choice to Be Proud Of

My Commitment to Sexual Purity

For the benefit of my future mate and children I do solemnly commit myself before God to the following biblical principles:

I resolve to . . . 'Forgetting what is behind . . . I press on towards the goal to win the prize for which God has called me heavenward in Christ Jesus.' Philippians 3: 13, 14.

When I am tempted I will . . . 'Flee the evil desires of youth, and pursue righteousness, faith, love and peace, . . . out of a pure heart.' 2 Timothy 2:22. Or 'Flee from sexual immorality. All other sins a man commits are outside his body, but he who sins sexually sins against his own body.' 1 Corinthians 6:18.

I will remember that . . . 'And he [God] will not let you be tempted beyond what you can bear. But when you are tempted, he will also provide a way out so that you can stand up under it.' 1 Corinthians 10:13.

I believe that . . . 'Marriage should be honoured by all, and the marriage bed kept pure, for God will judge the adulterer and the sexually immoral.' Hebrews 13:4.

In the future I pledge to live . . . 'a disciplined and prudent life, doing what is right and just and fair.' Proverbs 1:3.

Therefore, in honour of God's ideal for my life and my love and respect for God, I commit myself to refrain from all sex play and to remain sexually pure from this day forward, until I enter a biblical marriage.

_____   _____
Signature   Date

The Last Word

Where, then, does Smart Love begin? Not when you begin dating. Rather it begins somewhere in an unending circle of living and giving and growing daily into the will of God for our lives. Welcome to the winner's circle!

notes

Dating for Beginners

[1] Dr James Dobson, *Bringing Up Boys*, (Tyndale House Publishers), p. 99.

Chapter 1: Making Friends with Yourself

[1] Extracted from *The Strong-willed Child*, (Tyndale).

[2] Family Information Service: 'Healthy Alternatives to Relationships for Teens – Breaking the Cycle of Violence in Family and Dating Relationships'.

[3] Bruce Larson, *No Longer Strangers* (Word), p. 11.

[4] Morris Rosenberg, *Society and the Adolescent Self-image*. (Princeton University Press), pp. 193, 194.

Chapter 2: The Dating Game

[1] *PREPARE*, Enrich Inc., PO Box 190, Minneapolis, MN 55440.

[2] Neil Clark Warren, *Finding the Love of Your Life*.

[3] Jeannie Echenique, 'Early Dating May Lead to Early Sex'. *USA Today*.

[4] Maynard R. A. (Ed.) *Kids Having Kids*: *A Robin Hood Foundation Special Report on the Costs of Adolescent Childbearing*.

[5] Centres for Disease Control and Prevention. Fertility, Family Planning and Women's Health: New Data from National Survey of Family Growth. *Vital Health and Statistics*, 23 (19).

[6] Centres for Disease Control and Prevention. Sexually Transmitted Disease Surveillance, *Morbidity and Mortality Weekly Report*, 7 (2).

Chapter 3: Breaking Up is Hard to Do

[1] Family Information Service, 'Healthy Alternatives to Relationships for Teens – Breaking the Cycle of Violence in Family and Dating Relationships', p. 48.

[2] *Ibid*., p. 49.

[3] Dick Purnell, *Building a Relationship that Lasts,* (Here's Life Publishers) p. 15.

Chapter 4: The Young Adult's Number One Dilemma

[1] Joyce Brothers, *The Brothers System for Liberated Love and Marriage*, (Peter H. Wyden), p. 19.

[2] *Ibid*.

[3] *Ibid*.

[4] *Ibid*, p. 22.

[5] John James and Ibis Schlesinger, *Are You the One for Me?* (Addison Wesley), p. 198.

[6] Nancy Van Pelt, *Smart Love, a Field Guide for Single Adults*, (Fleming H. Revell), p. 128.

Chapter 5: Touchy Situations

[1] Susan Crain Bakos, 'The Sexually Assertive Woman', *Ladies' Home Journal.*

[2] Schuster, M. A. *et al*, The Sexual Practices of Adolescent Virgins: Genital Sexual Activity of High School Students Who Have Never Had Intercourse. *American Journal of Public Health*, 86 (11).

[3] *Sexual Health Today: Exploring the Past, Preserving the Future Through Choices Today.* The Medical Institute for Sexual Health, p. 112.

[4] *Sexual Health Today, Ibid*. p. 113.

[5] *Sexual Health Today, Ibid*. p. 112.

[6] Josh McDowell and Dick Day, *Why Wait?* (Here's Life Publishers, Inc.), p. 61.

[7] Sol Gordon and Kathleen Everly, 'Increasing Self-esteem in Vulnerable Students . . . A Tool for Reducing Pregnancy Among Teenagers'.

notes

Chapter 6: Close Encounters of a Dangerous Kind

1 McDowell and Day, *Ibid.*, p. 284.

2 *Ibid.*, p. 295.

3 Michael J. McManus, *Marriage Savers*, (Zondervan), p. 92.

4 *Ibid.*, p. 65.

5 Michael J. McManus, p. 65.

6 Centres for Disease Control and Prevention. Sexually Transmitted Disease Surveillance, *Morbidity and Mortality Weekly Report*, 7 (2).

7 Institute of Medicine. *The Hidden Epidemic – Confronting Sexually Transmitted Disease* (edited by Thomas R. Eng and William T. Butler), (National Academy Press), p. 37.

8 National Institutes of Health. *Cervical Cancer: NIH Consensus Development Statement*, Online, 43 (1), 1-30.

9 Marsha F. Goldsmith, 'Sexually Transmitted Diseases May Reverse the "Revolution" ', *Medical News and Perspectives*, 255; 13: 1665-1672.

10 Lewis J. Lord, 'Sex with Care' US News and World Report.

11 Eng and Butler, *ibid.*, p. 33.

12 *Sexual Health Today. Ibid*, pp. 121.

13 Lai, Y. M. *et al*. Human Papillomavirus Deoxyribonucleic Acid and Ribonucleic Acid in Seminal Plasma and Sperm Cells. Fertility and Sterility, 65 (5), 1026-1030.

14 Diane Hales, 'The Facts of Love', *Ladies' Home Journal*.

15 *Sexual Health Today, Ibid.*, p. 83.

16 Erica Lumiere, 'Women and AIDS', *Ladies' Home Journal*.

17 E. F. Jones and D. J. Forrest, 'Contraceptive Failure Rates Based on the 1998 NSFG', *Family Planning Perspectives* 24, No. 1.

18 Focus on the Family, *No Apologies – The Truth About Life, Love and Sex*, (Tyndale), p. 106.

19 As cited in 'How AIDS Can Be Spread', *Message* magazine supplement.

20 McDowell and Day, *Why Wait?* p. 257.

21 *Ibid.*, p. 261.

22 Nancy Van Pelt, *The Compleat Courtship*, (Review and Herald Publishing Association), p. 117.

23 Myron Harris and Jane Norman, *The Private Life of the American Teenager*, (Rawson, Wade Publishers), p. 104.

24 'Teen Pregnancy in the US – A Fact Sheet', US House of Representatives.

25 Mishell, D. R., Contraception. *New England Journal of Medicine*, 320 (12), 777-787.

26 *Sexual Health Today, ibid.*, pp. 127-128.

27 *Sexual Health Today, ibid.*

28 Michael J. McManus. *Ibid.*, p. 65.

29 Debra A. Bell, 'Helping Women Overcome Abortion Effects', *Virtue*.

30 Eugene J. Kanin and David H. Howard, *American Sociological Review* 23, no. 5:558.

31 McDowell and Day, *Why Wait?* p. 286.

32 Marianne K. Hering, 'Believe Well, Live Well', Focus on the Family.

33 Michael J. McManus (*ibid.*) As quoted after appearing on the 'Focus on the Family' radio programme.

34 Bryan Strong and Christine DeVault, *The Marriage and Family Experience*, 3rd ed., p. 223. See also Ira Reiss, 'A Multi-voiate Model of Extra-marital Sexual Permissiveness', *Journal of Marriage and Family*.

35 *Sexual Health Today, ibid.*, p. 173.

notes

Chapter 7: Tough Topics

[1] Nancy Van Pelt, *Smart Love*, pp. 237, 238.
[2] Sally Peters, 'Anal Sex May Be Increasing Among Adolescents', OB/GYN News.
[3] HIV Infogram. 'Update on Sexual Transmission of HIV', Public Health, Seattle and King Country.
[4] *Sexual Health Today*, *ibid*., p. 53.

Chapter 8: A Choice to Be Proud Of

[1] *Sexual Health Today*, *ibid*., p. 185.
[2] *Sexual Health Today*, *ibid*., p. 186.

The world-renowned family-life expert gives her top tips on marriage, relationships and parenting.

Nancy Van Pelt

To Have & To Hold

A Guide
to Sucessful Marriage

Top tips for achieving a
successful and happy
marriage.

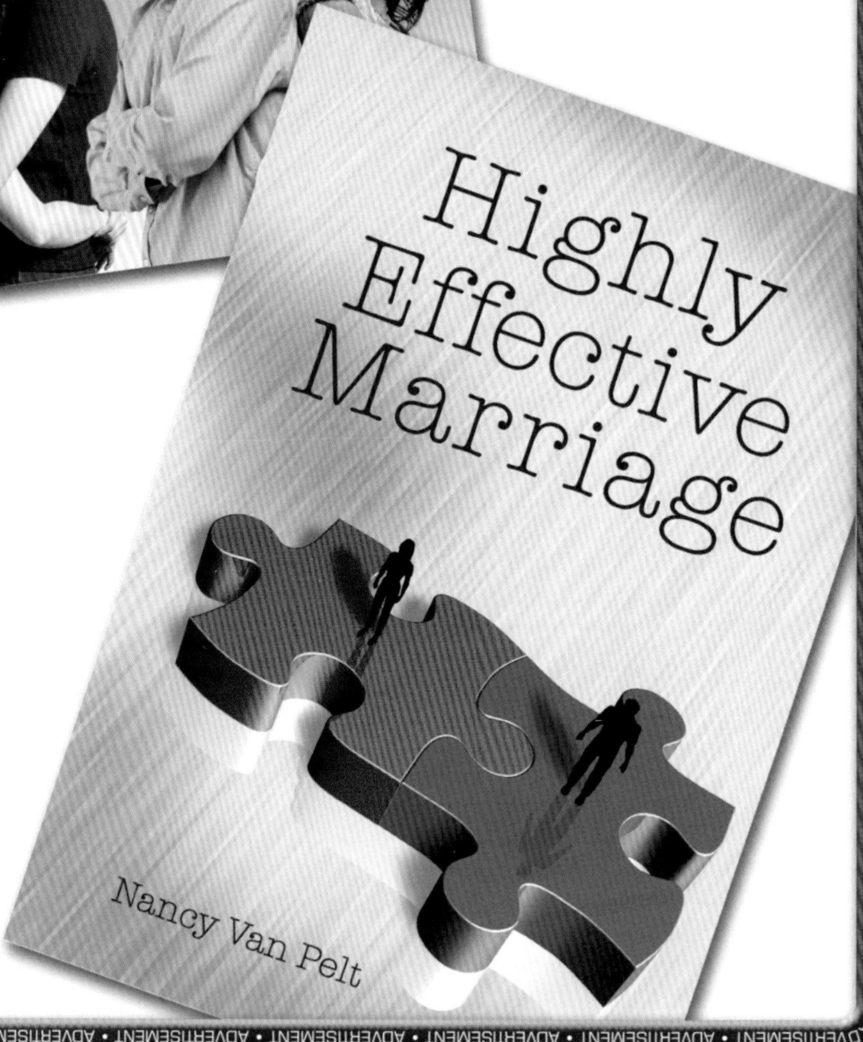

Highly
Effective
Marriage

Nancy Van Pelt

Sound advice to help you navigate your way
through the minefield of parenting.

Train Up a Child
Nancy Van Pelt

Highly Effective Marriage — Nancy Van Pelt

WHAT WOMEN SHOULD UNDERSTAND ABOUT MEN — Nancy Van...

To Have & To Hold — A Guide to Successful Marriage — Nancy Van Pelt

PARENTING TEENS — Nancy Van Pelt

CHARACTER UNDER CONSTRUCTION — Nancy Van Pelt

DANGEROUS RELATIONS — Nancy Van Pelt

Train Up a Child — Nancy Van Pelt

WHAT MEN SHOULD UNDERSTAND ABOUT WOMEN — Nancy Van Pelt

For more information or to order any of the books advertised here, please contact your local ABC Centre.

Botswana
Adventist Book Centre
PO Box 378, Plot 1024, Ledumadumane
Mogoditshane, South Botswana
Tel: 397 3639, 393 1506

Ghana
Home Health Education Service
PO Box GP 1016, 39 Gamel Nasser Ave.
Accra, Ghana, West Africa
Tel: 021 223720

Kenya
Home Health Education Service
PO Box 42276, James Gichuru Rd off
Gitanga Rd Nairobi, Kenya
Tel: 020 3877586

Malawi
Home Health Education Service
PO Box 1119, Kabula Hill Road
Blantyre, Malawi • Tel: 01 620264

Mauritius
Vie et Santé
10 Paul Badaut St. Rose Hill, Mauritius
Tel: 230 246 5343

Nigeria
Eastern Nigerian Union Mission of the
Seventh-day Adventist Church
Home Health Education Service
PMB 8003, Unuo Cham, Abia, Nigeria
Tel: 082 353871/2

North Western Nigerian Union Mission of
the Seventh-day Adventist Church
Home Health Education Service
PO Box 207, Ikeja
524 Ikorodu Road Maryland
Lagos, Nigeria • Tel: 01 4936863

South Africa
H.H.E.S. Distributors NPC
PO Box X20709 Bloemfontein, 9301
South Africa • Tel: 051 403 6900

Tanzania
Adventist Book Centre
Tanzania Adventist Press
PO Box 635, Morogoro, Tanzania
East Africa • Tel: 0232 604374

Uganda
Home Health Education Service
Uganda Adventist Centre
PO Box 6434, Makerere Road, Opp. Law
Development Centre, Kampala, Uganda
Tel: 041 540783

Zambia
Home Health Education Service
PO Box 38539, Cusa House, Ground floor
room 3, Cairo Road, Lusaka
Tel: 01 228404

Zimbabwe
Adventist Book Centre
PO Box 573, 114 Herbert Chitepo Street
Bulawayo • Tel: 09 61845/6

United Kingdom
Adventist Book Centre
The Stanborough Press, Alma Park
Grantham, Lincs., NG31 9SL
Tel: 01476 539900

United States of America
Review & Herald Publishing Association
55 West Oak Ridge Drive, Hagerstown
MD 21740 • Tel: 301 3933000